BLOODTIES

TED KERASOTE

NATURE, CULTURE,

BLOODTIES

AND THE HUNT

RANDOM HOUSE
NEW YORK

Library of Congress Cataloging-in-Publication Data
Kerasote, Ted.
Bloodties: nature, culture, and the hunt/Ted Kerasote.—1st ed.
    p.   cm.
ISBN 0-394-57609-8
1. Hunting—Philosophy.   2. Hunting—Psychological aspects.
3. Hunting—Social aspects.   4. Kerasote, Ted—Journeys.   I. Title.
SK14.K47   1993
799.2'01—dc20   92-56824

Manufactured in the United States of America
on acid-free paper
98765432
First Edition

BOOK DESIGN BY FRITZ METSCH

for home

AS A WAY OF THANKS

MANY PEOPLE GAVE GENEROUSLY OF THEIR TIME AND KNOWLEDGE, their food and their homes while I researched this book. My debt to them is enormous; my appreciation for their kindness will always remain.

I wish to thank particularly Henning Thing, formerly the director of wildlife management for the Greenland Home Rule, and now at the Danish Polar Center. Henning helped me find a suitable village in which to live, arranged transportation, and was a constant gloss on Greenlandic customs and society. Sven Nielsen, the headmaster of the Kullorsuaq school and my primary translator, and his wife, Emilie, opened their home to me, answered hours of questions, never lost patience. Edvard Nielsen also gave of his time, shared his music, and made me laugh. Nicolai Jensen took me back in time. From Upernavik, Karsten Meyer helped minimize the cost of my lodging while in Greenland, making a very expensive trip financially lighter, and Paul Alex Jensen provided a singular insight into the ways of the Greenlandic hunters. And to all the people of Kullorsuaq, *kujanak,* thank-you, for sharing your lives with an inquisitive writer.

Several biologists helped me to understand arctic ecology. Randall Reeves, of McGill University, never tired of talking about narwhals, and introduced me to many other researchers. Ian Stirling, of the Canadian Wildlife Service, explained the fine points of polar bear behavior. Thomas Smith, of the Canadian Department of Fisheries and Oceans, critiqued the section on ringed seals. Ted Granger, now retired from the Canadian Department of Fisheries and Oceans, and Michael Bradstreet, the director of the Long Point Bird Observatory, outlined the interrelationship of predators and prey along the ice edge.

In Alaska, Fran Mauer, of the U.S. Fish and Wildlife Service, Arctic National Wildlife Refuge, has been a constant sounding board and a good friend over the years. In Wyoming, I wish to thank Bruce Smith, of the U.S. Fish and Wildlife Service, National Elk Refuge, for our many helpful discussions, Steve Cain, of Grand Teton National Park, for reviewing some of my ideas on the park hunt, and Steve and Marylynn French, of the Yellowstone Grizzly Foundation, for increasing my knowledge of bears. Jim Halfpenny, of the Institute of Alpine and Arctic Research, has been a fine instructor of ecology and tracking. Brad Stelfox, formerly Director of Research at the Teton Science School in Jackson Hole and now at the Alberta Environmental Center, increased my knowledge of hoofed mammals.

Without the assistance of the late Lloyd Zeman, of Safari Outfitters in Cody, Wyoming, and Rosohotrybolovsoyuz (The Russian Hunting and Fishing Union), much of the section on trophy hunting could not have been written—both opened doors and enabled me to travel to Siberia. Bob Kubick, Paul Asper, Don Cox, and Ali Üstay were especially cooperative in explaining their thoughts on trophy hunting, as was C. J. McElroy. They have my appreciation for fielding many sensitive and personal questions. Vance Corrigan was generous in sharing his knowledge of the history of sheep hunting. Bruce Keller, a former vice president of Safari Club International, was not only receptive to the idea of this book and introduced me to hunters in that organization, but was also candid where others have been mute.

Although their story doesn't appear in this book, as I once thought it would, the Hayden family, of the Sheenjek River in the Arctic National Wildlife Refuge, showed me the sort of subsistence life-style that predominates across the boreal zone of arctic America. For their hospitality, both in summer and winter, while caribou hunting, on the trap line, and through the deep cold of a January in the Brooks Range, I will always be indebted and have fond memories. The pilot of the Arctic National Wildlife Refuge, Roger Kaye, the bush pilot from Fort Yukon, Roger Dowding, and the flying schoolteacher, Roger Wegel, also helped me to see aspects of Alaskan bush life for which I'm grateful.

In Wyoming Bob Ciulla introduced me to a side of hunting that I would not have otherwise experienced, and Benj Kaghan and Michelle Sullivan gave me the opportunity to present my ideas on hunting and gathering through lectures at their respective organizations, the Teton Science School and the Snake River Institute. Dawn Iveson, of the Teton County Historical Society, reviewed some of the material on hunter-gatherers, and Ruth Valsing, my research assistant, and the librarians of the Teton County Library—Micki Cook, Nancy Effinger, Teri Krumdick, Chickie Allin, and Sidney Smith—helped with months of searches and photocopying. Clarrisa Smith taught me more about gathering plants for food and medicine. From California, Tom McIntyre always engaged me in lively and thought-provoking discussions; from Montana, Tony Acerrano pressed the finer points of the philosophical debate on environmental ethics; from Washington, Susan Ewing provided perceptive criticism; and from Oregon, Barry Lopez gave me some invaluable points on doing research in the arctic. Jay Cassell and Tom Paugh, my editors at *Sports Afield,* have given me great freedom in addressing subjects whose themes were later incorporated into this work. They have my abiding respect for being courageous. Without the many, many early days that I spent with Peter Vasilas and Steve Booth, on the water and in the woods, the questions of this book would never have unfolded.

I am also indebted to Wayne Pacelle, Heidi Prescott, and D. J. Schubert, at The Fund for Animals, for their warm reception, their openness, and their willingness to engage in good-natured debate over many issues about which we disagree. Tom Regan at North Carolina State University and J. Baird Callicott, at the University of Wisconsin–Steven's Point, took time out of busy schedules to review their ideas with me.

Nick Lapham, of The Wolf Fund, read and critiqued the entire manuscript, as did Kim Fadiman. I wish to say a special and very deep thank-you to Kim, who pushed my thinking into subtler and more precise channels, and who has been a great intellectual and outdoor companion over the years.

In brief or ongoing dialogues, each of the following people also helped clarify my thoughts: in Wyoming, Len Carlman, Tucker Smith, Gene Ball, Mardie Murie, and Irene, John, Hope, and Nicolia Rallis; in Colorado, Steve Andrews, Bill Liske, and David Chrislip; in Alaska, Kimberly Johnson and Donald Novak; in Bhutan, the Tulku of Gantey Gompa; and in Nepal, David Shlim, Robin Houston, Pam Poon, and Chukinima Rimpoche.

Without the kindness of Donald and Gladys Kent, and Scottie and Daphne Dejanikus, who made living and working in Grand Teton National Park possible, this book wouldn't have taken shape in the same way. George and Elpis Kerasote never faltered in their enthusiasm and love. Elizabeth Kaplan, my agent, and David Rosenthal, my editor, supported me through the long haul. Elizabeth helped name this book.

To all of them, many thanks, *namaste, tashi delay.*

And especially to Richard Nelson—friend and kindred spirit.

Finally, I must mention those teachers who have brought humility and compassion to my life. They are Michael Chandras, Kathie Stirling, Sheila Sandubrae-Davis, Trisha Scott, and Little Sparrow. In this role, the animals and country of the Yellowstone have been my most constant companions. Any misinterpretations of their teachings, and of the help so many have given, are my own.

CONTENTS

ABOUT THE NOTES

TEXT FOUND WITHIN QUOTATION MARKS OR IN BLOCKS THAT I DIDN'T personally record is cited at the end of the book. These notes are arranged by the page number on which the quoted material first appears, followed by the passage's opening words.

PROLOGUE

MY BACK FENCE HAPPENS TO BE THE SOUTHEAST BORDER OF GRAND
Teton National Park. The boundary curves around our settlement of
houses and corrals, surrounds the village, and continues to the big bend
of the Gros Ventre River, where it meets the Teton Forest. We are an
inholding—inheld within the park, which is bounded by national forests, stretching north to Yellowstone and beyond. Out my windows, I
can see its southern boundary.

Marked by long, cold winters, high mountains, and big mammals, it's
a natural order in which agriculture has been a recent arrival. Those who
lived here before me gathered roots and berries, and, of necessity, depended on the flesh and blood, as well as the hide and fur of animals to
survive. I have tried to respect their knowledge.

In my freezer there's the meat of an elk, the being whom I consider the
distillate of this country. As I defrost one of his steaks this February
morning, the thermometer reading minus twenty-two degrees, a crys-
talline stratigraphy appears throughout his meat. It's as fine and lovely
as the ice flowers on the kitchen windows. When thawed he smells
faintly of what he ate last summer: grass and sedge, wildflowers, stream
water. He smells of this place, which, when I eat him, becomes an inholding within me. I guess to another I must smell of him, and of this
place as well. We have joined and it's the hunting that creates the con-
junction.

Living in the Gros Ventre Range to the east, he was what those with
a taste for discriminations call a "wilderness elk." Just to the west, "park
elk" are more visible. Spending the summer within Grand Teton Na-

tional Park, these animals migrate each fall to their winter range on the
National Elk Refuge, down valley and outside the town of Jackson. Like
wilderness elk, park elk are hunted. In fact, if I wanted to apply for one
of the park's "reduction" licenses, I could shoot my winter's meat almost
from my back fence, drive a pickup to the carcass, and skin it out on my
porch. I've never tried this particular way of converting *Bromus,* the grass
on which these elk feed, into me. I'm certain that the conversion
wouldn't work, at least not in the way this place wishes it to. Instead I go
into the mountains, roaming valleys and ridges that I have learned on
foot. This sort of hunting, along with eating local wildflowers and putting in a garden by the side of the cabin, has been my way of tasting the
gravity that holds me to this place.

As the years pass, all three activities take more of my time and an
ever-increasing commitment to what most people consider "living off
the land," and which I have come to think of as "living with the land."
I have to admit, though, that it is the hunting and gathering, rather than
the planting, that still pull at me the most, but for different reasons than
when I was younger. When I first began to hunt, I assumed that the pull
was born from the long hikes in the high country, the stalks, and the
exciting closeness to large wild animals, an excitement that gardening
could never reproduce. But when I began to gather wild plants for food
and medicine, I realized that a far deeper compulsion than excitement
was moving me when I hunted. Whether it's gathering meat, or berries,
or roots, eating from the wild entails a different relationship with the
earth than does agriculture. As a farmer you reap what you have sown; as
a hunter-gatherer you reap what the land provides from her pagan solici-
tude. A different sort of work is traded, and another humility created,
when plants and animals you can't buy or raise build your flesh.

I say all this as someone who grew up hunting, who renounced it for
its violence, who became a vegetarian, and who eventually went back to
hunting . . . certain creatures, that is. Of many animals, I can ask no more
than a photograph. Logically, I can't explain why this is so—why it's all
right to eat goose or grouse, but not swan or sandhill crane. Some of my
neighbors who hunt and gather understand the paradox of these senti-
ments concerning the pacts we make with certain animals, and the labile
answers to the question the reluctant taker of life most often asks—How
can I, who walk erect and manipulate tools, find respectful ways to interact with those who don't?

Some of my nonhunting neighbors propose one answer for this question. Taking the lead of the civil rights and feminist movements, they say that killing animals—whether for food or sport—is an expression of a long-standing patriarchal culture's enslavement of a minority group that must be ended. Animals, like others who have been disenfranchised, must be given rights.

The hunters reply that hunting, along with procreation, is the oldest expression of our genetic nature, and that those who hunt, rather than being bloodthirsty killers, are actually more concerned with preserving healthy, sustainable wildlife populations than those animal rightists who would sever all connections between humans and animals. Hunting is a legacy that should be passed along.

At the local potlucks—the chili marked "meat" and "vegetarian"— I have drifted away from these heated discussions. In a climate of political correctness, its attendant backlash, and the general campaign to convince the nonaligned to vote for a particular agenda the idea of our first accord with animals has been lost. Up until very recent times, this accord entailed our utter dependence upon animals and our recognition of that dependence through ritual and veneration. Grazing animals fed people who in turn fed predators, scavengers, and the decomposing organisms of the soil. Human nutrients then fertilized the grass that fed more grazing animals. This fated circle was one of the holy cycles of the planet.

Diminished and unsung, it continues to enfold us: Whether we're buried or have our ashes scattered to the wind, we, like the rest of the animal and plant kingdoms, end up as fodder for those tiny funerary recyclers—the insects, bacteria, and fungi. Our companions in death, they deserve our respect as much as grizzly bears and dolphins.

For a long time—most of my adult life—I have thought about how we might relearn to venerate these cycles of eating and being eaten, of recombination and transformation, especially as we destroy the wild and rural landscapes where these cycles operate most visibly.

Having queried many who claim knowledge about the subject—environmentalists, animal welfarists, sport and subsistence hunters, and spiritual leaders from many faiths—I found that those who made the most sense to me were the Buddhist monks who live high in the mountains of Asia. Sitting at the feet of these lamas, I heard them say that killing animals for food wasn't necessarily immoral, but that it was acting with disharmony and one should give it up. With enough pain in the world, they said, a person should try to do the least harm possible.

Their words gave me a starting point. What exactly does *the least harm possible* mean? Does it mean becoming a fossil fuel vegetarian— those people who with a clear conscience buy vegetables at the supermarket, never realizing that America's factory farms, intensively subsidized by petroleum from the wellhead to the combine and on to the interstate highway system, inflict an enormous toll on wildlife as they grow and deliver such seemingly benign products as cereal, bread, beans, and milk? Or does doing the least harm possible mean becoming an organic farmer, growing everything one needs alongside one's house? Could it mean hunting and gathering the animals and plants of one's bioregion?

Thinking of these alternatives, and all their potential combinations, I have wandered widely, often visiting canyons where I found other quiet and instructive voices. There, in the red sandstone, the people who called the West home for thousands of years had etched petroglyphs of bighorn sheep and elk. These inscriptions were their way of honoring the creatures who had given them life, of apologizing for the deaths they had caused, and of asking these animals to give themselves again so that human life might continue. In one of these shrines I asked those who walked the land I now walk, and who hunted the animals I now hunt, if killing for necessary food could really be acting with disharmony, as my Buddhist friends had claimed.

In that quiet cul-de-sac their voices were laconic. I heard, "Drawing is necessary," and this puzzled me. Then I noticed that from the flank of one sheep came a mortal arrow and what appeared to be streaks of red. In my heart I knew what the voices meant, but I asked anyway: Was being mindful of death's red flower—revering it, lamenting it, celebrating it—the necessary state of mind that makes the taking of animal life different from murder or the mere cropping of a "resource"? Was it what makes hunting ethical? Could it be what allows people to express their natural as well as their cultural inheritance? But they made no reply to my questions, though they may have, and I missed it. The wind had begun to blow.

Walking from the canyon, I continued to listen to the wind, the moving grass, and the slickrock's mumbled voices seeming to say, "Attend. Attend." I understood their counsel as advising witness, which is what I did, travelling around the world and living with three "cultures" who continue to hunt: arctic dwellers who must hunt to survive; trophy hunters who have made hunting into a competitive sport; and those hunters who can't be conveniently placed in either group, but who hunt because they believe that the practice makes them a more mindful member of their bioregion.

After a while, I realized that I was searching for someone who might still be drawing.

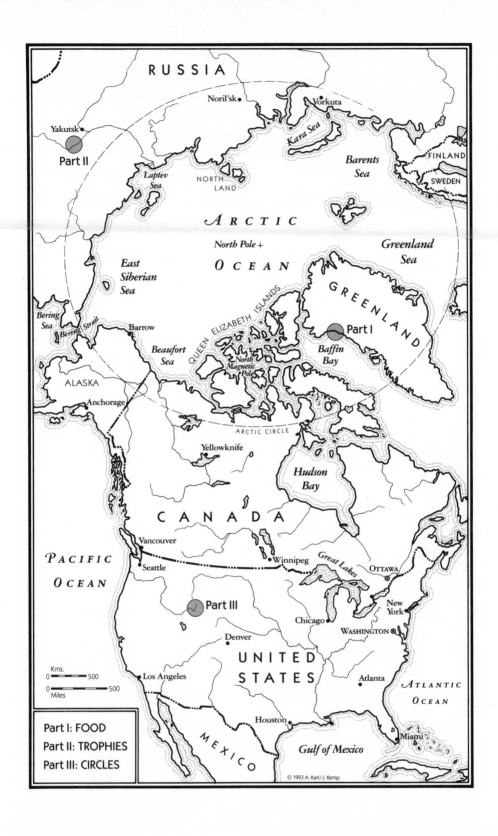

RUSSIA

Noril'sk•   •Vorkuta

                                    Kara Sea

Yakutsk•
                                                    FINLAND
Part II   *Laptev   NORTH   SWEDEN
                   Sea*   LAND*   *Barents
                                                     Sea*

              *East   A R C T I C
              Siberian
              Sea*   North Pole +   *Greenland
                                                                 Sea*
                                    O C E A N
*Bering   G R E E N L A N D
Sea*   Bering Strait• •Barrow   **Part I**
            *Beaufort   QUEEN ELIZABETH ISLANDS   *Baffin
ALASKA   Sea*   North   Bay*
                                Magnetic
•Anchorage   Pole

                                              ARCTIC CIRCLE

                 •Yellowknife
                                        *Hudson
                                         Bay*

         C A N A D A

PACIFIC   Vancouver•
OCEAN   •Winnipeg   *Great Lakes* OTTAWA ◉
               Seattle•
                                                              New
                                                              York•
                                        Part III
                                                    •Chicago
               •Denver   WASHINGTON ◉
                         U N I T E D
Kms.   S T A T E S
0 _____ 500
0 _____ 500   •Los Angeles   •Atlanta   *ATLANTIC
Miles   OCEAN*

                              •Houston
                   M   Miami•
                     E
                       X I C O   *Gulf of Mexico*

┌─────────────────────────┐   © 1993 A. Karl / J. Kemp
│ Part I: FOOD   │
│ Part II: TROPHIES   │
│ Part III: CIRCLES   │
└─────────────────────────┘

PART I

FOOD

I have killed you because I need your skin for my coat and your flesh for my food. I have nothing else to live on.
ABNAKI HUNTER

O N E

———➤➤◄◄———

"*U*UTTOQ . . . UUTTOQ . . . UUTTOQ.*"

Seals, seals, seals, said Nicolai Jensen, kissing the air with his five puckered fingers, indicating, across Kullorsuaq's frozen bay, how it would look when the basking seals of spring sunned themselves on the ice.

A stringer of white plastic jugs hung from the corner of his porch and he leaned above them like a captain at a taffrail, looking across the frozen strait to the mountainous island of Kiatagsuaq, over whose summit the weather often came. Sixty-four, and one of the village's three oldest hunters, he wore no hat or gloves this clear, calm morning, the March sun still low on the horizon. A thermometer read eighteen below zero. His short black hair was turning grey; his head was blocky; he was square and tough and weathered, dressed always in a blue anorak, baggy trousers, and the sealskin boots of Greenland called *kamit*.

Still leaning on the porch rail, he watched the icebergs glistening. A small wisp of cloud came off the inland ice as if it were carrying some portent, and he looked at his huskies, pegged in front of the porch among urine stains and frozen turds, seeming to gauge whether they were ready to travel. Three unchained husky pups ran between the sleeping dogs and down the short hill to the shoreline where a wave of ice hung suspended as it had frozen last fall. They gamboled back up the smoothly packed ramp of snow, under the kayak rack where two green boats rested upside down and the skeleton of a third lay cockpit to the sky. Inside the unfinished frame, appearing to be asleep, were two dead husky pups waiting to be skinned for their fur, often used for the linings of *kamit*.

"Hee-hee-hee," laughed Nicolai, tripping his fingers through the air and miming the puppies scampering. Then he looked at the cloud again, his eyes scanning a nunatak around which two tongues of ice calved into the frozen ocean. For hundreds of miles along this northwestern coast of Greenland the ice cap meets the sea, leaving no habitat for caribou, musk-ox, or people. Kullorsuaq's thirty-odd dwellings stand in a south-facing cove on a small island, six miles from the mainland.

"*Sila ajunngilaq!*" exclaimed Nicolai, turning away from the cloud. Good weather. Since he had a pacemaker installed four years ago he no longer hunted. Still, each morning he watched the weather.

"*Kaffi?*" he asked.

When I nodded he led me through the mudroom, past the lined-up *kamit* and running shoes of his children and grandchildren, and into the kitchen where a halibut defrosted in a basin by the foot of a kerosene stove.

The kitchen was about ten feet long by eight feet wide and contained little: a counter where food was prepared; a tub for melting ice into drinking water; a half-dozen duffels and cardboard boxes piled on the far wall. I sat on a stool by the entry while Qitora, Nicolai's wife, and Sara, his daughter, both in their nightclothes, dressed Sara's two children and picked up the sleeping quilts from the living room floor, a common arrangement in the small shacks of the village where three generations often shared one roof.

Being the good host, Nicolai swept a hand to the vacuum bottle on the counter. After I poured myself a mugful of coffee and returned to my stool, he sat on a chair by my side and awaited the clearing of the living room, where he wanted to show me some of his books. Lighting a cigarette, he inhaled briefly, only into his mouth, before blowing out tiny puffs of smoke. It was his way of obeying doctor's orders—no more smoking and no running alongside his dogs. When I asked him if the Danish doctors would allow him to fish he shook his head and laid a hand to his chest. "Tick, tick, tick, tick," he said, like a metronome. Then he charaded pulling a halibut to the surface on a long line. "Tickticktick-tickticktick!" He threw his hands in the air, letting his head fall back and his tongue hang out of his mouth. "No more fishing!" He laughed.

Qitora, her face impassive, her long black hair without a trace of white, motioned us into the living room. Despite her typical Inuit features, the probability was high that, like virtually all the villagers, she had some European ancestry, a result of visits by European whalers and missionaries since the 1600s. In fact, almost none of Greenland's inhabitants can claim unmixed, aboriginal blood and most have dropped their ancient names—Miteq, Nulialik, Orulo—for Scandinavian ones, Norway and Denmark having had a presence in the country extending from the late 900s (when Eric the Red founded the first colony) until 1979 when Denmark granted home rule. Indeed, economic, governmental, and social bonds between Greenland and Denmark are still inseparably interwoven and, in all probability, will remain so for many years to come. Universally, Greenlanders also prefer to be called no more than that, "Greenlanders," rather than Eskimos, a word of Algonquian origin meaning "eaters of raw flesh," which has fallen into disfavor, or Inuit, the term used by natives of the eastern Canadian Arctic, meaning "people."

The living room, as the kitchen, was painted a faded yellow. In one corner stood another kerosene stove and next to it were a VCR and a TV, flanked by two large windows overlooking the frozen bay. A dozen photographs decorated the far wall above the sofa: kayakers paddling toward icebergs; narwhals, shiny as black marble, surfacing in a lead; a mother, father, and young boy, leery of the camera, sitting before a sod hut. (It was Nicolai himself in the sepia photo, ten years old in the mid-1930s.) Then, back in the present again, the color photos showed men in white anoraks and women in embroidered *kamit* standing on the steps of a church for a wedding; they gathered in a small schoolroom for a graduation; they sat on the hill above the village, eating raw seal liver at the annual summer feast. On the opposite side of the room from the VCR and TV, arranged vertically in two pairs of oval frames, were some Audubon-like paintings of tropical birds. Between them hung the giant head of a polar bear surmounted by a dime-store print of Jesus leading a flock of sheep from the clouds.

Sitting up and yawning on the sofa, Nicolai's second oldest son, Lars, wiped the sleep from his eyes. A head taller than his father, he had the same jet-black hair and eyes but was more slightly built. Like Nicolai, the thirty-two-year-old Lars was also known as a great bear hunter, a renowned kayaker, and an expert with the harpoon. He had been longline fishing in the south for money and had been home only a few days. Like his father, he too had but three teeth in his mouth, which gave him a comical grin. He jumped up, tackled me around the waist, gave me a twirl, and deposited me on the sofa next to his shy and pretty girlfriend, Jensigne.

"*Qanorippit?*" I said to both of them. How are you?

"*Qaaa,*" Lars replied, correcting my pronunciation.

"*Qaaa.*"

"*Naamik,*" he said. No.

"*Qaaa,*" coached Jensigne, pushing back her long black hair.

"*Qaaa,*" I said.

She shook her head.

Nicolai, from his place on the floor by the end of the sofa, leaned over its arm and put his face close to mine. He had been eating the sugar cookies that Qitora had placed on the coffee table, an offering to guests that had recently replaced seal meat, and the reason, along with poor dental hygiene, that many in the village had lost their teeth. Now, when Nicolai opened his mouth trying to show me how to place my tongue, all I could see was masticated cookie between his single upper and two lower canines.

"*Qaaa,*" he bayed.

"*Qaaa,*" I repeated and everyone burst into laughter. In unison, including Sara's children, they shouted "*Qaaaaaaaaa,*" miming my accent.

Sara took over from across the room. "*Qaaa,*" she repeated softly, rounding her mouth. Lean, with large strong hands, she preferred living with her parents rather than with the father of her children. When her brothers were gone, it was she who laid the seals on the meat rack outside.

Screwing up my mouth, I duplicated her expression. "*Qaaa.*"

"*Naamik!*" everyone shouted. No!

Sucking my tongue into the back of my throat, I made a strangled croak that sounded like nothing they had been saying—"*Qqqquu-uaaahh!*"

"*Aap! Aap! Aap!*" Yes!

Nicolai poured me another cup of coffee and took out what he had promised to show me—his books, photographs, and harpoon heads. I sat on the floor by his side, and slowly so as not to miss anything he leafed through a volume about narwhals, written in Danish and illustrated with pen-and-ink drawings. He laughed at the depictions of the whale from the 1500s and 1600s that reinforced the legend of the unicorn, and gave a nod of approval to the most recent drawings, showing the portly cetacean, fifteen feet long with an additional eight feet of tusk coming from the left side of its snout, its mouth turned upwards in a perpetual grin. A few pages later he paused at his own portrait. Perhaps West Greenland's most famous living hunter, he had been rightfully included in this book on narwhals. "Nicolai Jensen," he said, touching his chest as if I might have missed the striking resemblance or was unable to read his name beneath the drawing. At a page showing a narwhal being born he laid the book in his lap. Pursing his lips, he imitated the newborn's high-pitched cries and demonstrated, by ducking and raising his head, how the mother narwhal pushed her calf to the surface for its first breaths. Steepling his hands and pumping his palms together rhythmically, he then mimed how baby narwhals were made: the adult whales standing on their tails and facing each other as they mated. In July, he said, the young were born. Within minutes, they breached twice on one side of their mother, dove under her, and breached twice on the other. His right hand, the newborn, swam under his left. Pointing to his eyes, he said, "I have seen it all."

On other occasions he had told me how he had kayaked up and down the fjords of this coast and sledded many times across its most salient feature, the enormous, uninhabited bight, two hundred miles wide, where the ice cap fell to the ocean between coastal mountains. Euro-Americans call it Melville Bay. The Greenlanders have named it Qimus-seriarsuaq, "the big place for dog sledding." He had once even been capsized by a narwhal and survived. But he never mentioned these great journeys or dangerous moments while hunting unless I pressed him. Now, without prompting, he swept his right hand across the room, creating the surface of the sea. His left hand breached through the air. As his knuckles escaped the water, Nicolai's right hand cast an imaginary harpoon at them—the whale's vertebrae. Not forward or back, he said, pointing to his fingers and then to his wrist, but right there, at the knuckles—the kidneys. He touched his own spine for emphasis. If the harpoon struck there, when the narwhal dove, the *avataq,* the float, and the *niutaq,* the drag, would be at the correct angle to tire him quickly.

Motioning to the kayak rack outside, Nicolai asked Lars to bring in some harpoons. Lars returned with two. Hafted from wood, they had different heads and foreshafts—one made from bronze, the others from ivory. Each trailed sixty feet of running line. About the second, Nicolai said one word, *"Usuk."* In case I had forgotten my Greenlandic vocabulary, he pointed to his crotch. The foreshaft was made from the penile bone of a walrus. Taking a moment to refresh my memory, he pointed to Qitora and said, *"Utsuut!"* vagina. He wiggled his fingers between his legs and laughed. Then he pointed to Lars. Shaking his head sadly, he measured a half inch between his thumb and forefinger. "Hee-hee-hee," he chortled and added, "He still doesn't have any children."

"Me . . ." He struck himself on the chest and waved a hand around the room, taking in his family. "Me . . ." He spread his hands about a foot apart then clasped them around an imaginary cylinder thick as a salami. He nodded happily while his wife, daughter, and grandchildren broke into uproarious laughter.

Lars twirled a finger by his temple and said, "He has a bad mind."

"And you?" asked Nicolai.

I knew that being serious wasn't the way to get on with him. I put one hand at my crotch and the other below my knee. Shrieking, he threw his hands in the air and choked with laughter. He had to take several sips of tea before we could return to the subject of harpoons.

Lars held up a piece of wood that looked like a narrow scapula. It was drilled with holes that fit pegs on the shafts of the weapons. When he fitted the device to one of the shafts, I saw in a flash that it was an atlatl, a throwing board. He jumped up and began to make stealthy paddling motions. Suddenly his eyes opened wide and he peered into the distance. He put a finger to his lips, laid down the imaginary paddle, and picked up the atlatl-mounted harpoon in his right hand. Undulating his left arm through the air, he said sharply, *"Qernertaq!"* Narwhal! Literally, the word means "greyish-black." Sticking his tongue from his mouth, he made a loud, moist, exhaling noise—the spout of the surfacing whale. His arm continued to undulate; his eyes fixed on it with intense concentration; he reared back with the harpoon and came forward. "Phomp!" he cried, indicating a strike. His left arm dove; his eyes stayed fastened to the spot where the whale had sounded. When it surfaced he raised a rifle and shot. Then he came back from where he had been—hunting on the ice edge. He smiled and said *"Qernertaq"* the way a fundamentalist Christian would say, "A-men."

Proudly, Nicolai said, "I taught him how to make harpoons and kayaks. His brother Nathaniel, too."

From beneath the VCR he pulled a blue toolbox. Placing it between his legs, he opened it and found a harpoon head, shaped like the others he had shown me but made from wood, its point broken off long ago. He said that it dated from the 1600s. He then showed me a newer head, made from bronze, half-finished, and the bar out of which he had fashioned it. A walrus tusk also lay at the bottom of the box along with his tools—chisels, knives, and small saws. From a cotton bag he poured a score of walrus teeth, each an inch long and a quarter inch in diameter, blunt at both ends, smooth and cool in the hand. He pointed to the necklace around Sara's neck so I knew what they were for.

In the meantime Lars had fetched a cardboard suitcase from the kitchen. Sitting opposite his father and me, he took a dozen orange-colored snapshot envelopes from it. One by one he handed me photos. There was Lars in his kayak, the horizon line between sea and sky indistinguishable, his boat seeming to float off the edge of the world. It was early spring, the weather stormy, the ice just beginning to open. Then he was standing on the ice edge, alongside a stream of blood trailing from the blue lead. The blood ended in the mounded shape of a narwhal, around which stood a half-dozen other hunters holding long knives and grinning. In the next photo Lars hoisted the tusk and glistening, decapitated head of the whale into the air. But it wasn't the same animal. In the background the light had changed. The sky was full of bright golden clouds. It was the long light of summer and he had caught another narwhal. Months went by—three more envelopes: Lars in a speedboat, the wake white and straight across the grey water of Melville Bay . . . a soccer match on a brown dry field . . . Jensigne and he, mugging under party streamers. Then a young boy offered a tiny seal to the camera. Lit by the low sun of September, his face was ruddy, as was the bloody little seal. Two envelopes later, Lars pointed to humanlike tracks on the grey pack ice. It was *nanoq,* the polar bear, hunting in the dim light of winter. Noses down, tails up, the huskies trotted along his spoor. Faster they went. They began to bark. There he stood! Sniffing the air, the bear turned and disappeared among the blocks of ice. Lars pulled out his knife and cut five of the eleven dogs loose from their traces. They bolted after the bear, who wheeled and swiped at them. Bounding up a hummock, the bear turned again. The dogs bit his legs, and the bear whirled round and round. Lars stopped pawing the air. Calmly, he raised an imaginary rifle. Thirty feet from the polar bear, he shot him in the neck. The next photo showed a couple of bears lying on their backs in the midst of crimson snow, as Lars and another hunter, wearing fluffy polar-bear trousers and bulky caribou parkas, eviscerated them. In the last envelope summer had returned. Seals perched on floes, looking appealingly at the camera before being shot, and there was Nicolai, laying out thick pieces of narwhal to dry on the shoreline rocks of an island. In the last photo Nicolai sat by the water, holding a child on his knee while offering her a tender piece of raw meat. As I handed the photos back to Lars, he said, "It's too bad I'm going to Savissivik." This was the village on the other side of Melville Bay where his girlfriend's family lived. "If I were staying here, we'd go hunting."

"We'd go right now," said Nicolai emphatically, "if my heart were okay. It's a shame. A shame! These days we have so many lazy hunters in the village that you'll see almost nothing."

Sara, who had been doing more hunting than either, made no offers.

For knud rasmussen, the great explorer of arctic america, Kullorsuaq was a staging area. As he said, "When I was a child I used often to hear an old Greenlandic woman tell how, far away North, at the end of the world, there lived a people who dressed in bearskins and ate raw flesh. . . . [T]he thought of them was always with me, and the first decision I came to as a man was that I would go to look for them."

The son of a Danish missionary and a woman with native blood, Rasmussen grew up in southern Greenland, playing with the children of hunters, driving a sled, and speaking the circumpolar language of the Inuit. At fourteen he left Greenland for Denmark and graduated from Copenhagen University. He had the dreamy eyes of a poet and the lean, high-cheeked features of a Norse hero. Which he was.

At the beginning of the twentieth century, he sailed north, building a hunting and mail hut on one of the islands near the present site of Kullorsuaq. The archipelago became the jumping-off point for his eventual sled crossing of Melville Bay, the first in anyone's memory—Dane or Inuit. On its far side he found the mythical Polar Inuit, visited previously only by British whalers and the American, Admiral Robert Peary, during his exploration of Greenland's north coast and quest for the pole. Unlike these first visitors to the world's most northern inhabitants who came by ship, Rasmussen arrived by sled and was greeted as an equal; nor did he think of the Polar Inuit only as suppliers of furs in exchange for manufactured goods and as workhorses to assist his geographical ambitions. Although he built a trading post, which he called Thule, and began to map a significant portion of America's northern coastline, he was an ethnographer at heart, recording the legends, technology, and mores of almost all the arctic peoples from Greenland to the Pacific. Having been born into the idiom, he was able to immerse himself completely in the life of the Inuit—a life that was changing rapidly and whose isolation would vanish completely after World War II.

During the conflict the United States built an airbase at Thule and enlarged it during the cold war that followed. Eventually radar stations were erected across arctic Canada and Alaska, the building of this Distant Early Warning System, the DEW Line, exposing nearby Inuit communities to modern technology more quickly and more profoundly than had whaling or the fur trade. Within two decades the bush plane and snowmobile supplanted the dogsled, and the powerboat the kayak; everywhere the rifle continued to replace the harpoon.

Greenlanders, however, didn't mechanize to the same extent as their Canadian and American relatives. A xenophobic Danish colonial government kept most of the country isolated from foreign influences, and topography precluded the use of machines—bush planes couldn't land on the unstable sea ice and rocky coastlines, and snowmobiles were seen as a liability on long journeys; a dog team could be fed on seals. It also became apparent that powerboats and rifles weren't the best tools for hunting narwhals, one of the more important animals in the Inuit's diet. Narwhals are particularly sensitive to the noise of outboards and sink quickly when shot. In northern Greenland, especially during the winter and spring, when narwhals, polar bears, and seals are pursued on a combination of sea ice and open water, the old hunting tools—kayak, harpoon, and dogsled—remained.

One of the most isolated communities of the region is Kullorsuaq, pronounced *Ku-slah'-swock.* Thirty hunters and their families live on the island, whose name means "the big thumb"—each steep headland and deep cove of the island climbing to a central, eighteen-hundred-foot-tall rock obelisk that, from the sea, resembles a giant digit stuck into sky. No plane connects the Kullorsuaqians to Thule, two hundred miles to the north, and its weekly military flight to the United States. If the people of Kullorsuaq want to visit their relations across Melville Bay, they must go by dogsled, as in Rasmussen's day, or by powerboat during the brief summer.

Travel in other directions is also limited. To the east of the village lies the ice cap, second in extent only to the one covering Antarctica, and devoid of people except for a few scientific-research stations. To the west is Baffin Bay, four hundred miles wide, frozen eight months of the year, on the far side of which are the islands of arctic Canada. To the south it's three days journey by helicopter and small plane, a thousand miles, to Greenland's capital and commercial center, Nuuk. Until 1989 communication between the village and the outside world proceeded at the leisurely pace of the nineteenth century—by ship and by dogsled. In that year helicopter service began and a satellite telephone was installed.

As far as I could discover, few nonnatives had spent any time on the island since Knud Rasmussen built his little green hunting shack a few kilometers up the coast from where Nicolai Jensen now has his, and went out on journeys much like this one, which he described in *Across Arctic America.*

With his friend Inugtuk, Rasmussen had been standing above a seal's breathing hole for four hours while his thermometer registered minus fifty-eight degrees Fahrenheit. Very early, before light, the two men had drunk a jug of boiling seal's blood filled with blubber and had set out across the ice with the dogs whose job it was to scent where seals had kept open small holes to breathe.

Inugtuk had scraped away the new snow from one such hole and chipped out the fresh ice that had accumulated since the seal's last visit. Then he took a long, curved "feeler" made of horn, and thrust it in the hole to ascertain the exact position of its bore and thus the position of the seal's body as it would come up to breathe. This would determine the direction of his harpoon thrust. Two more steps were necessary before beginning the long wait. The snow was repacked over the ice to dampen any sounds from the surface and a feather of swan's down was suspended from the forked sinews of a caribou's foot in the top of the hole, the idea being that as soon as a seal would come up to breathe, the feather would quiver and the hunter could strike.

Because of the low temperature and the wind, Rasmussen's wait seemed interminable. However, it wasn't as long a vigil as it might have been. "There are men who have stood for twelve hours on end," the explorer observed, "in the hope of bringing back food for the hungry ones at home."

At last, another of the hunters in their party struck a seal and they hurried over to share in the communal meal of liver and blubber, eaten kneeling around the dead animal. "For myself," said Rasmussen, "I always felt there was something touching and solemn about this ceremonial eating of the first meat on which men's lives depend."

Thirty years later, in the same region of the Northwest Territories, another arctic traveller, the Frenchman Gontran de Poncins, saw the rite repeated and recounted it in greater detail in his autobiographical tale, *Kabloona*.

> I can describe the scene, but how can I convey its solemnity? There was a hush as Tutannuak picked up his snowknife, made a small incision in the abdomen of the seal, put in his hand, and drew out the liver, all red and smoking. The five hunters knelt in silence as he proceeded. He put the liver down on the seal and cut it into six slices, one for each, and he set a slice on the snow at his place and before each of the men who knelt, still as in prayer, in that circle. Next he cut and laid beside the liver six chunks of blubber. Six men, members of the hungriest and most voracious race on earth, were motionless in the presence of the greatest delicacies known to the palate of their race. . . . Behind the men sat the dogs, quivering with greed, their eyes on the seal, but no less still and motionless than their masters. Here, before me, six men and their dogs sat worshipping the sea from which they drew their sustenance, like sun-worshippers adoring the source of light and life.

The deity who represented the sea, and whom they respected, was addressed by various names across the arctic—Sassuma Arnaa, Sedna, Takanaluk Arnaluk—but her role was everywhere the same. In human shape, she had been a young girl who had refused all offers of marriage. At last she was seduced by a seabird, a fulmar, disguised as a handsome young man. After living with him for a while, she was rescued by her father. The fulmar wasn't happy at losing his bride and pursued them, raising a terrible storm, at which point the father acted horribly. Terrified that his boat would sink, he threw his daughter overboard to lighten it. She clung to the gunwale, pleading to be taken on, while he chopped off her fingers, first the tips, then the next joints, and finally her palms and wrists, all of which turned into seals, walruses, and whales as they sank into the sea. The girl sank to the bottom as well, where she now lives, ruling over all the marine creatures who feed the people of the arctic.

If hunters are well meaning and treat animals with respect, taking only what they need and paying homage to the sacrifice their prey has made, the mistress of the sea continues to send her creatures to them. If, on the other hand, people ignore the taboos associated with the killing, cleaning, storing, and consuming of animals—for example, never mixing the meat of land and sea animals—the mistress of the sea will hold her animals close to her blubber lamp, the site of their reincarnation, causing people to starve until they mend their ways or an *angakkoq,* a shaman, travels down to her and makes appeasements. Around the world, varying with individual hunting cultures, such restrictive practices have formed the accord that people have made with the beings who sustain them.

A person used to buying food at the grocery may find such taboos incomprehensible. Even Rasmussen, raised in Greenland and an old hand at self-supported sled journeys on which some of his companions had died, could not truly understand the power of taboo until he paid a visit to his friend Aua's hunting camp on the Melville Peninsula north of Hudson Bay. He had frequently questioned Aua about what seemed to him "highly complicated and meaningless observances," only to have his inquiries deemed unreasonable by his host.

On this night, however, Aua rose to his feet and led Rasmussen outside his hut. Pointing to the storm-driven clouds, the hunter said, " 'Look . . . snow and storm; ill weather for hunting. And yet we must hunt for our daily food; *why?* Why must there be storms to hinder us when we are seeking meat for ourselves and those we love?' "

Aua then led Rasmussen around the settlement, showing him several more instances of hardship and suffering: weary hunters who had been unsuccessful; children shivering without food; and a woman dying of lung disease. Why should it be so, he asked Rasmussen, and the explorer had no answer.

> "You see," observed Aua, "even you cannot answer when we ask you why life is as it is. And so it must be. Our customs all come from life and are directed towards life; we cannot explain, we do not believe in this or that; but the answer lies in what I have just shown you.
>
> "*We fear!*
>
> "We fear the elements with which we have to fight in their fury to wrest out food from land and sea.
>
> "We fear cold and famine in our snow huts.
>
> "We fear the sickness that is daily to be seen amongst us. Not death, but the suffering.
>
> "We fear the souls of the dead, of human and animal alike.

"We fear the spirits of earth and air.

"And therefore our fathers, taught by their fathers before them, guarded themselves about with these old rules and customs, which are built upon the experience and knowledge of generations. We know not how or why, but we obey them that we may be suffered to live in peace. And for all our angakoqs and their knowledge of hidden things, we yet know so little that we fear everything else. We fear the things we see about us, and the things we know from the stories and myths of our forefathers. Therefore we hold by our customs and observe all the rules of tabu."

Aua's plaint was not unique. Across the arctic, Rasmussen heard versions of this story, linking the Inuit's conciliatory hunting, butchering, and eating practices to self-interest. Ivaluardjuk, another of Rasmussen's companions, summarized it best. "The greatest peril of life," he said, "lies in the fact that human food consists entirely of souls. All the creatures that we have to kill and eat, all those that we have to strike down and destroy to make clothes for ourselves, have souls, like we have, souls that do not perish with the body, and which must therefore be propitiated lest they should revenge themselves on us for taking away their bodies."

Sitting at my kitchen table, eating sugar cookies and bent over a map of the coast, Nicolai Jensen moved his index finger from island to island. "This is where the ice edge is in March," he said. "And here it is in April and May. In June it will be here." He touched the western tip of Kullorsuaq.

"My favorite time is after Easter, when we go to Qârusulik and there are seals everywhere. *Puissi . . . puissi . . . puissi.*" Lightly, Nicolai touched his finger around the island, a three-hour sled journey from the village, while using the Greenlandic word for a seal swimming in a lead—*puissi.* Just a few days before he had called them *uuttoq,* the word defining a seal sunning itself on the ice. Obviously, he had jumped ahead a month, to a time of more open water.

"Many, many seals in May." Taking another sugar cookie, he added, "They are really my favorite food, and not because they're healthier. When I'm travelling with people from south Greenland I notice that they get colder than I do because they eat European food and I eat seal. Seal meat is what I grew up on. I couldn't live without it."

"Do you do anything special then—when you kill a seal—to thank it? A ceremony perhaps."

"A ceremony?"

"Or some gesture. For instance, I met a hunter in Upernavik who said that when he skinned a seal, he never took its tail, because if he did it would be his last. Maybe he thought the soul of the seal still needed its tail to swim, but he wouldn't say. And this man, he remembered a hunter even older than himself who, when he killed a seal, would throw one of its whiskers back into the sea. But he had no idea why he did it. I have read, too, that some of the Inuit used to give a seal a drink of fresh water, as a way of thanks to it and the sea mother."

"Oh, the sea mother . . ." Authoritatively, Nicolai sat back in his chair. "Of course we all know about her. But she is just something that was made up a long time ago. We teach about her in school; the children learn about her. But she is a myth. I won't speak about what others do. I myself use only one tradition, given to me by my father, and I will tell you about it. At midnight on the winter solstice the earth shakes a little bit, so little that you can hardly feel it. At exactly this hour I go down to the shore and make a hole through the ice. With my lantern I look at the kelp and see which way the current is pushing it. If it is streaming to the east it means it will be a winter of good weather, not so many storms, and easy seal hunting. But if the kelp is streaming to the west, the winter will be stormy with few days to hunt, and we'll have hungry times. This tradition has no religion attached to it. It's only good sense."

"Have you ever seen someone throw back the bones of a *puissi* from the ice edge and say, 'Bring us more seals'?"

"I have heard of such things being done," said Nicolai, "but really no one believes in them anymore. They are done perhaps in fun. In the seventeen hundreds Christianity came to Greenland and put a stop to all that."

WHEN HANS EGEDE, THE NORWEGIAN-LUTHERAN MISSIONARY, SET foot on the southwestern coast of Greenland in 1721, wanting to Christianize the natives while also searching for the lost Norse settlers who hadn't been heard from since the 1400s, he was dressed in black and looked imposing. Seeing him deferred to by the seamen (he was also head of the trading mission sent out by King Frederick IV), the Inuit took him for an *angakkoq,* a shaman, and addressed him by that name. Egede, however, bent on reaching Greenland for over a decade and now finally standing upon its shore, didn't hear *angakkoq,* shaman; he heard *angisooq,* a word his inadequate printed glossary defined as "great." When they asked him if his God, about whom he so lovingly spoke, was also an *angakkoq,* he said most certainly, God was indeed great. This was a bit of an error.

Not that it didn't serve Egede's ultimate purpose. For five thousand years the Inuit had flourished in the earth's harshest environment by being technologically adaptable and spiritually circumspect. The kayak, the dogsled, the toggled harpoon, and the igloo enabled them to travel, hunt, and live with a great deal of comfort. But given the ever-present uncertainties of weather and the migrations of animals, they also lived in fear—not so much of death, as Rasmussen's friend, Aua, had explained, but of suffering. The *angakkoq*—reading the clouds, travelling to the spirit world, overseeing the keeping of taboos—became the mediator between the reality of daily existence and all those phenomena that couldn't be readily understood and caused them to suffer. He was the community's explainer of the unknown; he was its insurance policy.

Even though Egede eventually realized his error, he made no attempt to dissuade the Inuit from their notion that he and the God of the Danish-Norwegian church were superior forms of the many roles the traditional *angakkoq* played—doctor, teacher, spiritual advisor, and mediator. When a sick Greenlander asked him to blow on his stomach where it hurt, as any good *angakkoq* would do, Egede complied, creating goodwill. However, unlike the traditional *angakkoqs,* Egede also had at his disposal iron, wood, knives, guns, and tools. Here was an *angakkoq* of *angakkoqs,* one twice feared because he didn't stint on the use of force to bring home his teachings.

Ridiculing the Greenlanders' beliefs, he insisted they remove their amulets, which had protected them from evil for centuries. After all, if one had faith in the Lord—a Lord who promised eternal life—why did one need charms? Those who voluntarily took off their bones and feathers, and saw that no harm befell them, became convinced of Egede's power. Those who continued to wear them in secret risked his temper. About one such individual, the missionary said, "I had to give him a few blows across the back (for nothing can make them see reason except beating and punishment, which I have to practise occasionally, having found that this worked)." If Egede were still disobeyed, he threatened the Inuit's lives. Such tactics were eventually adopted by his son Niels who, finding some of his parishioners unswayed by exhortation, took recourse to what he called his "usual method": a sound flogging and turning the offender out of the house.

It was an uphill battle. The missionaries had little comprehension of the flexible schedule a hunting economy demanded. Instead of seeing the Inuit as good providers for their families, setting out to sea to hunt whenever necessary, Egede called them "slothful and brutish" and rooted in a "wandering and unstable way of life." On the other hand, the Inuit couldn't understand some of Christianity's anomalies, not the least of which was Jesus' being killed by the very people he was sent to save. Why had the supreme *angakkoq* allowed his one and only, great and compassionate *angakkoq* son to be slain? Or how could they, to whom Egede referred as "God's children," be refused baptism because they had two wives? When the missionary told them that they would of course be baptized if they got rid of one wife, the hunters were incredulous. The cast-off woman would starve without a hunter to provide for her, they told Egede. When he replied that this, too, was an example of "God's will," the hunters went away dumbfounded. Could this be a kind God?

Frequently, ill feeling arose between the Inuit and missionaries over daily routines. What is this Sunday of yours, the Inuit wanted to know, on which hunting must be prohibited? If during the previous week there had been stormy weather, keeping them shorebound, and they now had no food, how could they *not* go hunting? On the other hand, if they took meat from the cache of a neighbor and were thrashed for the deed, they couldn't understand why they were being punished. The word *stealing,* when applied to food, had no meaning for them—when the hunter from whom they had taken some seal meat had none, he would of course visit the meat cache of anyone who did. Such sharing had kept Inuit alive for centuries. Far better to share, or hunt on Sunday, than to pray for daily bread. On this point the head of the infant Greenlandic church finally capitulated, changing the Lord's Prayer to read, "Give us this day the seal meat we need."

Over the next two centuries the missionaries who followed Egede succeeded in Christianizing the entire country. They didn't prevail because their prayers were perceived as more effective than the spells of the *angakkoq*'s in preventing blizzards and starvation. Nor did they win over the Inuit because their Christian heaven was seen as more appealing than the various hereafters the Inuit themselves had conjured: a place under the sea, full of sunshine and many animals to hunt; or an eternal soccer game in the sky where souls, transformed into northern lights, kicked a ball made from walrus skin stuffed with feathers.

Rather it was the marvelous tools the missionaries provided on this earth—firearms, steel knives, long-lasting needles—that persuaded the Inuit to convert to Christianity, or *seem* to convert. A practical people, they rolled their eyes, murmured psalms, nodded their heads, and exchanged their amulets for the Bible. The goods they received in the bargain—the increased leverage they now had on the natural world—made *Sila,* the great weather, less intimidating and the times of starvation less frequent. They gained some control over the randomness of nature, and, in the process, generation by generation, youngster by youngster, inevitably lost their belief that every rock . . . every cloud . . . every seal had its own particular soul, its *inua,* whose power had to be respected and with some small but heartfelt gesture propitiated.

"Nobody here believes that rivers, mountains, and the sea have a spirit," said Nicolai Jensen, taking one last sugar cookie.

"As for the bearskin in my house, it has no particular meaning. This one was hunted by my eldest son and given to his mother as a gift."

F O U R

————>><<————

IN APRIL WE WENT BEAR HUNTING. AS THE MOON CAME INTO FULL-
ness, in the first stable weather after several weeks of storm, we left,
sledding northwest into the icebergs, the pinnacle in the center of the
island becoming visible as we rounded the headland under which the
village was built. The wind was on our right shoulders, coming off
the ice cap, and we crossed foot-high waves of hard snow, running west.
Ahead of us, under the great blue bell of the sky, the features of the
coastline—islands, glaciers, and mountains—sprawled north to meet
the frozen line of the sea. Over that place, Thule land, a faint brown
smudge hung. It was arctic haze, crossing the pole from coal-fired electricity plants in Siberia.

Lars, busy repairing his sled and outfitting his girlfriend with travelling clothes for their journey to Savissivik, had been unable to go. I went
with my next-door neighbor, Peter Aronsen, a short, dark, and quiet
man who was one of the village's most accomplished hunters, even
though he had had the ill luck to lose his father at the age of eight.
Self-taught, he had taken over twenty polar bears and many narwhals,
one a rare two-toothed creature, whose cleaned skull and twin tusks now
stood in the corner of his small shack. He hoped to sell the ivory for a
large sum, he said, which would be particularly welcome, since his wife
didn't work and they were expecting their second child, and he also
supported his mother and his sixteen-year-old brother, Abi.

Unfortunately, Peter's lot continued to be harder than most. An in-
fected arm, caused by a prick from a seal flipper, had laid him low for
weeks, and his original dog team, all big strong animals from the same

family, had died in a distemper epidemic. The team he had now put together, by barter and the kindness of friends, was made up of small castaways who couldn't learn to work together. In a land where a man's dogs are his pride, this continued to be a source of humiliation for him. In fact, one day as I had stood on Nicolai's porch, watching Peter set out across the bay, the older hunter had charaded the mincing steps of Peter's small animals while disdainfully shaking his head and making a "tsk-tsk-tsk" noise of disapproval with his tongue. Then, pointing to the brutes staked out in his yard, he swelled his chest and made a muscle. "These are dogs," he said.

If anything, such setbacks made Peter work all the harder. He had discovered one of the most productive fishing spots around the island, bringing back sled loads of large halibut, and he often went exploring far off the coast in stormy weather when his neighbors were drinking coffee by their stoves. Which is what we were now planning to do, given the added incentive of Abi's turning sixteen while we would be on the ice. Taking on the role of the father he never had, Peter wanted to help his shy younger brother, a downy moustache just appearing on his upper lip, find his first polar bear. And the chances of this happening were good, he told me.

He mentioned this while running his fingers over a map of Melville Bay spread on my kitchen table, as if he might be feeling the ice edge where the bears hunted and the seals swam. "I know the moods of animals," he said, tracing his fingers over the headlands. "I can see the bears moving to the land and I also know exactly when they will go back to sea. I think the storm that has been blowing will have moved the ice edge closer and when the moon becomes full the leads will open. Then the bears will be there," he pointed far off the coast, "hunting seals. Besides . . ." He looked up. "I am tired of eating fish."

So on a cold windy day when all the other sleds in the village were parked at their usual spots on the ice, we set out. Peter had changed from jeans and a sweatshirt into sealskin boots, polar bear trousers, and a green, store-bought anorak lined with sheepskin—a compact, round-faced man with a bit of black moustache, zinging his whip in figure eights over the backs of sixteen squabbling huskies while I sat behind him.

Abi followed on his own sled, pulled by a team of eleven dogs. West, north again, finally northwest, we sledded through the icebergs, big as stadiums and eroded by wind and seasonal melting into the shapes of mountains and delicate arches. Nearly all the icebergs were tricolored: along their bottoms turquoise; on their tops dazzling white; in between the shade of water so long locked in cold that it had lost its earthly color and turned the pale blue seen around the edges of stars. Peter kept his distance, for blocks could calve from the bergs and the sea ice around them could be thin.

Soon we saw their birthing place, the Nunatakavsaup Glacier, a smooth expanse of ice rising toward the eastern horizon. At its snout rows of crevasses, looking like ripples in a sandbar, fractured into icebergs that fell into the sea. Blocks several hundred yards across were held precariously by one corner against equally large bergs, all of them defying gravity until the spring. The fjord into which they calved was crowded with rows of bergs. At its mouth, the bergs separated and floated west. Eventually some would reach Newfoundland, occasionally the latitude of Cape Cod, visitors from this white hole of the planet, this two-mile-deep plateau of ice, which, if melted, would raise sea level twenty-one feet, inundating Sydney, Athens, New York.

We turned our backs to the ice cap and to the wind, our legs hanging off the side of the fifteen-foot-long sled, its runners, cross-thwarts, and steering handles bound together with parachute cord. Once, cord made from the hide of a bearded seal would have been used for lashing and the cross members might have been driftwood, or the bones of whales, instead of milled fir shipped from Europe. In either case, the effect was the same. Over the drifts and small blocks of ice the heavily laden sled articulated sinuously. Against the upright steering handles Peter had placed the kitchen box filled with cooking pots, several Primus stoves, his vacuum bottle, a hatchet, and a bit of food—coffee, bread, and margarine. In front of the box he had stacked a layer of frozen halibut—food for the dogs and snacks for us—and covered the fish with several caribou hides. Because caribou don't live anywhere near Kullorsuaq, the skins had been bought or acquired through trading, either in Thule or in southern Greenland. He had tied the skins and fish in place with the yellow plastic rope now found all along the coasts of North America, and under the lashings he had slipped a *tooq,* the six-foot-long, wood-shafted chisel used to chip drinking ice off bergs and to make fishing holes in the sea ice. By its side were two harpoons and a pair of bolt-action rifles—a .222 Remington with a scope, for hunting seals, and a rusty 30-06 with iron sights, dating from 1917, for polar bear. Between the uprights he had hung a canvas bag in which he had placed extra mittens, a pair of binoculars, fish hooks, a foot-long butchering knife, and a pliers and saw for repairing the sled. Two plastic jugs, four gallons each, full of kerosene, hung from each upright, as well as the *taaltuaq,* a miniature sled, two feet long by a foot and a half wide, upon the front of which was hung a square of white cloth, now rolled up for travelling. In the middle of the cloth a slit was cut for the rifle barrel. Unfurling this "sail" and tying his rifle to the mounts behind it, a hunter slid the little sled before him on the ice. Thus camouflaged, he could stalk very close to a dozing seal. The harnessing of the dogs was also uniquely suited to the environment of the frozen sea. Each animal was joined to the sled by its own trace so that the team pulled in a fan, distributing the weight when crossing thin ice.

I sat toward the rear of the sled against the kitchen box, and Peter sat before me, yelling *"Eee-eee-eee"* for right, *"Eeeyoo"* for left, and *"Yüp-yüp-yüp!"* for get a move on!, all the while cracking his whip over a lazy dog who had begun to shirk, and the one or two clever ones who, trotting smartly, were merely keeping their traces taut without actually pulling against their harnesses. A white-and-black female with a raw pink nose refused to stop this trick, and Peter kept the whip singing over her tail. Weaving back and forth she tried to avoid his reminder. But she wasn't agile enough. Caught between the traces, she tripped. In a pinch, she was dragged beneath the sled and yowled as if she were being crushed to death.

Whistling the team to a stop, Peter jumped off the sled and dragged her from beneath the runners. *"Uummannaq!"* he yelled, booting her toward the other dogs. During the time I spent in Greenland I recorded many translations for this expletive, my favorite being, "Oh, you wretch! You strike a dagger in my heart!" Without any visible harm, the bitch scampered back to the team.

Peter shook his head in disgust, as if to say, "This is what I am reduced to." He then set about untangling the dozen traces, which had been woven into a giant braid by the huskies' weaving back and forth in the pack. Abi performed the same job. When the brothers were done, we had a cup of coffee, shared some bread and margarine, and were on our way again.

Two hours later we reached the island of Qârusulik and stopped at Nicolai Jensen's hunting house, perched atop a rocky promontory and facing the sound filled with icebergs. Here was the apron of rock on which he had been photographed, laying pieces of narwhal meat to dry; here was the little cove, now frozen, where one could spot seals all summer; here was the very place he had described so lovingly. We walked into a plywood shack, the walls painted green, the ceiling five and a half feet high. There were two bunks in a corner, a pair of binoculars hanging from a nail, a loaf of frozen bread on the counter, and the spine of a seal in the doorway, hardly any meat left between its vertebrae. Sitting on the bunks, we ate some bread and margarine. It was too cold to linger.

Just before leaving, Peter and Abi gave the dogs a few bites of narwhal blubber from a pile that lay outside the shack. Then with a *"Yüp-yüp-yüp!"* we were on our way. Within minutes we passed beneath the hut Knud Rasmussen had built at the turn of the century, and shortly thereafter we sledded by the granite headlands on the north end of Qârusulik. There the snow changed shape. The drifts became long and more widely spaced, miming the shape of swells on the open sea. We were now beyond the archipelago of coastal islands and were on the sea ice of Melville Bay. The east wind picked up balls of snow, displaced by our sled runners, and blew them toward the dogs so that we moved in a ground blizzard of powder. Only three icebergs remained ahead of us. Directly in line with the northwestering sun, they shone as if wet. Around them the frozen sea was covered with pink and purple glister that, running unimpeded to the horizon, fell over the edge of the world where it met the pale blue sky. Behind us the rock pinnacle of Kullorsuaq had become a shadowy finger merging with the coastline.

North the sun continued its long low arc. We followed it, reaching jumbled ice, head high, that blocked our way. Peter turned south, standing on the sled like a bareback rider in the circus, knees flexing, whip in one hand for balance, yelling steering commands to the dogs. A passage through the blocks ended in a cul-de-sac. We turned around and continued south. Peter looked depressed. He kept turning his head every which way, searching for a passage west, where he hoped to find open water. He said one word, *"Ajortooq!"* Bad.

Another lane of snow led through the jumble. We turned into it and it gave way to a smooth plain of ice running north. Peter sat down and steered toward the setting sun. Within the hour he stopped by a small berg shaped like a mound. Walking in circles before it, he thrust his *tooq* into the ice to ascertain its thickness. After many probes he grunted his approval. Eight hours after leaving Kullorsuaq we had arrived at our first night's camp. It was one degree below zero.

While I unloaded the gear Peter chipped a U-shaped bracket in the ice to tether the dogs. When they were staked, he began to slice off bite-size pieces from the back of a halibut, popping several in his mouth and handing some to Abi and me. Then we put the sleds side by side and, using harpoons for poles, erected a patched canvas sheet over them, guyed down to more U-shaped ice brackets. The joined sleds became our sleeping platform and were covered with caribou skins; a sheet of plywood, laid on the ice before them, was our kitchen.

Our shelter taken care of, Peter and Abi turned to feeding the dogs. With their hatchets, they chopped two of the flatfish into chunks while the huskies trembled and salivated. Then the men threw the fish into the air above the teams, and in a frenzy of growling and tearing the huskies gobbled their dinner in less than fifteen seconds. They were given no water—they ate snow during the winter months. Without another glance at their teams, Peter and Abi walked into the tent. I couldn't be so quick.

Over the ice cap the full moon had risen and, to the northwest, the sun skidded along the horizon, tinting the frozen sea the color of wild roses. When it set, the sky above it turned lilac, then lavender, then a clear and profound celestial blue containing one bright star.

Opening the flap of the tent, I saw that Peter was already pouring boiling water into a Melitta filter. I sat on the caribou skins and smelled the coffee. He handed me a piece of bread and some raw halibut. Opening my compass and using its mirror, Abi looked at his new moustache. "Today he is fifteen," said Peter, "tomorrow sixteen." Abi closed the compass and shyly looked at his hands.

Filling a mug with coffee, Peter took a sip and gazed at the taut roof of his tent. "*Nuannerpoq,*" he said. Delightful.

I had forgotten we had been looking for polar bear.

Peter hadn't. The next morning he stopped the dogs after ten minutes of running and climbed a berg tall enough for a vantage. Pointing west where a grey line of vapor hung along the horizon, he said "*Imaq,*" literally, "the sea." In this case he meant leads, the channels of water that open in sea ice. But between us and the cloud were miles of jumbled ice. We sat, glassing for close to an hour, seeing many shapes that looked like bears but no real *nanoq.* For the time being, it was intriguing enough to imagine bears roaming out there, not as was once supposed, floating clockwise around the pole, but in stable, regional populations—hunting, mating, being born, and dying—faithful to a home territory. If there is one animal that best represents adaptation to the arctic, in both the Inuit as well as in the white person's imagination, it must be the polar bear—*Ursus maritimus . . . nanoq . . .* the bear of the sea, the color of snow. Its shape is taller, lankier, and more streamlined than that of the grizzly; its canines, enabling it to tear apart its almost exclusively flesh diet, are longer and sharper; its claws are shorter, allowing it to run more effortlessly on ice. Its fur isn't true white but shades of cream. Sometimes, along the coast of Hudson Bay, I have seen bears whose hips and legs were full of rufous highlights.

"Let's go," Peter said, waving to the ice jumble before us. On we sledded, trying all day to find a way through it. Up and down we bounced, on and off the sleds we climbed, freeing the runners from where they had snagged on blocks the size of cars. Once Peter had to chop a passage with his ax; once the tow yoke, to which all the traces were attached, broke; once the sled tilted so far on its side that Peter and I fell over backwards. Standing up, he laughed so hard that tears came to his eyes. Then he jogged after the huskies who had kept pulling.

As we sledded, I watched the shapes of the small bergs in the distance, catching a glimpse of bearlike ice, which made my heart beat faster. Few sights are more exciting than glimpsing what biologists like to call the "largest nonaquatic carnivore in the world." And few wildlife sightings more profoundly reveal the limits of human physiology. Here is a creature, whether a small female of three hundred pounds or a large male of fifteen hundred who, with no more than its fur and fat, moves comfortably through an environment in which we can survive only through the use of technology and, in times past, the bear's own fur. Little wonder that we have envied them.

In all probability the first Asian people who reached arctic America learned new ways to hunt seals by watching polar bears, who preceded them from Asia about 200,000 years ago. With enormous patience, the bear will wait for hours above a seal's breathing hole; it will use blocks of ice to conceal its stalk; and when no terrain features are available behind which to hide, it will walk slowly toward a basking seal, sometimes crouched, sometimes immersed in the channels of water that form on top of the sea ice in the summer, until it is within forty feet of the seal, occasionally as far away as ninety—then it charges. Some authors, such as the great storyteller and Rasmussen's partner in the Thule trading post, Peter Freuchen, claim to have witnessed polar bears' covering their black noses with their paws to conceal them from prey. The majority of researchers have never seen the trick, though I have sometimes observed a bear snoozing with a paw over its nose, seeming to shield its muzzle from the wind. Other observers have theorized that the bear's black nose is actually a form of deceptive camouflage—lost in the surrounding whiteness of the bear's fur, it appears, to the seal being stalked, as another seal in the distance.

Most of these techniques of stalking and camouflage are ones that native hunters have used and still use. The bear, of course, does them one better, being able to swim effortlessly beneath the water and burst upon the ice to kill a seal with a blow of its paw. Old carvings, depicting streamlined bears seeming to fly, are not poor renditions from unskilled artists. They are representations of the bear caught in one of its two elements, swimming and hunting, in the way human hunters no doubt would have wished to emulate.

Watching the cloud hanging on the western horizon, I thought of what might be taking place at the edge of the leads: a bear rushing a seal, grabbing it, biting it many times on the head, dragging it away from the water, then beginning its meal of blubber. Almost always bears prefer to eat only the fat, which gives them the most caloric return for the energy they expend in stalking their prey. To live well, an active, adult bear needs an average of eleven pounds of seal fat per day, much of it ac-cumulated during the spring. In this time of increasing light, it will hunt ringed seal pups, first by sniffing out their subnivean birthing lairs and crashing down upon the roof with both forefeet, later by stalking the newly weaned and still naïve pups as they bask on the ice. During this active hunting season some bears can increase their weight enormously, laying on the fat stores they will need to last through the open water of summer and early fall, when hunting becomes difficult. Ian Stirling, of the Canadian Wildlife Service and one of the foremost polar bear re-searchers in the world, notes that one female, darted in December, weighed 213 pounds. By the following August when she was recaptured, she weighed 992 pounds.

With the arrival of the warm months, bears stranded on land go through a period of fasting and "walking hibernation," a physiological state in which the chemical composition of their blood resembles that of hibernating black bears. For a good part of the day, they'll doze on their backs, feet in the air, rising to eat little more than kelp and coastal grasses, grazing on these plants like cows. In fact, rooting in a patch of kelp, shoving their heads into the seaweed and tossing it into the air with their snouts, they have seemed almost porcine to me. However, the re-semblance ends there—bears can lissomely turn the entire end of their noses at right angles to their facial plane to catch a scent as they doze. Then they'll suck and nibble at the air, drinking it in and appraising it for prey, carrion, and danger.

Sometimes one can see these summer bears walking idly through flocks of molting, flightless geese without a glance at what appears to be an easy meal. Besides being in a state of "walking hibernation," there is another reason for their seemingly lethargic behavior. One of the most well insulated of all mammals, a polar bear must be careful not to over-heat and waste energy. At its normal walking speed of 2.5 miles per hour its body temperature remains a fairly constant 98.6 degrees Fahrenheit. But at less than double that speed (4.2 miles per hour), its temperature goes up to one hundred degrees and it uses thirteen times the amount of energy it would if resting. No wonder bears swivel their noses without moving their heads, refrain from chasing geese, and even in the winter seem to plod slowly across the ice. The bear's susceptibility to overheat-ing is also another reason why human hunters have been successful at running them down with dogs. The bear quickly overheats and must stop.

When not forced to gallop the bear is marvelously adapted to its environment—its ears small to conserve heat, its paws large to act as paddles as well as to spread its weight on thin ice. In the water, the bear's four-inch-thick fat keeps it warm. On land, an underlayer of dense fur and a more open layer of guard hairs protect it from arctic gales. The guard hairs are hollow and won't mat when wet. Shaken, they easily toss off water before freezing. In addition, the guard hairs reflect and trans-mit much of the sun's visible and near-infrared radiation down through the bear's pelt where it is absorbed by its black skin, causing a rise in surface temperature well above the bear's core temperature. The hairs then serve a secondary function of trapping the heat emitted by skin, forming a layer of insulating air within the pelt. D. M. Lavigne, another Canadian biologist who did some of the original research in how polar bears trap heat in this fashion, points out that this phenomenon isn't unique to the bears, but is also found in seals and even some subarctic plants and "wooly bear" caterpillars.

In the early 1970s Lavigne and his colleague, Nils Øritsland, found that the pelts of several white animals, including harp seal pups and polar bears, also absorb much of the ultraviolet component in sunlight, a phenomenon that led to practical applications. When photographed from the air with normal film, white bears on white snow were frequently difficult to recognize. But when their habitat was rephotographed using UV-sensitive film, the snow, which reflects UV, appeared white. The bears, which absorb UV, were rendered black. Because large areas of the arctic, particularly in the former Soviet Union, have never been photographed from the air with a mind to finding polar bears, an accurate circumpolar census still does not exist. However, extrapolating from Alaskan and Canadian surveys, Ian Stirling estimates that there may be as many as forty thousand bears circumpolarly, and points out that the species is not endangered as some believe. Periodically, biologists from each arctic nation meet to share and publish information about polar bears under the auspices of the Species Survival Commission of The World Conservation Union, but at the present time there is no unified, circumpolar management scheme for the species. In fact, how bears are treated varies greatly.

In both Norway and Russia polar bears are protected. In Canada each management unit is allowed a quota and only Inuit may take bears, though they may sell part of their quota to sport hunters as a way of generating cash. The sport hunter must be guided by an Inuit and travel only by dogsled. If he is unsuccessful, that portion of the native hunter's allowance is cancelled and not reissued. "What this means," says Stirling, "is that through the sport-hunting program, more benefits accrue to the Inuit while fewer polar bears are killed."

In the United States, sport hunting for polar bears—done mostly with the use of aircraft—was terminated in 1972 under the Marine Mammal Protection Act. Today only natives may hunt polar bears in Alaska, for food and clothing.

Greenland's regulations are similar to those of the United States. Polar bears can be killed only by residents who, like Peter Aronsen, have subsistence hunting as their primary occupation. Between one- and two hundred bears are killed each year in Greenland—data is scanty—about twenty of which are taken by the hunters from Kullorsuaq. On the average, two bears fall each season to Peter.

Now, as we entered a long oasis of flat ice, he stood on the sled, raised his binoculars, and glassed a wide arc ahead of us. Within a few minutes his intuition proved correct as he spotted a seal basking by its hole. For a moment, looking for bears was put aside. He stopped the huskies, pulled on his white anorak, assembled the shooting sled, and began to stalk. He had gone only a hundred yards when a dog barked and the seal dove under the ice like a gopher going to ground. He glared at the dog, then gave a shrug. Without another word, he resumed our steady pace, wasting no energy discussing what might have been.

As the sun set we reached another unremarkable spot amidst tossed-up ice and camped. In our tent, Peter lit a candle on an overturned pot, and said, "Yesterday Abi was fifteen, today he is sixteen." A few minutes after this ceremony both men were asleep—still in their clothes, curled knees-to-chest on the caribou rugs, the Primus going full blast.

The next day when I asked Peter if they ever used sleeping bags, he laughed. What if a polar bear attacked the dogs, he asked, or the ice opened and you had to strike camp? You'd be in a fine mess, wearing only your long underwear while lying in a sleeping bag. He motioned to my sleeping bag on the ice, where, overcome by the kerosene fumes in the tent, I had slept. I said no problem: He would shoot the bear and I would take his picture. He looked at me for a long second, then gave a great laugh.

Unable to force a way west, we turned south and passed giant pans of ice until late in the afternoon. Then we climbed a small berg and glassed for open water. Landward and to the south a flotilla of icebergs clustered; to the far west stood two spindly towers of ice surrounded by a horizon-to-horizon jumble of blocks. Just beyond them the elusive grey line of vapor still beckoned. But the open water beneath it was out of reach. Shaking his head in disgust, Peter returned to the sled and made some tea. While a pot of ice melted on the Primus, he looked to the south, seeming to formulate a plan. Abi dozed on his sled. Neither man seemed to notice the skyscape unfolding from the way we had come: Long arms of cirrostratus clouds arced toward the distant coast where sharp black peaks thrust from a promontory called Tutulissuaq, "the big headland of caribou." Above the mountains hung delicate puffs of orange cloud. The ice and mountains were wild yet delicately lit.

"*Kusanartooq,*" I said. Beautiful.

Peter looked around and nodded. He had other things on his mind.

Six hours later, our faces liverish-purple from the wind and cold, we made camp by a berg that looked indistinguishable from the thousands of other ice humps we had passed. "This is where I camped in January," he said, and to prove it he dug a blue plastic jerry can from the snow.

We pitched the tent and fed the dogs the last of the halibut. The sun went down in a huge red mushroom cloud, and while Peter and Abi melted ice I decided to be helpful. I climbed the berg to glass the frozen sea, and saw nothing. When I returned, Peter looked at me quizzically.

To lighten his somber mood I held out all five fingers of one hand and said, "Five *uuttoq*." Five basking seals. Raising the fingers of my other hand, I added, "Two *aaveq* and one *nanoq*." Two walruses and one polar bear.

He gave me a dumbfounded look, and almost reached for his rifle, before throwing his head back and roaring with laughter. From his sled Abi looked up, and Peter told him what I had said. He smiled. Then I saw Peter staring at the iceberg I had climbed, his expression more serious.

Pointing to the berg, he led me to its edge and gestured to my ascending footprints. Clearing away the snow just inches from the tracks I'd left, he revealed a gap between the flat sea ice on which we stood and the sloping side of the berg. In the opening, large enough to admit a human body, was the dark sea. He pointed to me; he made a precipitous motion into the gap; he crossed his arms and swept them away from each other in the universal gesture of disappearance. Then probing with an imaginary *tooq*, he emphasized the need to inspect such ice before stepping on it. Without further ado, he walked back to the tent and made coffee.

In the morning the sky was streaked with cirrus clouds. Peter climbed the berg, studied the four horizons, and said that by tomorrow it would be storming. Since we were almost out of food, and the chances of getting seals were slim, he wanted to go home. He pointed to the southeast where Kullorsuaq's black finger poked over the horizon.

We broke camp and sledded toward the distant shore, stopping in the late afternoon at the small rocky island of Qutdleq, where Peter camped with his family during the summer. While Abi stayed with the dogs, Peter and I climbed the shoreline cliffs covered with ramps of ice. On a flat headland overlooking the bay we found what he had wanted to show me—the backbone of a narwhal he had harpooned the previous season. As we turned over the bones, two ptarmigan flew off, croaking.

Making toward the far side of the island, we walked through rimed grass and windswept rocks. On a stretch of hard snow, Peter stopped. I was behind him so I didn't immediately see what he was looking at. When I came up to his shoulder, he had one finger pointing to the ground and a smile on his face. A line of bear prints wandered across the snow and disappeared into the rocks.

"*Nanoq*," he said, adding that the tracks were two or three weeks old.

I looked at them. Right here the polar bear had stood. The tracks were almost twelve inches long. I looked up and followed the spoor with my eyes, wishing to see what we had been searching for, and knowing we wouldn't.

Peter stared at me with his usual mute face. Then he pointed at my watch, by which I gathered that we had to go. I turned and he shook his head. Taking my wrist, he pointed to the month on the watch's face. Then he rolled his hand through the air, indicating future time, while saying the name of the next month and the next. He gestured to the tracks, once again saying April, May, and June as he swept a hand to the sea, indicating the way we had come. Touching his eyes, he pointed to the tracks again, and raised an imaginary rifle, making the sound of a shot.

Oh, now I understood. There was no need for disappointment, for there was much time. If not on this trip then on the next, or a month from now . . . at some point on his circuits across the sea ice, his path and a bear's would cross. He raised the imaginary rifle and fired again. The end was inevitable, given his patience, his skill, and his continuing need . . . as well as the ways of the bear: to hunt seals; to frequent open water; to be curious. He stood before me, his polar bear trousers opalescent in the hazy light—wrapped in bears.

Then he pointed to the bay. There were also his nets to check. If he hadn't been lucky with bears, he might be with seals. But when we reached the nets, suspended under the ice to catch and drown seals during the dark winter days, they were empty. After he and Abi reset them, they raced each other toward the black pinnacle of Kullorsuaq, already vanishing in the lowering clouds.

Later that evening, as I brought a chunk of ice into my shack, I saw Peter carrying a halibut from his cold-storage shed. He had the frozen fish on one shoulder, and he waved with his free hand, semaphoring, "Good night," and what only could be taken for a resigned, "Fish again."

THE MORNING PROVED HIS FORECAST ACCURATE. IT WAS SNOWING SO hard that I could barely see the bay. An east wind blew off the ice cap; flags stood straight out from their poles; the paths through the village drifted over. As I sat at the kitchen table, finishing my notes from our trip, the shack swayed and the table trembled under my hands. It was a monumental wind, a wind like few I had ever experienced.

Curious as to its real strength, I walked through the double entry and opened the outer door, which was instantly jerked wide. I held on to the knob and flew after it, grabbing the porch rail so as not to be blown away. My hair stood out from my head, and my left ear, facing into the wind, instantly filled with snow. I hauled the door closed and had to pry the snow from my ear where it was packed solid. This was too interesting not to investigate, and I also needed some bread. I dressed and plodded to the store through the drifts, the wind driving me from behind, pushing me over the piles of snow and making me trot in the clear stretches. Around the shacks it raised tornadoes of powder, which enveloped me, driving snow up my nostrils.

At the KNI—Greenland's equivalent to Canada's Hudson's Bay Company—a plump woman sat behind the checkout counter; otherwise the store was empty. Four aisles of packaged and canned food, fishing supplies, tools, rifles, and household goods stretched to a back wall where there was a cooler with some vacuum-packed milk, a chest freezer holding meats imported from Denmark, and bread from southern Greenland. On a clothes rack hung some parkas and a few dresses so plain they would make a European woman weep for her Greenlandic sisters. In one corner stood some narwhal tusks from the previous season.

It being March and the last shipment of food having been received in September, the two main aisles were rapidly emptying of their choice items—cans of apricots and fruit cocktail, beets and peas—leaving nothing but pasta, rice, coffee, tea, boxes of müesli, sacks of sugar, and a never-ending supply of cookies, gingerbread, gumdrops, licorice, jujubes, and several varieties of chocolate bars—what the Danish dentist, who had just completed his yearly visit a few weeks ago, called "a catastrophe."

Here the villagers spent part of their disposable income, earned either through seasonally selling fish, sealskins, and *mattak* (the whale's skin and a centimeter of underlying fat), or through working at one of the few municipal jobs—garbage collector, clerk, handyman. The cost of housing and medical care both were low, construction loans (said not to be repaid during these times of depressed seal prices) were available from the national government, and Denmark's legacy of socialized medicine had been retained when Greenland achieved home rule. In addition, other benefits were available: disability payments for those injured while hunting or fishing; welfare for those families unable to meet a minimum yearly income; and loans to purchase boats and outboards. All of which softened the enormous prices of the goods in the KNI. The little plastic sack I took home, containing a few cans of vegetables, a microscopic packet of coffee, a box of cereal, and a loaf of whole wheat bread, cost nearly twenty dollars. Of course, we were far closer to the North Pole than to anywhere most of this food had been grown and packaged. Some of the villagers hardly ever purchased this much, seeming to buy no more than coffee and tobacco. Others could be seen spending a hundred dollars at a time.

As I stepped from the KNI's entryway snow burned my cheeks and filled my collar. I had not put on my anorak and I felt naked, the wind cutting through three layers of long underwear and two pile jackets. When I reached the path, going east to my house and fully exposed to the bay, a gust rocked me backwards, knocking me to my feet. Snow blew under my eyelids and blinded me. When I had wiped my eyes clear, everything—houses, sleds, kayak racks—had disappeared. I knelt in a world of total whiteness and felt my body go numb. When the gusts passed I could vaguely see the path, and I recollected how people, in days gone by, had been forced to bivouac in their warm parkas and trousers for a few hours, or even a day or two, when they had only been going from one igloo to another. Dressed as I was, I wouldn't have survived. Finally reaching my shack, I noticed that Abi's sled was gone from his porch. He was out tending his long lines.

I hung my clothes to dry. I made some coffee. Warmed by the kerosene stove, I sat and read. Surrounded by wind, the world obscured by clouds, I listened to the words this land, and its storms, had created.

> *You earth,*
> *Our great earth!*

said the Inuit, Padloq.

> *See, oh see:*
> *All these heaps*
> *Of bleached bones*
> *And wind-dried skeletons!*
> *They crumble in the air,*
> *The mighty world,*
> *The mighty world's*
> *Air!*
> *Bleached bones,*
> *Wind-dried skeletons,*
> *Crumble in the air!*
> *Hey-hey-hey!*

How uncaring the arctic must have seemed to these people before they had frame houses, kerosene stoves, and the KNI. How they must have worked for their sustenance, fully aware that, like the creatures they ate, they would be turned to dust by the implacable wind. No wonder their paradises were filled with beneficent sunshine and endless animals to hunt. But I wondered if they could have enjoyed such a heaven for long, devoid as it was of the earth's many passions. Uvanuk, an Inuit woman, thought not.

> *The great sea*
> *Moves me!*
> *The great sea*
> *Sets me adrift!*
> *It moves me*

Like algae on stones
In running brook water.
The vault of heaven
Moves me!
The mighty weather
Storms through my soul
It tears me with it,
And I tremble with joy.

How many times did I read her words during that day of wind and snow? With nowhere to go, how long did I study a full-page photograph of a soapstone figurine, five inches tall—an Inuit man, head bowed, shoulders bent, knees buckled, face weary and staring down at the ice. He dragged a harpoon in his right hand; his left held a knife. Around his hood and across his chest some rope was looped. Passing over his shoulders, the lines went to a small seal, curved across his back, and it was hard to say where the man left off and the seal began. There was also no telling how far the hunter was from home. His face was impassive, registering neither proximity to nor distance from wherever he was going. His back, it seemed, would never straighten. The ropes, it seemed, would never be undone, unbinding him from that seal, all seals, his way.

I had looked at this photograph many times before, but I don't think ever so closely as on this day—the storm rushing by outside and I longing to know what the mind inside the figurine had thought, and knowing how little I knew of the great weather, of the ties that bind, and perhaps how much less my neighbors, also in their warm houses, understood if one compared their knowledge to that of their great-great-grandparents.

The storm lasted two days, startling me when it quit. Suddenly my shack seemed very quiet. Walking to the windows, I saw a light, calm snow falling and the Greenlandic flag on Nicolai's house drooped along its staff. By dusk blue holes appeared in the cloud cover, and the next morning the sun's warmth gave no knowledge of the wind-driven cold.

At about eleven, I walked to the sled-building workshop and sat on the bench alongside it. On the ice a few huskies crooned; they were answered by a team staked farther along the shore. Otherwise, silence hung across the bay. At the red shack behind Nicolai's house, a birthday flag had been run up its pole. Two figures, bundled in their parkas, came down the path and went into the shack for tea and cookies, and to leave a few coins as was the custom. Out on the bay, a teenage boy pulled a sled toward the bergs, going for ice to be chipped and melted into water. The sky was a pale blue and so silent that it hummed.

Appreciating the sunshine on my face, I waited for Edvard Nielsen, one of the schoolteachers, who had a break between classes at this time. Soon he came down the hill from the school, hands in his pockets and whistling a tune. As always, he wore a purple stocking cap and a denim jacket with chrome skulls on the shoulders. Halfway down the steps carved in the snow he slipped. Without taking his hands from his pockets, he did a neat pirouette and skied to the bottom. He sat down next to me with a cocky nod.

"Nice recovery," I said.

He gave a shrug, indicating that it was no big deal.

"*Qanorippit?*" I asked. How are you?

"I'm JUST fine!" He lowered his mirrored sunglasses so I could see the twinkle in his eyes. A thin ponytail hung over his collar and I noticed that he had sewn another patch on his jacket, displaying an enormous hand flipping a middle finger.

"*Takkuuk! Sila kiaguppoq,*" I attempted. See, warm weather. And it was—four degrees above zero, but pleasant enough in the glare of the April sun to sit without hat and gloves.

"You bet!" he answered, then without further ado he got down to our usual business of trading new words. "What does it mean, 'Jerk my chain'?"

Having been schooled by Nicolai, I found the idiom easy to explain.

"And what is a dork?" From his jacket pocket he took out a miniature English-Danish dictionary. Holding it out like a piece of trash, he said, "Hopeless! A disaster!"

Clearly, his English was improving faster than my Greenlandic. He had a wonderful ear for languages, and, in addition to being a teacher, was a fine musician, a real wizard at the electronic keyboard, as I had discovered at one of the school dances. Music had also spurred his curiosity about faraway places, and I was able to answer some of his questions. Had I ever visited Asbury Park, The Shore, and E Street, he asked, the places Bruce Springsteen had made famous? What did they look like? Why was the Big Apple called the big apple? Had I been to Woodstock?

Yes, I had.

If a cross between James Dean, Robin Hood, and a Hell's Angel could have put on a reverential look, Edvard did. Someday he would like to see all these places, he had said, San Francisco too, but he doubted he ever would. Like so many Greenlanders, he had no way to accumulate the money it took to travel. In fact, he didn't even have enough to build himself and his wife a house of their own. They shuttled between his in-law's fairly well furnished home and his parents' squalid little shack that reeked of seal. His father, great hunter though he was, had many children to support, and had never gotten financially ahead as had his father-in-law, a schoolteacher. So I wouldn't misunderstood what he was saying, Edvard added that he, too, hoped to be a father soon; so far, however, he and his wife had been unsuccessful, which bothered his wife more than it did him. I had had an inkling that this was the case. A freckled woman with auburn hair, she wore her emotions on her shirt-sleeve, in her case a leather motorcycle jacket. In the pecking order of catalogue clothing, bought from Europe, her jacket was at the very top. Sometimes I would see the two of them, sitting here and passing a ciga-rette between them like a vow, while her eyes hung on the children walking by.

"A dork," I explained, "is me wearing a snowmobile suit instead of polar bear trousers."

No lights went on in Edvard's pale green eyes (inherited perhaps from his Danish great-great-grandfather), so I leafed through the large dictio-nary I carried to these meetings: inept; gauche; a maladroit. He was still not clear, but would be temporarily satisfied.

"Your words, please," he said.

"Wind."

"Easy—*anore.* You could have looked that up."

"Just checking. How about *uummannaq*?"

He chuckled and said, "You are a bad person."

Though I was disappointed with his version of this colorful expletive (Oh, you wretch! You strike a dagger in my heart!) I let it pass. I had a more important question to ask, one that had been troubling me during my stormbound days. Why had no one, outside of Peter and Nicolai, offered to let me accompany them when they went hunting?

He gave me a curious, suspicious look and leaned closer. Looking over the tops of his mirrored sunglasses, he said, "Can I trust you?"

I said he could try.

He leaned even closer as if there might be spies about. "Are you from Greenpeace?"

When I told him no, he said, "Are you sure?"

"Would someone from Greenpeace eat fish and seals, and have a fur hat and caribou *kamit*?"

He gave me a toothy leer. "I trust you," he said. "But the other hunters, who haven't talked to Sven like Nicolai and Peter have, they think you are from Greenpeace. And Greenpeace we all hate."

Sven Nielsen was the only European who lived in the village. A Dane and the headmaster of the school, he had been living in Kullorsuaq for fifteen years and was married to one of Nicolai's daughters. Acting as my other translator, he had introduced me to Nicolai and Peter but, busy with school and familial responsibilities, hadn't approached any of the other hunters. Now I understood why my reception had been cool.

Ever since the late 1970s, when Greenpeace mounted its campaign to end the clubbing of juvenile harp seals in Newfoundland, Greenlanders began to suffer economic hardship. Although the campaign wasn't mounted directly against subsistence hunters in the arctic, little distinction was made on the part of Greenpeace between harp seals in Newfoundland and ringed seals in Greenland, northern Canada, and Alaska. To make matters worse, harp seals are called "Greenland Seals" in Danish. In Europe the semantic confusion was exacerbated by an ad campaign that showed the harp seal pups (called "baby" seals by the media), staring from magazines with great soulful eyes. When Brigitte Bardot added her talents to the "Save the Seals" campaign, few people in the south gave much thought to an arctic hunter camped on the ice, trying to feed his family and earning some extra cash by hunting an entirely different species of seal, the ringed, which numbers in the millions. Greenpeace wasn't interested in finding out or publicizing the differences between the two hunts.

The organization (along with groups that included the International Fund for Animal Welfare, the Friends of the Earth, and the People's Trust for Endangered Species) helped to convince the Common Market to ban seal-pup products and the entire international market in sealskins promptly collapsed. Given those "baby" seal eyes, what woman wanted to be seen wearing any sealskin coat? In Greenland the average price for the skin of a ringed seal was 148 kroner in 1979. In 1986 it was twenty-five. Trying to forestall economic ruin, the Greenland Home Rule took two measures. It began to subsidize the purchase of sealskins from hunters, which somewhat maintained pre-Greenpeace prices, and it began an anti-antiseal campaign, distributing information in EEC countries about subsistence hunting in Greenland. In short, the campaign stated that ringed seals were the species commonly taken in Greenland and that harp seals arrived in the country's waters only as sub- and young adults. By then they had lost their white coats and rather than being clubbed to death, as was done in Newfoundland by commercial cash hunters, they were shot while swimming as was any other summertime pinniped, by subsistence hunters whose primary motivation was procuring food. Needless to say, the anti-antiseal campaign had only a small impact on European communities bent on preserving distant, virtually unknown animal life, which they didn't view as table fare, as they did cattle or chickens. In the late 1980s a small economic turnabout was achieved by the initiation of a joint venture between the Greenland national tannery and an internationally known Danish clothing designer, Lars Hillingsoe. The tannery started producing very thin and soft skins and Hillingsoe used them in an entire new line of haute couture.

Which really missed the point, said many Greenlanders. The point was to have southerners understand that eating agricultural products and livestock wasn't an option in the arctic . . . that Greenlanders couldn't live like Danes or Parisians or people in Miami. Even if one disregarded the fact that asking northern peoples to give up their traditional diets was another form of imperialism, where would northerners get the money to pay for a diet totally composed of such processed foods? They had enough trouble scraping together the cash for fuel, ammunition, and a few amenities. If subsistence hunting was the only way, outside of welfare, to exist in those regions of the far north that offered no employment in mines or oil fields, why not also sell sealskins to make a little cash, which could buy people the few tools they needed to hunt and enjoy some of the comforts southerners enjoyed? To which the hard-line Greenpeacers answered that if Greenlanders wanted to be more than aboriginal hunters—that is, if they wanted to sell their excess skins on the international market, use guns and outboards in addition to harpoons and kayaks, and eat a few southern foods—then they had to live or die by the market. This is a point worth considering, if the market had been allowed to base its decision on all the facts, which Greenpeace had done its best to hide. Round and round the argument—over seals, whales, and polar bears—continues to this day.

"Will you tell the hunters I'm not from Greenpeace?" I asked Edvard.

"Yes." He looked across the bay. "Will you come hunting with me? I and some other young hunters will be going to Tutulissuaq for seals and bears as soon as school is finished."

I realized I had been undiplomatic in not considering that he, too, was a hunter.

"Of course."

"School is finished on May tenth," he said, "and I will be done making my sled." He paused and fell into a series of non sequiturs. "I am thinking of becoming a full-time hunter. . . . There are many great hunters in this village. . . . It was my grandfather who taught Nicolai." He took a breath and leaned against the shack, frustrated that he couldn't find the right English words. "Our parents tell us that the future is in working," he said slowly, "that hunting is too hard. They tell us to be schoolteachers. Next year there may even be a fish factory in the village, which will hire some of us. I don't think, though, that hunting will ever die in this country."

He looked across the frozen bay to the headlands of Kiatagsuaq—snow gullies and black granite cliffs rose to a windswept plateau that merged into the ice cap.

"If you hunt all summer," I asked, "will you go back to teaching school in the fall?"

He gave an imperceptible shrug. "That is not free. Being a hunter is being free in nature."

"Have you done much hunting?"

"*Aap!*"

"Seals?"

He gave me a disgusted look that implied I must be kidding.

"Ice bear?"

He nodded "absolutely," then said, "I would like to get a narwhal this summer. But I don't think I'm old enough yet."

Before I could ask him why not, he stood up and said, "I need to buy some cigarettes."

"Will you tell me about your ice bear and about the trip to Tutulissuaq?"

"Tonight," he called. "I will come by."

He didn't.

—>>—<<—

EDVARD'S NOT KEEPING THE APPOINTMENT WASN'T UNUSUAL. HALF a dozen things could have delayed him, as they had in the past. He could have remembered that he had wanted to work on his sled; he could have needed to spend time with his wife, or mother, or father, or father-in-law; he could have been listening to music, or practicing at his keyboard; or he could have forgotten, or just not meant to come at all.

Likewise, on several occasions, Peter Aronsen had said that on such and such a day we would go hunting. On the agreed-upon day he packed his sled and went off by himself, leaving me frustrated and puzzled. Over time, as I continued to read about other white people's attempts to understand the culture of the arctic, and the more I let the days go by without trying to orchestrate events, I came to realize that what was socially binding for an American or European was not for a Greenlandic hunter.

Perhaps the paws of his dogs had gone sore and he believed that they would be further injured by carrying more weight; perhaps he had an intuitive suspicion that two people would compromise the seal stalking he planned to do; perhaps he had argued with his wife and wished to be alone on the ice. Off he drove. Once it was suitable to take a writer hunting; now it was not. No explanation necessary. At eleven in the morning, sitting on the bench by the sled-building hut, Edvard had said, "Tonight I will come by." At eight in the evening other events precluded his visit. As I eventually discovered, if I had not been at my shack as I had promised, Edvard would have gone off whistling, not feeling disappointed or slighted. Understanding this took quite a while. But I had lots of time.

Often I would visit Sven Nielsen, the boyish schoolteacher with grey-ing hair rumpled on his forehead, and soulful eyes. His large glasses gave him a perpetually surprised regard, and he had the slow, careful move-ments of someone who has been tall, clumsy, and shy his entire life.

On this day I found him at home, after school, braiding dog harnesses on the carpet of his living room floor. Because of his position as headmas-ter of the school, Sven and his wife, Emilie, had the largest and most well furnished house in the village, with amenities few others could afford—a large storage tank for water, an old but serviceable refrigerator, and much store-bought food in addition to the seals and birds Sven hunted.

No surprise that their house was almost always full of visitors: Their food was plentiful and delicious; they had many curiosities—novels, picture books, and carvings; and Sven was very good at one of the vil-lage's favorite games, chess. He had also organized a video rental club, loaning the movies out for five kroner each (eighty U.S. cents), the money generated being used to acquire more videos from the district capital of Upernavik.

Everything else aside, being keeper of the videos made his living room a busy place, for in a village of thirty-six households there were nineteen VCRs. In fact, it was by video that the villagers received their visual news of the outside world—every three weeks a taped report of national and international events was flown in by helicopter. So strong had the pull of news and movies become that, in Sven's opinion, the first item people bought when they had disposable income was now often a VCR instead of an outboard motor.

Standing up, he held out a harness and said, "I thought I would get my dog things ready."

I had a feeling that Sven might be cherishing this rare, solitary mo-ment and I offered to come back another time.

"Oh, no, no," he said. "Please, have some coffee." He gestured to the ever-present vacuum bottle on the dining room table, empty mugs wait-ing around it. As I poured myself a cup, an old woman came in. Stooped with arthritis but with a lively greeting, she handed Sven a new pair of *kamit*. The outer boots were made from bearded seal, the inners were lined with the long fleece of Greenlandic sheep.

"More things to get ready," said Sven when the woman had left. He tossed the boots on an armchair where a pair of polar bear trousers lay, their seat torn and obviously waiting repair. "They are seven years old," he said about the trousers. "Usually they last only four years, but they are expensive to replace." He did a quick calculation. "Six hundred fifty dollars U.S. Once you've tried them, though, you don't want anything else. They aren't very heavy, and if the weather is warm they don't feel so warm. If the weather is cold they keep you hot."

"Did you get the bear?" I asked.

"I have never seen one alive."

Perhaps he saw the surprise on my face.

"According to tradition," he explained, "I have gotten one. In 1979 I was at the ice barrier with three other hunters who saw this bear swimming in a lead. They shot it from their kayaks and dragged it back to camp with their boats. Since I was a member of the sledging party, I was also considered to have gotten the bear and was entitled to part of it. This was done in the traditional way. The hide and meat were divided into four portions and one of the hunters turned his back upon them while a second hunter pointed to one of the piles. The man with his back turned called out another of the hunter's names. And that portion went to the man named. And so on until all was gone."

"That seems clever."

"Most meat is divided this way, except ringed seals, which are hunted individually and belong to the hunter who shoots them. In the case of narwhal, the hunter who first harpoons it gets the major portion along with the tusk. If a second hunter puts in a killing blow, he receives the second largest portion, and the rest of the meat, blubber, and *mattak* is divided among the other hunters who are along." He paused, glancing at the dining room table. "Would you like a game of chess?"

When we had settled over the board and made our opening moves, I asked about the blubber I had seen outside Nicolai's hunting shack on the island of Qârusulik. Was it left behind because kerosene and electricity had replaced fat lamps?

"Yes," said Sven. He lit his pipe, studied the board, and brought out a bishop. I could see that, three moves into the game, I had more than likely already lost it.

"They do use some of the blubber," he added. "But you can't feed dogs only fat. They get sick, and it takes so much kerosene to melt it down and sell it that it's not economic. It's not done."

He gave a philosophical shrug and explained how the village's proposed fish factory and freezer plant would create a healthier economy. Presently people caught no more fish than they and their dogs could consume. But if they could freeze halibut during the winter and spring, selling it when freezer ships came in the summer, they would have more disposable cash. This would do more than buy them luxuries, like motorcycle jackets and running shoes. It would prevent the waste of animals, particularly belugas, the white whales who migrated along the coast in the fall. Then, said Sven, laying aside his pipe, some hunters lost their heads and killed many of the whales, selling only the *mattak* to the KNI for a very high price, and abandoning the meat because the store, lacking large freezer facilities, couldn't buy it all.

Sven gave another of his shrugs. "The old hunters in the village would say that in their day such things never happened. A successful hunter stored the meat under rocks at the hunting sites and came back to the village to get others, and everybody would share the whale. Now, some hunters get a little greedy. They don't have much money and they see the whales as cash. It's not good, but it's human." Uneasily, he glanced at his pipe, then at me, hoping that I would understand.

When I made no reply, he said, "Many things have changed. Many things. When I came here in 1975 I think there were no more than two or three powerboats. Now everyone has one. There wasn't a single telephone. Now there are twenty-eight." He lit his pipe, filling the room with smoke. "And the school was only half its present size. We had no helicopter or pier." He motioned toward the shore and his face became nostalgic. "It was very romantic."

Without much confidence, I brought out a knight, and Sven matched my move. At this moment Emilie walked into the living room, her stomach bulging out of her white ski parka. She and Sven had had their first child when she was seventeen. She was now twenty-nine, and this was to be their fourth. Her black hair fell around her shoulders, she had a dazzling smile, and she appeared content, smug, and radiant all at once. A little sharply, she asked Sven if he had invited me to dinner. When he said no, which I gathered was what she had expected, she immediately made the invitation.

While she began to work in the kitchen, Sven chased my king around the board, explaining how the best-off families in the village were those that kept their offspring to a reasonable number (perhaps seeing Emilie made him think of his growing family), and in which the wife worked at some municipal job and the husband hunted. In this way they could afford to build a larger house, buy some store-bought food, order entertainment and dress clothes from Europe, but still carry on some of the old life—sledging, eating seals, and wearing traditional clothing while on the ice. "A good mix," he said. Finally, he cornered and dispatched me.

In the meantime Emilie had turned some seal ribs into a stew mixed with potatoes and rice. The ribs were the color of dark wine, the fat on their outer side thick, their bones delicate like a lamb's. She had gotten the ribs from her father's meat rack.

Joined by their two almost-teenage daughters and their young son, we sat down to dinner. Meqo, a little plump and resembling her grandfather, Nicolai, giggled at my struggling Greenlandic. Magdalene, thin and with Danish features, kept her eyes on her plate. Four-year-old Harold ruled his end of the table with an iron fork, waving it at his father, who was obviously no disciplinarian. Meekly, Sven took his son's cuffs, wagging a finger at him when he shouted.

After dinner, as Sven and I harnessed his team and set off to check his long lines, he proved no better with his dogs than with his son. They greeted him with an uncommon friendliness, jumping up to lick his face. Handling his whip amateurishly, he waved it over their heads, shouting at them to lie down, a command they ignored. He had changed into his torn polar bear trousers, a heavy sweater covered by a dirty anorak, and a fur-lined hat with huge earflaps. Compared to the compact Greenlanders, he looked like a giraffe in arctic costume.

As he began to harness the dogs to his sled, they ran the traces around his legs and tripped him. He asked me to stand in front of them as a distraction while he clipped them in. Finished, he picked up his whip, stepped aside, called "*Yüp-yüp-yüp!*" and jumped immediately on the sled, which, unburdened by any gear, rocketed by me. I leapt for the uprights and just caught one. Dragged along for fifty feet, I finally managed to haul myself onto the sled, losing my hat in the process. Miraculously, it caught on one of the uprights. As I retrieved it, I saw several young boys on the ice football field doubled over with laughter.

"You will hear about that," he said.

At his fishing spot, fifteen minutes' sledding around the other side of the island, we chipped out the ice that had formed in the hole, and hauled up a thousand meters of line by putting it over our shoulders and walking it across the ice. We found no halibut. Sven baited the hooks, threw the scraps to the dogs, and dropped the line back into the dark sea. Tying off the line to an ice stanchion, he gave the hole a last custodial look, and repeated his undisciplined harnessing job. I wasn't so foolish this time. I got on the sled, noticing with some concern that Sven had put his whip out of reach as he clipped in the traces. The instant he let go of the last dog, the team jumped forward. He shouted to stop; they broke into a gallop; he lunged for his whip and threw a hand toward the uprights, managing to grab the crossbar.

"Stop!" he yelled.

Gleefully, the dogs rushed on.

Dragged behind the sled, his *kamit* bouncing over the ice, Sven hauled himself over the crossbar and fell in a heap. The sled bounced wildly. Pulling his hat from his eyes, he lashed out with his whip and stopped the dogs. When he regained his breath, and straightened his hat, he said, "I'm glad *that* didn't happen at the village."

We exchanged places, I to the rear, he forward. Getting the team moving, he asked, a little shyly, "Does Peter ever have trouble with his dogs?"

"Sometimes he can't get them to stop." This was the truth.

Sven smiled. "I don't feel so bad then."

At home we found Emilie knitting on the couch with Harold sleeping on her lap. Sven made a fresh pot of coffee and while we waited for it to drip I looked at the walrus and polar bear skulls on the sideboard. Sven had told me that he had lowered the head of the walrus off the dock one September and that the sea had frozen before he could pull it back up. When he retrieved it the following June, the head had been picked clean by the fish. I took the walrus skull off the shelf and stared into its face. Stodgy in life, it appeared very carnivorous in death. Almost unconsciously my eyes were drawn to the narrower and even more predatory-looking skull of the polar bear. Putting down the walrus, I lifted the bear skull and opened and closed its jaws.

The daggerlike upper canines fit precisely against the lower ones, the twelve incisors meshing neatly upon each other. Again I moved the jaws, the hinge at their back rocking like a polished gimbal. Bringing its snout to my nose, I opened the bear's mouth and imagined the hundreds of seals who had gone down these jaws, and the mind who had stalked them. I brushed his smooth skull and thought of what it had stored: the smells of seal, narwhal, and walrus; the movements of tides, leads, and wind; and of the wanderings of other bears. Sven's oldest daughter, Magdalene, had been built partly on the flesh of this very bear. Her mother, Emilie, had been built on other bears just like him, who had been built on seals, going back . . . back . . . back to the time when Emilie's ancestors had walked across the Bering land bridge, eight thousand years ago.

"It's beautiful, isn't it?" said Sven, handing me a cup of coffee.

I agreed that it was and replaced the skull on the shelf.

"Come here," he said, leading me to the bookshelves on the opposite side of the room where he kept some old carvings. There were ivory needles used to bind up the wounds of harpooned seals so that their blood, more valued for food in the old days, wouldn't be lost, as well as fishhooks made from the bones of common murres. The centerpiece was a troll-like ivory statue called a *tupilak*. Originally *angakkoqs* made these creatures by fastening together the parts of a dead animal, or even a human being. The *tupilak* was brought to life by the *angakkoq* and sent on a mission to kill a specific person for revenge.

"Nicolai carved some of these," said Sven, "but not so much carving is done now. There are too many other diversions." He smiled because of what he was about to offer—exactly one of those diversions. "Would you like to see a video?"

I took an armchair and a few moments later we were watching a movie in which two detectives busted a Chicago coke ring. After the third violent car chase, Sven said, "The children in the village think that in America all you do is shoot each other from cars."

At one in the morning, with thanks for the long visit, I left and turned up the hill toward the helicopter pad, trying to walk off some of the coffee and gunfire. The sky was clear, calm, and tinged with lavender. I sat on the headland with my back to a big rock and looked down at the tiers of scattered houses. I counted thirty-five dwellings in all, plus the community buildings. Just beneath me stood the church and school. Below them, going toward the bay, was the tiny post office shack and Sven's house, and along the shore were the propane storage hut, the generator unit, the long red KNI building, and the rusted petroleum tanks. On the ice, a dozen sleds were parked with their sleeping huskies. Beyond them the neat rectangle of the ice football field waited for the following day's practice. A few hundred yards beyond the field, icebergs marched up the bay, disappearing toward the ice cap and the mountains.

My eyes came back to the village and found the white bearskin hanging on a rack above Simon and Lea's storage shed—she the manager of the KNI, he her hunter husband who had taken me fishing several times. The ideal economic unit, as Sven had said. A few weeks ago Simon had gotten this bear in the same area where Peter, Abi, and I had been hunting, but between his visit and ours, the ice had shifted and closed. And so the skin hung there, a reminder of both skill and luck, as well as my introduction to polar bear meat, which was tender, rich, and surprisingly delicate in flavor. The skull of the bear now sat on the corner of Simon's porch, staring, as I did, to the sea.

I wondered why the hunters kept these skulls—was it something more than the beauty of bone . . . respect, say, for a finer symmetry than human hands could fashion? When I had posed this question to Nicolai he had given me a gruff answer. "We see seals all the time, bears not so often. That is why we keep them."

Later I had repeated his words to Paul Alex Jensen, a friend of mine in Upernavik. He was no relation to Nicolai, but had travelled with him on many hunts. Like Sven, he was a *qallunaaq*—a foreigner, a Dane—and also married to a Greenlandic woman. He had been in the country for nearly twenty years, was fluent in the language, and known among the people as one of the few whites to have become skilled at harpooning narwhals from a kayak. In fact, he had supported his family for years as a hunter, living with the Greenlanders on the sea ice, day in and day out, so perhaps he knew what he was talking about.

"Oh, Nicolai . . . Nicolai," he said, shaking his head. "He is ashamed to admit that he might even think of animals as sacred, or that he has any ceremonies. The Greenlanders will never reveal what they think to you, and never to me. Maybe never even to themselves. The missionaries, they took everything away."

SEVEN

—>><<—

A FEW DAYS LATER EDVARD INTRODUCED ME TO ANOTHER HUN-
ter—one in the the middle ranks of the village, who came and went
unheralded, of whom no one ever said, as they did of Nicolai or Peter,
"He is great." Everything about him was average—his height, his
plump nut-brown cheeks, his button nose, and three Confucian hairs
straggling from his chin, even his name, one of the most common in
Greenland, Lars Olsen. The only thing different about him was that he
was a master of hunting *uuttoq,* basking seals, with the *taaltuaq,* the
shooting sled and sail.

He was twenty-five, married to a woman named Justine, six years
older than himself and quite a bit larger, a fixture at the KNI's cash
register. She had a fifteen-year-old daughter from a previous marriage,
two young sons by Lars, and a third on the way. Six years ago her first
husband, having just harpooned a narwhal, was surprised by a walrus
who rose up alongside his kayak. It was the very sort of aggressive rogue
bull who makes a habit of pursuing seals and hunters. Justine's husband
was dragged beneath the surface and never seen again.

Misfortune continued to plague the family. Three years later a
younger brother was lost in a speedboat accident—all that was found was
his capsized craft. The two men's disappearance into the arctic sea had
informed Lars. While on the ice, he was extremely alert, watching every
horizon with a wariness that far exceeded a hunter's careful glassing for
prey, and at home he sank blissfully into the enjoyment of his house's
security—his boys curled between his hip and Justine's back, a pile of
novels, a cup of coffee, and an overflowing ashtray by their bedside. He

had never travelled beyond Upernavik, he said modestly, two hundred miles to the south, and didn't expect he ever would. No, neither had he crossed Melville Bay. He looked distressed when I asked him this, as if I were tempting fate to make him recount long sled journeys. Perhaps if he had a reason to cross Melville Bay, he said shyly, he would. His eyes slid away from mine. They were humble and friendly, without plans or guile.

Wearing polar bear trousers, sealskin boots, and a white anorak stained with blood, Lars tromped down the stairs to the living room where I waited. His house stood on the hill overlooking Nicolai's shack and was painted a cheery yellow. In the windows of the living room Justine had placed some potted geraniums, bravely turning their red silk flowers to the snow. Atop the video was the inevitable polar bear skull.

He had been one of only three hunters to kill seals in April, and he had the jaunt of success in his step. He also wore a new canvas hat, lined with imitation fur, and as we went out the door he picked up a pair of skis that he had carved from fir planks the previous day. Sealskin was tacked to the undersides of each ski, allowing them to slide forward but not back. He put them over his shoulder, saying that he had made them for the soft ice we might encounter. They would keep his boots dry and possibly save him a dunking. At the sled he placed the skis on a rack he had also built, a nice touch that secured them out of the way, yet ready.

Nine huskies pulled us away from the village, which was quiet and still, the kids in school. A lone old man, looking like a ball of fur in his trousers and caribou parka, sat on his sled in the middle of the bay and jigged for arctic cod. Puffs of clouds obscured the sky; haze lay on the ice cap; the light was pallid and hard to gauge as to season, neither winter nor spring. Going south, we passed the tip of Saarlia Island, where a ptarmigan flew along the windswept hillsides and a raven soared and cawed lightly. An hour later, we rounded the western headland of Kia-tagsuaq, and sledded east under three enormous black walls of granite, separated by steep couloirs filled with snow. When I checked my watch against the map, I noted that we were travelling at 5 miles per hour.

Shortly, we crossed a three-foot-wide lead, the dogs leaping over the slushy water without breaking stride. The lead extended southward across the bay, southward as far as we could see toward Nuussuaq, the large headland on the southern horizon where clouds were building and moving toward us.

At an apron of rock Lars stopped the dogs, and we climbed above the bay, spying a seal—a tiny black speck—far out on the lead. Without hurry, Lars descended to the sled, had some coffee and cookies, then started the dogs along the lead, raising his glasses periodically to watch the animal. It disappeared when we were still a half mile from it. Lars continued toward a small iceberg, which we were able to climb after he had chipped hand- and footholds up its side with his long knife. Straddling the narrow top like mountaineers on an arête, we searched far across the ice. Two seals lay to the east of the lead and several more seaward, minute black shards among the bergs. Inland rose spectacular coxcombs, their prows jutting to the south as a beam of pale yellow light shone upon them from a break in the clouds.

"*Uuttoq . . . uuttoq . . . uuttoq,*" Lars said excitedly, sweeping his hand across the ice, his eyes watering in the wind.

Still he didn't hurry. We slid down the berg on the seats of our pants and had more coffee and cookies at the sled. Then he cleared the traces methodically, cursing in a low guttural voice when one of the dogs yelped. Giving his equipment a thorough visual inspection—rifle lashed against the caribou hides, shooting sled hanging from the uprights, skis on their rack—he finally stared at each horizon. Only then did he start the huskies off with a soft cluck, aiming for the two seals on the landward side of the lead.

Twice we walked through drifted snow, making it easier for the dogs, and once Lars stopped, looking for a good minute at the seals through his binoculars. They lay two hundred yards apart, the one on the right raising and lowering its head, the one on the left not so vigilant.

When we were five hundred yards from them, Lars stopped the sled a last time, laid his glasses on the caribou hide, and lashed them in place so they wouldn't be lost during his stalk. Then he bound his rifle to the shooting sled, mounted the sail around the barrel, and put five cartridges in the magazine. Taking a can of silicone lubricant from the kitchen box, he squirted some mist into the rifle's chamber, and bolted a cartridge home. As if checking off the final item of a mental list, he stared at the weapon's safety and engaged it.

Now both seals raised and lowered their heads, their rear flippers bobbing so that they looked like black gulls on a beach. Lars set out after the right one, the sail and rifle held before him. When he was halfway to the seal it raised its head, and he stopped, waiting until it resumed napping. Soon Lars was down on all fours, pushing the sled ahead of him and stopping when the seal looked up.

With only a few changes in equipment, the scene before me could have been observed several hundred years ago. Then the hunter wouldn't have crouched behind a white sail and a rifle. He would have carried a harpoon and raised his legs to imitate a seal's waving its flippers. He might also have donned sealskin, making himself look like another seal. The seal being stalked, catching a glimpse of such a camouflaged hunter, might have thought, as one hunter told me, "Ah, another *uuttoq*. Another pair of eyes to watch for polar bears," and have gone back to dozing. Onward crawled the hunter until he was within a harpoon's throw of his dinner. Some hunters, Nicolai Jensen being one of them, tell of getting so close to a seal in this way that they were able to reach out and slay it with their knife.

Lars crawled closer, his rear in the air . . . closer and closer. Through the foreshortening of my binoculars, it appeared that the muzzle of his rifle would actually touch the seal. Still he pushed on. Suddenly, he lay down. A few seconds later the seal jerked convulsively, as if diving for its hole. Its rear flippers paddled in the air, but the seal itself went nowhere. Then I heard the shot, like the ping of steel.

Up until this point the huskies had been sitting with their ears perked, watching Lars's progress. At the sound of the rifle they leapt forward and ran toward their master. Another shot sounded. Lars jumped up, sprinted toward the seal, and dragged it away from its hole by its rear flippers. When the dogs arrived, he led them off twenty yards. There they sat, whining uncontrollably.

The haul-out hole, which now lay between the dogs and the seal, was about fifteen inches in diameter and a foot deep. When I looked in it, I saw slush covering the sea. Around the hole the seal's body heat had melted the ice, which held the imprint of its five claws in several places. A bright crimson stain, big as a place mat, lay two feet from the hole, and a drag mark of lighter-colored blood led off to the seal itself.

It was a male, about three feet long, dark grey and covered with black rosettes, giving the impression of a jungle cat, an impression strengthened by his feline face: Long pearly whiskers sprouted from his cheeks. His nostrils—vertical slits—curved away from each other, like a closing and opening quotation mark placed back to back, and his eyes were big, slightly ellipsoid, and liquid black, topped by five brow hairs like a spare bouquet. His ear slits lay parallel to the line of his body; his fore flippers were pressed to his sides; only his gaping mouth disrupted the smooth lines. In the middle of his bristling teeth lay his grey tongue, spotted exactly like his coat with black flowers the size of pennies. His fur was wet and his body pliant—in fact, it was hard to feel where muscle and bone began. Lying on the ice, and discounting his predatory face, he resembled nothing so much as a furred slug. When I touched his throat, my hand came away warm.

Lars showed me where one bullet had creased the nape of the seal's neck, paralyzing him, and the second had entered behind the left flipper, exiting behind the right one, killing him. Looking up with a troubled expression, he said that his rifle was "bad." Going to the sled, he tore off the side of a cracker box, ran it out seventy yards, and stuck it in the snow. Then he lay behind his rifle, shot at the target, ran to it, came back, adjusted the scope, and shot again.

While he tuned his rifle, I thought of this ringed seal, whom the Greenlanders called *puissi* in the summer and *uuttoq* in the spring. For biologists it is *Phoca hispida.* He had spent a good part of his life under the ice being as much a predator as the man who had shot him. Using "the skylight effect"—the dim light that filters down through the ice— he had been able to sight his prey, predominantly arctic cod, about eight inches long, and also zooplankton. In addition, his whiskers and eyebrows, more technically called vibrissae, acted as pressure sensors, detecting the turbidity caused by fish. Swimming behind a cod, he would stretch out his head until his vibrissae touched the fish. Then he would suck the cod into his mouth and swallow all in one motion.

During the winter he had abraded the underside of the ice with his foreflippers to form breathing holes. Alongside some of the holes, large enough to pull himself through, called "hauling out," he had dug resting lairs in the snow. Not much larger than a seal, a resting lair can be fifty degrees warmer than the ambient temperature when occupied, which is how seals survive arctic gales when they're above the ice. When they're in the frigid water, three inches of fat keep them warm.

In just such a lair, a female ringed seal gives birth to a yellow-white, downy pup. After a month, it will begin to forage on its own, but it will stay near the breathing hole of its mother's den, where it can be found lying next to her as she molts, using the heat of the spring sun to speed the annual process. Typically, no more than a few basking seals will be found around a single breathing hole, so as to have a clear escape route from polar bears.

It is these evolutionary strategies for coping with the arctic environment that have made ringed seals, the smallest of the arctic pinnipeds, into fairly solitary creatures. Being loners has also spared them from the commercial hunting that such gregarious species as harp and fur seals have suffered. In response to these strategies, Inuit hunters have had to develop meticulous hunting techniques—standing for hours above a seal's breathing hole, harpoon poised or rifle aimed, and in the spring crawling across the ice with harpoon or rifle ready. Using these methods, Inuit have kept themselves alive for centuries while barely denting the population of ringed seals. They remain the most numerous of any pinniped, numbering an estimated 2.5 to 6 million individuals. Still, this fact must have been little consolation to the seal who now lay on the ice, soon to be our dinner.

Lars fired at his target nine more times before he was satisfied. Then he closed the bolt and pulled the trigger, listening for the click of the firing pin on the empty chamber while marking it in his mind—empty. He was the most careful hunter I had ever met.

After lashing the assembled shooting sail and rifle to the sled, he let the dogs run to the seal's hole and lick the blood. While they were occupied, he dragged the seal onto the sled and bound it to the front thwarts. Clucking the dogs into a walk, he headed inland. While he stood and glassed, I poured him a mug of coffee, which he drank without taking the binoculars from his eyes, the snow so smooth, and the huskies pulling so steadily, that he didn't spill a drop. Suddenly he lowered his glasses, pointed toward the cliffs, and said, "*Uuttoq*," smiling like a farmer standing in the midst of his fields.

He redirected the dogs slightly to the north, and when a third of a mile from the seal, he began to stalk. However, he got only a few hundred yards before the seal dove.

We continued toward the island before us, Inugsuligssuaq, and turned into the strait separating it from another, lower island, Inugsulik, on whose landward side a yellow shack stood, commanding the sheltered bay and a wide vantage: to the north the black walls of Kiatagsuaq; to the east the jutting coxcombs; to the south the frozen bay . . . icebergs . . . the cliffs of Nuussuaq, wavering in mirage.

After parking the sled on the sloping beach, Lars bypassed the hut and walked up the rocky slabs behind it. We could see several *uuttoq* in the distance. We unloaded the sled and started out, taking only the rifle and supply bag. During the next three hours Lars stalked three seals and got none. Each dove before he could fire.

We returned to the hut, tethered the dogs, and without preamble he took his long knife and carefully skinned the seal. When done, he chopped a hole in the sea ice and rinsed the pelt, working the blood out of the fur with his bare hands. Then he hung it from the *tooq* to drip for a few minutes, before folding it in thirds, hair side out. In the meantime I took the caribou sleeping hides and kitchen box up to the shack. It contained no more than a counter, a bench, and one window with a broken pane patched with flapping plastic. Old rags, seal bones, rusted batteries, newspapers, and empty sardine cans covered the floor. I pushed the litter into a corner, primed the stove, and fetched a pot of seawater.

Lars had gone back to the carcass, flaying off its blubber and setting the pink slabs aside. With the animal on its back, he opened the abdominal cavity, revealing the entrails in their well of dark blood. Cutting off the heart, he split it in half and patted it in the snow, propping it open to drain. Then he pulled out the small intestine, looping it like a lariat over his left hand and slicing each loop with one-inch cuts. As he pulled the intestine through his clenched fist, the contents jumped from the incisions. He laid the intestine by the heart and washed his hands with snow. Next, he cut away the liver and placed it in the center of one of the flanks of blubber. Kneeling by the slab of fat, he sliced off a thin piece of liver, popped it in his mouth, and chased it with some blubber.

"*Mamaq!*" he exclaimed, tasty, and offered me some, his round face beaming.

The liver reminded me of metallic seawater; the blubber was slippery and hard to bite, almost like margarine but greasier; in fact, it was almost tasteless.

"*Mamaq!*" I said, and he handed me some more.

Returning to the carcass, Lars chopped most of it into pieces, which he tossed to the dogs along with the offal. They erupted into a frenzied free-for-all, and he watched a minute before wading into their midst. Leading a small female aside, he fed her individually. Cowed by the males, she hadn't gotten a single piece. Then he again knelt by the liver and blubber and fed himself big pieces of each. The huskies, done with their meal, their cheeks stained with blood, looked on dismayed.

Finally, he gave his stomach a contented pat. Standing, he set about preparing our dinner. He cut a half-dozen ribs from the remaining quarter of the seal, and taking the heart and small intestine, climbed to the hut. The stove had warmed it, and we hung our outer clothes from a line. Beneath his polar bear trousers and anorak, Lars was dressed in blue athletic warm-ups.

Within a few minutes the heart was boiled. It was fibrous, a little salty, and delicious. In a few more minutes, Lars laid the steaming ribs on one of the sturdy grocery bags from the KNI, imprinted with a map of Greenland, showing the store's locations beneath the motto *"KNI— eqqarleriinnut tamanut"* (KNI—for the whole family). We crouched around this plastic plate, sucking the meat off the bones. The seal tasted like mutton gone to sea—thick, greasy, and with a hint of kelp. Holding ribs in his teeth, Lars whisked his knife past his lips, cutting away the blubber, which he left on the bag.

When the intestine was cooked, he took it outside and sliced it into three-inch pieces, which he piled on another slab of blubber. He handed me a piece. Surprise! It tasted like squid dipped in wasabi sauce.

Soon clouds began to cover the sky from the southeast, obscuring first the ice cap, then the coxcombs. We went into the hut, sat around the hissing stove, and finished every last bit of seal. Taking his binoculars, Lars stood in the doorway and glassed across the bay, which was rapidly disappearing from sight. Within an hour a strong, warm wind brought snow, obscuring even the nearby sled from view.

Giving a sigh of disappointment, Lars hung his glasses on a nail, lay on the bench, and pulled a caribou skin over him. I got into my sleeping bag. During the night, which never got dark, he rose periodically to pump the stove and look outside. At five-thirty in the morning, we could see a thin yellow line under the clouds, and Lars said that we would watch what the weather would do. He brewed some coffee, turned off the stove, and stuffed a rag in the torn plastic covering the window to stop its flapping. Lying back among his robes, he opened a Greenlandic novel. I had an explorer's tale and burrowed into my sleeping bag.

Reading and dozing, I felt as homey as could be, our snug little shelter surrounded by ice and vast silence. All that could be heard was the sifting of the snow against the door, a sound so soothing that it made the quiet tangible, the way mountains at the edge of a prairie make it seem larger. Out of that silence came the words I read, spoken by a Caribou Inuit, a hundred years older than we. "All true wisdom is only to be found far from the dwellings of men, in the great solitudes; and it can only be attained through suffering." I wondered if this shack qualified. Perhaps it did . . . but I doubted that I had ever suffered long enough, or that Lars had either, to attain the sort of wisdom the old hunter meant. In some ways doing what we were now doing—reading—disqualified us forever from that state of grace, for the literate person carries around with him a storehouse of experiences he has never had, a memory of places he has never set foot in—a world beyond his horizons where he can imagine assistance, no matter how tenuous, and a possible escape from his present, no matter how illusory. Those who have never read, or even seen a film, are wedded to the demands of their country in a much purer and inextricable way. Lars, without the means to leave northwestern Greenland, but with the knowledge of what lay beyond it, was one step removed from the old hunters' union. I was most distant of all.

By eight-thirty sheets of blue had unfurled across the northern sky, cirrostratus arced overhead, and five lenticular clouds, like a squadron of flying saucers, flew over the coxcombs. To the south a grey, sullen haze roiled. Lars said that he couldn't tell what kind of weather the day would bring.

We waited; the clearing part of the sky seemed to win. We set out to the south, approaching an *uuttoq* whom Lars had seen from the door of the hut. He wounded it and spent a long time probing the hole with his *tooq* without being able to retrieve it. Just before we left, he walked back along the trail of blood and looked into the hole one last time as if unable to believe that the seal wasn't there.

The wind increased and the clear half of the sky was pushed farther north. Glancing at the oncoming clouds, Lars said, "Let's go back to Kullorsuaq. The *uuttoq* won't stay on the ice with this wind."

At the hut we loaded the sled with everything except the blubber and several pounds of uncooked seal ribs, which, curiously, he left sitting on a plastic bag outside the hut. Just as we lashed the last bit of gear in place, the sun emerged, the wind died, and it grew warmer. Lars looked up, and with a mischievous smile said, "Let's stay." We unloaded the sled, walked up the hill behind the hut, and spotted two seals hauled-out in the bay. Off we went and after three hours of sledding and stalking we got neither—both dove when Lars was still hundreds of yards from them. Then the southern clouds turned ominously black and began to advance across the bay. We returned to the hut, loaded the sled one more time, and headed north toward home.

Soon glittering small snowflakes began to fall, although the sun's warmth could still be felt through the overcast. Not far beyond the strait separating the two islands, Lars saw an *uuttoq,* which was peering down into its hole. Shortly, the head of another seal emerged and the two animals touched noses.

Quickly, Lars drove the dogs toward the seal, counting, I suspected, on the falling snow and obscure light to conceal us. He grabbed the shooting sled and began his stalk at a trot. When the seal in the hole disappeared and the one on the ice looked up, he dropped into a crouch. A half minute passed . . . finally the seal lowered its head and dozed. Peeking around the side of the sail, Lars crawled forward. Closer he went, and still closer. It seemed impossible that the seal couldn't see him. Muffled by the wind came a sound like a door closing. The seal never woke up. Lars sprinted toward it, pulled it from the hole, lay down behind his sail, and pointed his rifle at the hole where he hoped the other seal would emerge. It didn't.

When the dogs reached Lars, he had already partially skinned the seal. It was a female, four feet long and tremendously fat, her flippers seeming too small to propel her great body. Why she hadn't moved was apparent. There was a neat hole above her left ear. On the other side, the bullet had taken out her right eye. On her face there was an expression of surprise— no more than a gasp—and I realized that the first seal Lars had killed, who had been paralyzed by a shot in the neck, had worn a very different expression: pain and what could only be called sadness.

Lars rinsed the skin in the sea, hung it on the *tooq* to drain, and lashed the carcass on the front of the sled. As he turned his back to the team and began to fold the skin, the huskies rushed the seal. Shouting, he grabbed his whip and beat them off; but as soon as his back was turned the largest dog, a brown and black bully, took a bite from the carcass. Lars yanked him away and kicked him in the ribs.

Keeping an eye on the dogs, he folded the pelt and stowed it next to the carcass. Then, taking a coffee filter from the kitchen box, he wiped his hands on it, picked up his binoculars, and scanned to the north. "*Uuttoq!*" he said with satisfaction, and immediately began to untangle the traces, preparing his team for the next stalk.

While he worked, I lay on the ice by the seal's hole and looked toward the south from where we had sledded: sea ice, mountains, clouds; a wide-angle view. Had she not seen the sled and dogs . . . the approaching sail? Obviously not or, if she had, they had meant no danger.

In another twenty minutes we were parked before the great black walls of Kiatagsuaq, disappearing upwards into mist and lightly falling snow. The little seal Lars had spotted lay only a few hundred yards ahead, waving a flipper in the air, rolling on its side, and dozing. Full of stealth and speed, Lars closed the distance, lay down, and shot almost immediately. The *uuttoq*'s head fell to the snow.

By the time the dogs and I arrived at the haul-out hole, Lars had the seal—a male, three-quarters the size of the female, and shot through the body—half-skinned. As Lars pulled the hide from the seal's back, it shuddered and emitted a horrible, enraged growl. Blood spurted from its mouth, and Lars slammed it on the skull with the butt of his knife. The animal lay still, and Lars looked very unhappy, completing the skinning with his jaw clenched. As he rinsed the hide, the carcass continued to quiver.

On we went around the western headland of Kiatagsuaq. There, almost on the shore and directly under its black walls, lay another *uuttoq*, still absorbing the sun's insolation, though the sky was the color of nails. Incredibly fast, as if he had been oiled with practice, Lars stalked it, slid into a prone position, and shot. The crack of his rifle, echoing from the cliffs, actually sounded like the report of a firearm. The seal staggered into its hole, and Lars looked up, beckoning at me to come faster. He didn't wait.

Running to meet the sled, he grabbed his *tooq* and ran back to the hole, which was sprayed with blood for ten feet all around. Probing gently, he stopped suddenly, and with great care chiseled away some ice from the edge. Pushing up his sleeve, he reached into the slush and came out with a flipper. A small seal followed, part of its mouth shot away, its eyes set in a quizzical regard, as if it were still trying to understand what had happened to it.

Without cleaning it, Lars fastened the seal in front of the kitchen box as a backrest for me, wrung out his sleeve, and whooped the dogs into a trot. Seaward, the icebergs became ghostly shapes and the coffee filter, which Lars had discarded several miles back, caught and passed us. Blown by the wind, it rolled out of sight. Cracking his whip gayly, he turned and said, "Much snow." You could have powered a spotlight with his smile. In the entire month of April he had taken six seals. Now he had gotten four in two days.

He whipped the huskies across a lead, the sled easily bridging it. Approaching the next open water, which was wider, Lars hesitated. Looking up and down the lead, he decided to press on. The huskies faltered at the edge; he snarled at them; they jumped for the far side and swam a bit before reaching firm ice. The sled just spanned the gap. As the dogs pulled it across, they lost their footing, and slowly, like a ship going down stern first, the sled began to vanish into the sea. Lars and I leapt off its front and hauled on the traces, while he yelled at the dogs to pull harder. With a suck, the water gave up the sled and we jumped on. The dogs shook themselves and broke into a trot.

The headland, rising into fuming clouds to our right, had provided a reference. Now—as we left the last rocks, and set out across the bay toward Kullorsuaq—all sense of place vanished. Everywhere it was white and ten feet away might have been ten miles. A hummock off the runner looked like a berg; the dogs disappeared into vapor. Keeping the wind on his right cheek, Lars whipped the dogs continually, for they wanted to turn downwind and head out to sea. Despite his calls and whipping, they did turn downwind, and he had to run alongside their left flank, kicking them so as to get them to mind. In the next hour, we jumped off the sled many times, finally resigning ourselves to running alongside the team to keep it pointed toward home.

Suddenly the hills of Saarlia Island loomed from the mist, exactly where they should have been on the left side of the sled. Without any more physical cajoling, the dogs ran along the shore. Panting, we threw ourselves on the sled, turned the headland, and saw the black finger of Kullorsuaq across the strait, like an X ray in the clouds. Straining at their harnesses, the huskies broke into a run.

At the village Lars staked the team, put the two skinned carcasses in a wood chest on the shore—the "cold boxes" where meat was stored—and began cleaning the third. In my shack, I hung my gear to dry, had some dinner, and several hours later strolled over to Lars's house to ask if we'd go hunting again tomorrow. I found him walking back from the store with Justine. He had washed up and changed into blue slacks and a black aviator's jacket with the words FLIGHT LEADER scripted across the left breast pocket. He said that maybe the day after tomorrow we could go, for his sled needed repair.

In the morning all traces of the storm had vanished. The sky was a deep soft blue that reflected the mood of the village. Men in clean white anoraks hurried to their sleds, hailing each other. Others, having been tardier at anticipating the warm weather, stood targets against the headland and sighted-in their guns. It was easy to see who, like Lars, had already brought home meat. Trails of blood led from the frozen bay to the steps of their homes. The air was full of cheer. The *uuttoq* were back.

Looking for Edvard, I found his old mother, small and dry as a piece of sinew, flensing a sealskin on the floor of her shack. Using an *ulu,* the curved skinning knife of the arctic, she took off the fat so swiftly that it looked as if she might be scraping cake icing from a pan. She hadn't seen her son, she said, so I continued on to his wife's house where I found only

Hans, his father-in-law, tending a pot of seal ribs. A dapper man, deeply pockmarked, and with a little pot belly, he wore a vest and tie, his schoolteacher's uniform, even though it was the weekend. Stirring the bubbling pot, he offered me a plate of ribs. Edvard had gone to the sled-building shack, he said. After finishing my meal, I strolled down the hill and found Edvard lashing thwarts to runners, the purple tassel of his stocking cap falling in his eyes. His wife sat on a gasoline can, smoked a cigarette, and watched him with girlish love. I asked him if he'd do some translation between Lars and me when he was done, and he replied that he was too busy with his sled right now, needing to get it done by the time classes were over. Maybe in a few days he could help.

I wandered back through the village as boys and girls began to play their afternoon football game. Closer by, a sled driver chopped a frozen seal into pieces for his team, and two preschoolers ran in front of me, chasing a hoop with a stick. At the red house below my shack a dozen people, dressed in parkas, jeans, and high-topped running shoes, had gathered on the porch around two enormous pots of boiled seal ribs and a flank of blubber on which lay an *ulu* and a liver. They cut off pieces of liver; they gnawed at the ribs; they waved me closer and pushed food into my hands. Stuffed, I ate my third meal of the day. The afternoon lengthened, the dusk fell, and the football game, now made up of the village's teenage boys, went on and on. Ten o'clock passed and so did midnight. The sky was violet, the mountains ghostly. Still the footballers played, practicing for the upcoming play-off matches to be held in Nuussuaq. At about one in the morning plump teenage girls, wearing jackets saying BORN TO SKI and LOST IN NEPAL, emerged like moths from their homes and promenaded arm-in-arm through the twilight. One hardly ever saw them during the day.

In the morning the air was still balmy, and a dozen hunters sledded away from the village, yüpping at their dogs and cracking their whips. One household opened its windows and turned up its stereo. As Lars and I headed across the bay, the voices of Diana Ross and The Supremes followed us: "It keeps me crying baby for you, keeps me sighing baby for you, so won't you hurry, come on, boy . . . come see about me."

We rounded the headland and began to negotiate the jam of icebergs before the Nunatakavsaup Glacier. On the smoother ice beyond, we spied an *uuttoq,* which Lars stalked on skis and shot. Then we sledded around the north side of Amdrup Island, climbing its northern headland to glass the sea. Hundreds of square miles of ice surrounded us—bergs, pressure ridges . . . emptiness. Not quite. My eye had become better at finding movement. Along the coast a sled appeared and vanished, looking liquid in the blobs of mirage.

"From Thule," said Lars, pointing to the northern horizon.

We descended to the sled and he drove to the small island of Uvingassoq where there was another hunting shack. It became our base while the weather lasted. From its door we could glass the arms of three bays, see the glaciers calving into the sea and the jagged mountains of Tutulissuaq looming from the ice cap.

Our outer clothes hung on a line, we read and drank coffee, Lars going to the door occasionally with his binoculars. Perhaps one out of four times he would say, "*Uuttoq!*" and we'd scramble into our parkas, run down the beach, harness the dogs, and sled away.

The hut was even more squalid than the last, filled with years of rags, cans, newspapers, and kitchen leavings. The midden heap by its side contained everything from the skulls of seals to the flywheels of outboard motors, and it was a relief to leave the littered shore and climb the rocky ridge above. There an enormous view unfolded: glaciers, nunataks, and mountains in one direction, the frozen plain of Melville Bay in the other. Across it, sleds moved like tiny centipedes. From that vantage the name Qimusseriarsuaq, "the big place for dog sledding," seemed the right one to use.

At the very top of the ridge, against an upright wall of rock, someone had placed a slab of granite to form a seat protected from the wind. From this bench I could look from one horizon to the other, and from the roof of the shack below to that of Knud Rasmussen's across the strait.

Sitting in the nook, huddled in my parka, I thought of this insightful man at one of his low moments, when he dropped his stoicism and confessed to being less than pleased with his surroundings. "As I sat eating the rotten fish," he wrote, "which was spread out on an unappetizing floor, the horrible filth of which is indescribable, and conversed with my lively hostess, it did seem to me for a moment, perhaps because I was overtired, that work among primitive peoples is not all pleasure. You have to live *with* those whom you wish to describe. If they are swine, you must live with them in their swinery."

His hostess, messy though she was, proved an excellent storyteller and repaid him for his discomfort. On just such an evening, laying aside his standards and his wish to institute reform, he translated one of the many myths of the arctic, which he rarely found to be fairy tales with happy endings. On the contrary, many of them proved to be harsh lessons, grounded in a land that forced its inhabitants to pay for their errors in judgment with their lives, where the boundary between filth and food could vanish as easily as the one between happiness and tragedy.

One of his favorites was about the foolish raven who, wanting to marry two geese, neglected their counsel and didn't rest himself before their migration. Flying far out to sea, he grew weary, and though his wives spread their wings for him, they soon saw their flock-mates speeding out of sight. Not wanting to be left behind, they abandoned their new husband. The sea washed over him, carrying him down. . . .

A raven flew overhead, looking down at me and croaking, "Karock, karock." I laugh, I laugh. "Karock." Still, a raven laughs.

And there was the one about the bear who took care of a woman, heartbroken because she had lost her child. She stayed in his house while he fed her and cared for her, asking of her only one promise—that if she returned to her kind she would never mention that she had lived with bears. But when she arrived at her home, she was unable to hold her tongue. As the bear had feared, her kinsmen drove out in sledges and surrounded him with their dogs.

And what of the starving man who ate his wives . . . or the child who cannibalized his parents? So much horror, so much sadness, so much loss . . . so much pleasure, so much . . . daylight in which to do anything one cared . . . so much darkness out of which demons grew—all of it decided so long ago, at the very beginning of time when the world was totally dark and water could burn, and people had only the light of their lamps, fueled by water. In that time, said Rasmussen, quoting another Inuit storyteller, two old women were sitting by their lamp and talking about what to do with all this darkness.

" 'Let us be without day,' one of them said, 'if at the same time we may be without death!' . . .

" 'No,' said the other one, 'we will have both light and death.' "

And that is what came to pass, though whether this was the wiser choice, no one has been able to tell.

By dinner snow was steadily falling. We crouched around the stove, chewing our seal ribs as the hut filled with steam. Later, we sat on the bench, neither reading nor talking. Mesmerized, we stared at the window where a wall of white flakes came up to the panes.

By morning the sky had cleared, bringing a remarkably cold wind from the north. Not weather for *uuttoq* hunting, said Lars, and we packed and left.

Pushed by the wind, the sled loaded with carcasses, we sped through the strait between Amdrup and Qârusulik islands. The wind rolled the previous night's snowfall into a ground blizzard; the bergs ahead shone incandescently; between Knud Rasmussen and Nicolai Jensen's hunting huts we met another sled, outward bound. It was one of the oldest hunters of the village and he was alone, his brown face creased with deep furrows, his body thin and bent over. He wore a smart blue anorak and luxurious polar bear trousers. Lars and he jumped off their sleds and stood talking in the wind, whips in hand as the snow blew around them. Lars pointed to the spots he had gotten seals and the old man noted each with a nod. There was a brief moment of silence. Then they jumped on their sleds and whipped up their dogs. The old man waved as we passed. On each lens of his mirrored sunglasses was a pink palm tree.

Two days later Edvard met me on Lars's porch where the flensed sealskins were hung to dry. Sold to the KNI, each would fetch Lars about forty-five dollars. The weather had turned mild again, and he sat on his porch rail, wearing only jeans, a red-and-white-checkered shirt, and a pair of new running shoes—mild, of course, being relative. The thermometer read twelve degrees Fahrenheit.

"Why did he choose to hunt in the bays," I asked, "instead of going out to the ice edge?"

"He doesn't have a kayak," Edvard translated, "to fetch seals from open water, and there are too many other hunters there. He prefers less competition and he likes to hunt *uuttoq*."

"Why did he go first south, then north to hunt? Did he know that one place would be better than the other at different times?"

"No. Sometimes he goes on whim, sometimes he just likes to explore new territory."

"What is the most seals he has ever gotten in a day?"

"Eight."

"Why did he leave behind the seal ribs that we didn't cook, on a plastic bag by the door of the huts? Was it for other hunters, or a gift?"

When Edvard translated this question, Lars looked at the ground as if ashamed.

"I have plenty of meat here," he said.

Edvard seemed uncomfortable at this, and I waited to see what would happen. With a shrug, he added, "There is much meat."

I let it be and asked, "After he killed each seal, I saw him bend over and touch it. What was he doing? Was it something special?"

"Yes, it was," said Lars, brightening. "I look to see where I have shot and if my aim has been true."

THE FOOTBALLERS RETURNED FROM NUUSSUAQ, HAVING WON THEIR
match. Greeted by friends and family, who shouted and fired guns, they
marched along the main path of the village, holding their trophy overhead and crying, "Hey! Hey! Hey!"

School finished for the year and fathers and their young sons, dressed
alike in white anoraks, set off hunting for *uuttoq,* pushing their sleds over
the widening fissure where the sea ice joined the shore. From the fissure
deep cracks, jagged as lightning bolts, radiated across the bay—indicating the coming breakup.

Already the southern hillsides had begun to melt, exposing boulders
and tufts of brown grass, discarded food packaging, seal bones, dog
turds, and oily seeps running from the blubber piles. The smell of rotting fish and feces drifted on the air, as well as a familiar but hard-to-
place sound—rising and falling, vibrating . . . birds! And not the
ever-present ravens. From boulder to boulder, carrying bits of grass in
their beaks, snow buntings flew. A little larger than finches, they were
plump, with grey backs and dapper black legs. *Plectrophenax nivalis. Snes-
purv* in Danish. In Greenlandic, *Qupaloraarsuk.* Spring.

Then a hunter arrived from down the coast, saying that the men from
Nuussuaq had taken the first narwhal of the season—at the ice edge far
offshore. Peter Aronsen loaded his sled with harpoons and kayak and set
off within hours. Edvard Nielsen's father and his uncle, Timotheus, left
as well, and so did Otto Danielsen and Lars Petersen. All had one thing
in common. They had been called "great hunters" by Sven, a title he gave
to only ten out of the forty hunters in the village, his criterion being that

a man not only hunted *uuttoq* and polar bear, but also narwhal with a kayak and harpoon. For whatever reason—because they wanted to travel light, or they knew that they might be bringing back much meat—none of the great hunters asked me to go along.

Walking through the village, I saw Nicolai, leaning on his porch rail and smoking a cigarette as he watched the men depart. He was waiting for Lars's return from Savissivik so they could go to their summer home on Qârusulik, and he looked as dejected as an old dog who could no longer run. He gave me a curt wave, not his usual beckoning to join him on his porch, and he turned and went inside.

At the sled building shop I found Edvard still lashing thwarts to the runners of his sled. Now that school was over I was hoping we could depart for Tutulissuaq and look for bears. But he said that he needed at least a week to get ready, and he had also heard that the snow was deep, so travelling would be difficult. Besides, some of the young hunters who were joining us had gone to the ice edge for narwhal. I had learned not to press him. "Let me know," I said.

Slipping on the melting path, I walked down to Sven's and found him napping on his living room couch. Rising, he asked me if I would like some coffee and a game of chess. While he put out the pieces, I told him of our delayed departure to Tutulissuaq, and with a surprising amount of bite he said, "Edvard is not a hunter."

"He plans to hunt all summer—like you."

Sven lit his pipe, cleared his throat, and said, "We will see." Having drawn the first move, I pushed out a pawn. He took a long time to contemplate his gambit as I watched two more sleds cross the bay. "Everyone is off for narwhal," I said.

"Yes. It's very exciting. Will you go with Peter?"

I mentioned that he had left the day before.

"They have their ways," he said, and frowned. Then he asked, "What about Lars Olsen?"

I reminded him that Lars didn't have a kayak.

"Yes. I forgot that."

"You do."

He shook his head. "I will retrieve seals that I have shot with my kayak, but I have never gone after narwhal. I am a teacher, not a great hunter." He thought a moment longer. "But Simon Olsvig lost his kayak in a windstorm last year and just the other week his rowboat was crushed in the ice. I know he would like to go to the ice edge, but he cannot without a boat. Perhaps we could make a party, and he could use my kayak." Absentmindedly, he moved a pawn, exposing his king.

I moved my queen and said, "Check."

"Ah!" He put down his pipe. "I have made an error."

Thinking of Simon using his kayak to get the newly arrived narwhals, he had—it was the only time I ever won a game from him. Afterward, we walked up the hill to Simon's house, and Sven described his plan. Simon, who had been sitting at his dining room table and glumly looking at the bay through binoculars, immediately beamed and seemed to grow larger before our eyes. Perhaps it was the thought of all the meat and *mattak* a narwhal would provide, or the money to be made from its tusk, or just the excitement of chasing them. In a deep voice, he called upstairs to his son, Karl, to get ready; he telephoned his wife, Lea, at the KNI, and asked her to bring home some food; he looked to his dogs parked on the ice, counted on his fingers, did a mental calculation, and said, "We will leave by this afternoon." Which we did.

Narwhals have a way of doing that to people, and not just to Greenlandic hunters. For at least two and a half thousand years, the genus they represent—*Monodon*, one-toothed—has tantalized our species as we have pursued them occasionally in fact and mostly in myth.

The first Westerner to describe them was the Greek physician Ctesias, who in 416 B.C. accepted an appointment to the court of King Darius II of Persia. He brought home tales of a single-horned creature, the asslike unicorn, who was swift, powerful, and possessed amazing properties. Those who drank wine or water from its horn were immune to epilepsy and the effects of poison.

Such lore was later corroborated by Aristotle, Pliny, and Aelian, all of whom added some single-horned creatures to the genus: the rhinoceros, the Indian ox and horse, and the bison. By the time of the late Middle Ages and early Renaissance, when narwhal tusks began to find their way to Europe from Greenland, providing "proof" of the unicorn's existence, the nobility of the continent began to spend enormous sums for their putative charms, carrying them about, as Odell Shepard writes in *The Lore of the Unicorn*, "on dark nights and in perilous places." Why royalty become dependent on these shafts of ivory that, several thousand miles to the north, were still being used as harpoon shafts is an interesting sidelight on the politics of the time.

During the Renaissance, Shepard explains, poison became the favored means of political assassination. As skilled assassins began to use substances that had delayed effects, the protection afforded by food tasters, the favored means of Roman emperors to foil poisoners, was diminished. Fearing for their lives, noblemen grasped at anything that ancient wisdom claimed might disclose a fatal meal or cup: snake's tongue, griffon's claw, toadstones, and the horn of the unicorn. Hung in dining halls and carried to the table by an officer of the household, the horn was touched to food or immersed in a drink. If it sweated, or its appearance changed in the least—poison.

Of course, many merchants who sold the horns didn't know from where they came and believed in the myth of the horselike unicorn as much as did their customers. Those who had discovered the true source of the horn—a whale from the northern seas—had little desire to reveal its origin and risk spoiling their profits.

Had most of the Continent's royalty known the origin of the horn they dipped in their food, they might not have been so eager to trust its prophylaxis. In Old Norse "narwhal" means "corpse-whale," supposedly because the pallid color of the narwhal's skin resembles that of a drowned human. However, in the water narwhals are anything but pallid. Their backs and sides are the color of fine black marble sprinkled with oblong white spots, and as the spots curve onto the lighter belly region, they merge and disappear. Young narwhals are grey and old males can become almost white.

Seen floating from the side, narwhals also seem, at least to me, a bit ungainly and even humorous, exhibiting the portly man's profile: a stout midriff, a small head, and a lean tail. While resting, the rear two thirds of a narwhal's body hangs down into the water at about a thirty-degree angle, and the tusk lies parallel to the surface. The corners of its mouth turn up, giving it a constant grin, and its flippers are short compared to most whales, a little over a foot long, and curved along the leading edge and rounded at the tip. It has no dorsal fin, only a ridge of fatty tissue— two inches high and about two and a half feet long—midway between its snout and tail. Its tail, I think, is its most beautiful feature. Deeply but smoothly cleaved, like a bosom, the four-foot-wide fluke is black on its leading edges and full of grey swirls like the reflections of clouds on a dark and placid sea.

For this creature, *qernertaq,* we now waited.

We had left at four in the afternoon, sledding through an incandescent snowstorm, the big wet flakes melting as they landed on the sleds. I rode with Simon and Sven followed with his white kayak lashed on his sled. Karl, Simon's fifteen-year-old son, brought up the rear.

Of all the hunters in the village Simon was the neatest. The tarp covering the floor of his sled had been washed of bloodstains; its ropes were coiled; the kitchen box was new. Not only was his own dress equally neat, it had a touch of panache: Besides the usual costume of polar bear trousers and anorak, he wore a blue ski hat with a green pom-pom. Compact and perfectly proportioned, with high cheekbones and a strong jaw, Simon might have been the first man to have set off for the New World from Asia—eyes clear and searching the distance, skin smooth and the color of good earth. He also had an ever-present smile, which may have been a product of his financial good fortune. Married to the manager of the KNI, he lived luxuriously while still being a hunter. In his rations were vacuum-packed cold cuts and Havarti cheese, and he wore a magnificent white turtleneck beneath his anorak.

After a couple of hours the snow tapered off, and the clouds began to disperse. Seaward of Kiatagsuaq, we turned north along a lead that had been sealed by the moving ice. Tossed-up blocks, like a jagged scar, pointed to the horizon. We followed this barrier for several miles until the lead reopened slightly and we were able to cross. Simon drove his dogs through the slush unassisted, then dragged at the harness of Sven's lead dog, who was reluctant to cross. Karl's huskies, too, needed coaxing. He stood on his sled, snarling at them with all the embarrassment of a teenage boy who wants to be an equal among men. In his beautifully tailored caribou parka and polar bear trousers, he looked like a great hunter, and of course he was brandishing his whip expertly, but inside his clothes, he was still a thin, young, self-conscious boy, raising his hand to his mouth when his voice cracked. When he laughed, which was often, it was a tinkling version of Nicolai's, "Hee-hee-hee."

We sledded west under the clearing heaven. As the hours went by, and the sun slid north, the light turned a soft, ambrosial blue. Simon stopped by a small berg and climbed it.

"*Imaq!*" he whooped, lowering his binoculars. The sea.

We joined him and saw in the far distance a pond of shining water, like a stain of quicksilver before a mountain range of ice.

"There will be seals," he said as we returned to the sleds. "And maybe narwhals." Making a breaching motion with his hand, he unlashed his rifle and laid it, muzzle forward, on the caribou skins. We set off, and as we drove toward the setting sun I thought of the narwhals who might be swimming beneath it.

As whales go, they aren't large. Without his tusk a male may stretch fifteen feet and weigh thirty-five hundred pounds. Females are a bit smaller. Generally, only males bear a tusk, on rare occasions two, each of which can be up to nine feet long. Very rarely, females will show one tusk, and even more infrequently, a pair. This—the unicorn's horn—is in reality an enormous tooth, erupting from the gum, protruding through the upper lip, and spiralling sinistrally. Most often tusks are creamy white in color, tending to pale canary yellow, and grooved to within a few inches of their polished tips. Though many have theorized on the cause of the spirals in the narwhal's tusk, no one has hit upon a conclusive answer.

If biologists remain murky as to the physiological origins of the spiralled tusk, they are clearer about its function. It is now generally thought that it is a secondary sexual characteristic used in social rituals to determine dominance. Narwhals have been observed crossing their tusks both above and below the surface and striking them against each other. When approaching head-to-head, they may be trying to gauge which tusk is larger. Such encounters produce head scarring and broken tusks—one narwhal has even been found with the point of another tusk embedded near the base of its own. Narwhals do not spear their prey with their tusks, as was once believed, nor do they ram boats.

In fact, their tusks may have evolved for a much more sensitive purpose—to transmit vocalizations. Like other cetaceans, narwhals make underwater acoustic signals: clicks that resemble the echolocation sounds of dolphins and which are almost certainly used for the same purpose, as well as both pulsed and pure tones (the latter like whistles), that may be social signals and the signature of individual animals. Interestingly enough, the tusk has its origin within a few centimeters of the nasal region that is considered by most researchers to be the emanating site of these sounds. One researcher, while handling captive narwhals, found that "when a captive bull narwhal vocalized, strong vibrations corresponding to the sound could be felt running down the tusk." These observations bring up an obvious question. Is the female portion of the population, largely tuskless, hampered in its ability to communicate? As far as we can tell, no.

As Randall Reeves, a Canadian biologist, has said, "I wish we knew more."

We do, but not much. Perhaps thirty thousand of these creatures live along the shores of western Greenland and throughout the Canadian archipelago. How many swim east of Greenland and across the Russian arctic is anybody's guess. Not many are taken. Canada's national quota is 527, allocated settlement by settlement. Presently no quotas have been set in Greenland. The hunters of Kullorsuaq take about twenty each spring.

Bearing just left of the setting sun, we now crossed a level plain of snow. At about midnight we came over a rise and saw the lead in the distance, a quarter of a mile wide, narrowing into a channel only a few feet across, which extended north, straight as a conduit. On the far side of the lead the bergs were lit pink, and above them flew a wavering line of marine birds. The water was very still, like high-gloss pewter, and reflected the bergs as a tarn reflects mountains. In another moment the air smelled of the ocean, and the dogs broke into a run.

A tent was pitched by the ice edge and two figures raised their hands—Otto Danielsen and Lars Petersen. We drove the dogs by their camp and on to the north a few hundred yards where we staked the teams. Simon, Karl, and Sven immediately lashed their rifles to their shooting sleds and pointed them toward the water, which was filled with a skim of slush.

While they made their preparations, I walked to the ice edge and looked down, noting that the seemingly solid platform of ice on which we stood was only about three feet thick. It was white in its upper third and a faint shade of turquoise toward its bottom. A skein of silver bubbles hung along its side, and beneath them the sea was a profound and limitless black. According to a chart I carried, it was twenty-two hundred feet deep, the home of cod, halibut, and catfish. The last, what the Greenlanders called *qeeraq,* was an ugly monster with gaping jaws, huge shoulders, and not much of a tail, only a dorsiventral flattening of its body—the last thing one could imagine eating. Yet its flesh was white and very tasty. There were shark down there, too, mottled and dusky, with rows of back-pointing, triangular teeth—Karl and I had hauled a seven-footer from his fishing hole a month before. Most of these creatures never willingly broke the surface—their only relationship to the air was as the prey of men and seals and marine birds, all of whom used the ice edge as their hunting ground: Men camped upon it; pinnipeds swam beneath its margins; flying over miles of ice, birds finally descended to its edge where they could feed. Far out in the lead common eiders splashed. Above them black guillemots, a small alcid related to the puffins, auks, and murres, passed in flocks that made the sound of rustling tissue paper in the still air.

Though I was reluctant to stick my head into the frigid water and see their brownish-green blur, I also knew that another life-form used the underside of the ice edge—algae with intricate skeletons made of silica, known as diatoms. Adapted to cold, they could produce oxygen through photosynthesis even under the low-light conditions that existed beneath the ice. During the dark winter it is thought that they survive by metabolizing nitrogen and carbon. They were the starting point for the oceanic food chain that supported all life along this coast.

Upon them crustaceans fed. These tiny, shrimplike creatures, collectively known as zooplankton, displayed a wide variety of sizes and adaptations. Some, like the half-inch-long *Onisimus,* could burrow into the ice; others, like the three-inch long *Gammaracanthus,* walked along its under surface; still others, *Parathemisto,* were upwelled and then, as some researchers believe, were able to maintain their position close to the ice edge to feed upon the algae sluffing off its bottom.

All these crustaceans were fodder for the arctic cod, a diminutive fish that reached eight or nine inches in length during its six-year life span. Adapted to the increased salinity and cold that occurred below the ice edge, and having a specially shaped mouth designed for sucking zooplankton off the under-ice surface, the fish inhabited crevasses within the ice itself. In turn, the smallest of the cod, a few inches in length, fed some of the marine birds like the guillemot. Frequenting the ice edge and diving below it, guillemots also ate zooplankton. The other bird in the lead before me, the eider, was waiting for inshore water to open. There, in the shallows, it could dive to the bottom and feed on the clams and benthic crustaceans that made up its diet. In the meantime, like the guillemot, it was receiving the benefit of the ice edge's shelter—in its lee it could escape the wind and enjoy warmer temperatures.

The arctic cod and crustaceans also sustained the ringed seals that Simon, Karl, and Sven had come to shoot. Narwhals fed on the cod, and polar bears ate both whales and pinnipeds. The people of Kullorsuaq ate all five varieties of ice-edge dwellers—fish, seals, birds, whales, and bears—the ravens and the arctic fox taking what remained. I was standing on an ecotone—a region of transition and mixing, a meeting ground, a connector of life-forms.

KA-POOOOM!

Simon lay behind his rifle. An instant after its report, the bullet creased the slush in the lead, going over the head of a seal who dropped immediately from sight. Simon stood up, good-naturedly scuffed the snow with his boot, and reached for another seal rib from the pot steaming in front of Otto and Lars's tent. I walked over.

A canvas tent had been erected over their paired sleds and from inside it came the sound of light snoring—Otto's younger brother, Marcus, had given up the vigil and gone to sleep. Before the tent, at the edge of the lead, four rifles on shooting sleds pointed toward the water, as did the bows of Otto and Lars's yellow-and-white kayaks. A few yards from the pot of ribs lay the carcasses of two seals, surrounded by blood-stained snow. At the corner of the tent lay a common eider, a *miteq,* its plumage more vivid than any I had seen. In the low light of the sun, its crown glowed jet black; its thick bill was golden; its breast was the color of rosewood; its cheeks ivory. Lying on the snow, the duck was as beautiful and unlikely as a bowl of fruit.

KA-POOOOM!

Eighty yards out in the lead a seal thrashed, staining the water a dark red. Lars, a tall, thin hunter, stood up from his rifle, slid into his kayak, and paddled off, leaving a glossy channel through the slush. He put a gaff through the nose of the seal and returned, keeping the towline between his teeth, so that if a walrus tried to grab the seal, he could let it go and not be pulled under. Paddling toward us, he seemed to be on an alpine lake, for the sun had set and the bergs behind him were lit by alpenglow.

Finishing a rib, Karl punted the gnawed-clean bone into the lead where it landed with a tiny sound—*tack!* A moment later we heard the muffled pops of gunfire—one, two, three shots, followed by another half-dozen, coming from the south.

"Oh, they are in a lucky spot," said Sven.

Lars slid the kayak along the ice edge, and Otto, roly-poly in his parka and polar bear trousers, grabbed the towrope. Within a few minutes the seal had joined the two carcasses by the cook pot. We strolled to our camp, and Sven took a position at the narrowing of the lead. Standing above his shooting sled, he lit his pipe and clasped his hands behind his back with an air of great contentment. Simon and Karl sat on a sled, their rifles an arm's length away. After brewing a pot of coffee, they opened some pâté and crackers and made dainty little sandwiches, their eyes never leaving the water.

"Do you think we will see a narwhal?" I asked.

"Maybe," said Simon, wagging his head in a gesture that seemed to say he was pretty sure that we would.

By two in the morning I could no longer stay awake. I threw my bag on the snow behind our tent, and when I awoke at eight I found two seals lying nearby. Simon and Karl had each gotten one, having slept, they said, only an hour. Sven was standing at the ice edge looking across what had enlarged into a bay. Occasionally the head of a seal would appear, but far out of range.

It was a beautiful morning—no clouds in the sky, the sun already high, the distant mountains rising from pearly hills of fog. Along the coast we could see from Nuussuaq to Tutulissuaq, a distance of nearly one hundred miles.

Looking for a narrower lead, we sledded north for a couple of hours until we found one that was only thirty feet across and just beginning to open slowly to the west. We stopped. A moment later a seal appeared, and Sven shot it. Here, Simon declared, we would camp for the day, shoot seals, and wait for narwhals.

The sleds were put together to form a couch, a stove was lit, and a pot of seawater brought to boil. Sven butchered the seal he had just taken, and Simon and Karl cut up the two from the previous evening. The huskies shivered in anticipation, their tongues playing at their lips as they whined and salivated.

Flippers, vertebrae, shoulder joints, intestines, hearts, livers—all got flung into the air above the dog teams. Growling and snarling at each other, ripping, snapping, and tearing, they ate their single meal of the day in a little over a minute. We took a little longer on our ribs.

Then Karl and Simon lay on their sleds and went to sleep, and Sven shot another seal and fetched it with his kayak. Afterwards, while our companions continued to doze, he sat on his sled smoking his pipe, and I reclined on my sleeping pad, my back against the runner. The sun was warm on our faces and the water sparkling blue—we might have been at the beach. Half-dozing, we watched the lead grow wider and wider. From a canal it became a pond, then a lake, finally a sound, what is called a polynya—a large extent of open water in the sea ice. Within an hour the far side disappeared, forming mirages that looked like trees. Looking up at Sven, I noticed that his face, lifted toward the sun and the minute breeze, was as serene as this gentle day. I mentioned that I had rarely seen a friendlier moment in the arctic, and he said that it was why he liked spring hunting so much—to be by the water, to kayak, to enjoy the long, warm days, and to run dogs all at the same time.

He gazed at the distant mirage and gave a sigh, which I took to be one of contentment, but then I noticed that his face had grown somber.

"But sometimes I become lonely for my homeland," he said. "Even here at the ice edge, and it puts me in a dilemma."

Emilie and his children didn't speak Danish, he said, and if he returned to Denmark they would be far more isolated than he was in Greenland.

"Don't you consider yourself a Greenlander after fifteen years?"

"No, I am a Dane, working in Greenland."

Before I could respond, Otto and Marcus on one sled, and Lars on a second, drove along the lead. Waving at us, they continued north.

"They are looking for narwhal," said Sven, "and this isn't a perfect spot." I could tell by the tone of his voice that he had closed the subject of his dilemma and had returned to immediate concerns. "There's no ice block to trap them so they can be harpooned."

"Will you try to harpoon a narwhal if we see one?"

"No. But I hope Simon will try with the kayak. But maybe he won't. He has gotten five narwhals, all shot from the ice, and maybe he will not want to start harpooning now. It is dangerous you know."

Perhaps I wore a dubious expression, for he elaborated. "Any of these hunters would choose to make his life easier if he could. I think that they would use a harpoon gun if they could bring it on the ice. Maybe they would even hunt by a helicopter if it were available." I made a skeptical face, and he qualified what he had said. "They work hard and they get tired. And it's dangerous. All they want, I think, is more money and more leisure time."

"Have you asked them?"

"They don't talk about these things. They don't—" he searched for the word, "speculate."

"What would they do with more free time?"

"The same thing everyone else does—entertain themselves."

"*Puissi!*"

Sitting upright, Simon pointed to the water. A very large seal paddled several hundred yards off the ice edge. Simon jumped up, grabbed his *tooq,* and ran to the ice edge. Putting the metal end of the *tooq* in the water and the wooden shaft in his mouth, he began to make a low moaning sound.

"He is trying to call the seal closer," whispered Sven.

The seal, however, didn't like what it heard. It dove into a bright patch of water and didn't reemerge for a long time. When it did Simon pointed at it, far off in the lead, and Sven lay down behind his rifle. The shot was low and the seal dove.

Standing up, Sven said, "I am not too good at that distance."

Then another seal appeared a hundred yards off. Dropping to the ice again, Sven bolted a round and fired. We could hear the wet smack of the bullet. He went to his boat, paddled out, and retrieved the floating seal, whom I dragged on the ice when he handed me the line.

There was a neat hole behind the seal's left eye; the right side of its head was blown away. She was a female with exceptionally long whiskers . . . then I noticed her chest pulsing. I put my hand on her heart and counted the throbs—seventy per minute—until they stopped.

In the meantime Simon studied two harpoons that he had placed in the ice. They were a dozen feet apart, and he sighted across their tops toward Kiatagsuaq, trying to determine if the ice we were on had moved. Then he looked to the lead, which had grown into a full-fledged bay. Six hours ago it had been only thirty feet wide. Now one flat iceberg, floating in the wavering mirage, could be seen on its far side.

We were on moving ice, he said, and we should go.

We broke camp and followed the other hunters' sled tracks along the lead. Within a mile the water disappeared under a berg, but we found it again on the other side, leading north. On the horizon, it joined a polynya, glittering in the sun.

Soon another lead crossed our route and forced us toward land. We went through a field of confused ice—Sven leading. At times we were out of sight of each other. An hour went by and a shot sounded ahead of us. When we reached Sven he was lashing a small seal to his sled.

We didn't get much farther before the sled tracks we were following vanished into open water. Already this new lead was a hundred yards wide. We turned right and within a minute found another lead opening before us, trapping us on a giant, floating pan of ice. A half sled length wide, it was visibly enlarging. Simon looked over his shoulder and yelled at Karl to hurry. We crossed the lead, entered some giant ice blocks, and found Sven overturned among them, futiley trying to right his sled. Simon leapt off our sled and began to pull at Sven's as if our lives depended on it. Everyone lending a hand, we righted the sled and its lashed-on kayak. Then we shoved and lifted the other two sleds through the blocks, and Simon forced his team ahead, shouting at Sven and Karl to hurry. Another half an hour of hard driving, and two lead crossings, brought us to a lead that made a sinuous curve toward where Lars and Otto had gone. Immediately we could see it closing and Simon stopped alongside it. He took off his hat, leaned against the uprights of his sled, and said, in English, "Rest."

The air was so still, and we were so hot from the work, that we not only took off our hats, but also our gloves and parkas as we waited for Karl. He didn't arrive for a long time, and Simon almost started back to search for him. But then he came into sight, a freshly killed seal jiggling on his sled. As he cleaned it, the lead by which we had stopped grew so narrow that within ten minutes we bridged it easily, and headed north toward the setting sun.

It took another hour to weave our way through a few miles of tall spindly bergs. When we emerged from the maze, the blue-and-white glare of the day had diminished and we found ourselves before the giant lake we had seen several hours before, the bergs on its far horizon topped by faint pink clouds. We drove to the ice edge and sledded along the water, Karl's and Simon's whips making golden hoops in the air. At the corner of the bay, the perfect spot to trap a narwhal as Sven had said, we saw the kayaks of Otto and Lars, pointing toward the water. Twenty yards back from the ice edge stood their tent. We, too, parked and camped.

No sooner had we staked the huskies than a seal rose in the water before us. Its smooth, glistening head turned left and right, its eyes wide. Falling behind his rifle, Simon shot over the seal. It dove and came up again a few yards away. Again Simon missed. The seal rose a third time and Simon hit it squarely in the head. Thrashing on the surface, the seal tried to dive while a fountain of its blood spouted and burbled. Finally, like a stove-in tanker, it lay still while a stain of blood washed away from it.

After Simon retrieved it, we all began to pitch the tent. Hardly was it erected, though, before a walrus surfaced off the ice edge. Simon, quicker to his rifle than Sven or Karl, opened fire on it, and with a slinky motion it submerged. Clucking his tongue, he smiled and shook his head.

The sun went behind a bank of clouds, turning the seascape a dusky grey. It became difficult to see the seals, who now rose in great numbers. Taking turns, Sven, Karl, and Simon lay behind their rifles, shot methodically, and paddled the kayak into the bay to retrieve the floating animals. As the twilight deepened, the seals vanished.

Catching his breath, Sven sat on his sled while Simon went into the tent to make coffee and Karl began to skin. In front of us lay a row of greenish-black carcasses, their fur flowered with spots. Beyond them the water skimmed over with slush.

Noticing me looking at the mangled heads of some of the seals, Sven took a cartridge from his pocket and showed me its soft-nose bullet, explaining that the expansion of such bullets killed the seal instantly with a large wound, but sometimes ruined their hides. Most of the hunters used nonexpanding, full-metal case bullets, he said, so as minimize damage to the hides, which they wanted to sell. But sometimes these bullets wounded and didn't kill. He preferred to ruin a hide and get the meat.

I stared at the last seal he had shot. Both its eyes were gone and two tubes of brain matter hung down its cheeks. It was a wound that seemed almost sacrilegious, turning the seal's expressive and curious face—its lights, its windows upon the world—into mush. And yet, for an animal who shows only its head above the water and whose instinct is to dive for its hole through the ice, the head shot kills instantly and cuts the hunter's losses. Was the harpoon—the seal writhing on the end of the shaft—any kinder? Was *kindness* the right word to use?

As I handed Sven the cartridge we heard a distant noise and looked up. From across the bay, at the horizon where another ice edge rose into bergs, came the sound of a large splashing and, unmistakably, as if transmitted through crystal, the long, drawn-out moans of whales.

Standing over a seal, Karl became immobile. His right hand grasped a big knife. Cocking his ear to the sea, he held the fingers of his left hand spread in the air. His eyes were so big that their whites shone in the dusk.

The sound hung, vanished, reappeared.

"*Atata! Atata!*" he cried. Father! Father! "*Qernertaq!*" Narwhal!

Simon threw open the flap, listened a second, then grabbed a cased rifle from where it lay in the snow. Wearing a huge smile, he opened the action of a rusted 30-06 and sprayed it with lubricant. He swayed his shoulders as if dancing. Sven began to assemble his harpoon. With a hopeful glance at Simon, he laid it and its float alongside his kayak. Silently paddling their boats, Otto and Lars appeared along the ice edge and drifted in front of our camp. Otto had a harpoon and rifle lashed to his deck, Lars only a rifle, for he hadn't finished the sealskin float he had been making.

For a long time we waited—not moving, not speaking. The bright spot in the northern clouds circled a little farther to the right, a little farther to the northeast, and the first pod of distant splashing moved south and another followed it from the far side of the bay. We searched the horizon with our binoculars but for a long time could see nothing, only hearing their exhalations and high-pitched squeals and sonorous moans. Then out of the mirage, a half-dozen whales breached, their backs mottled and silver in the dusky light. Along the distant shore, pod after pod followed them. In the meantime seals once again began to rise before us, swimming, diving, playing—unmolested. No one wanted to scare off the narwhals by shooting.

Three A.M. passed. Lars and Otto drifted in their boats. Karl, Simon, and Sven stood holding their rifles. An orange haze colored the eastern sky, and the singing of the narwhals grew louder as they curved around the southern shore of the polynya. In the distance, they began to come up our side of the bay. Soon their voices were coming from the air itself, making the whales seem like avian creatures instead of marine ones. The ice upon which we stood had begun to act as an acoustical resonator.

In another moment the narwhals became visible to the naked eye. Their black backs rose and fell against the white ice, accompanied by the sound of their spouting, and by their limpid calls, like geese on the edge of one's imagination, or coyote song far away in the moonlight, both intermingled and synthesized by water. I raised my binoculars. In the mirage where sea met ice, the narwhals appeared out of a sky-blue strip of ether and breached smoothly, their spines like gibbous moons, their flukes sliding back into a substance that seemed neither sea nor sky. Two more hours went by. A large and valuable hooded seal rose, inspected us, and disappeared without a shot being fired at it, though all the hunters looked at it with longing.

Then—spreading the slush without a ripple or a sound—three narwhals came toward camp. Simon and Karl ran down the lead with their rifles as Sven looked forlornly at his abandoned harpoon and kayak. Paddles light in their hands, Otto and Lars waited.

The whales sounded. Within a few seconds they rose again, only two hundred yards from us, a cow and a calf. The slush lifted over their backs and slid down their sides without breaking. They seemed frictionless. The third narwhal followed and sounded. Within a few seconds two more whales came up the lead, a hundred yards off from where Simon and Karl had hidden themselves in some ice blocks. They headed directly for Otto and Lars and the two men grew visibly tense but didn't do anything except hold their paddles. When we next saw the whales they were far offshore and heading away.

Ten minutes later . . . thirty minutes—who could tell as the splashing and singing continued to fill the air—three more narwhals swam along the ice edge, not fifty yards off. Karl, who had returned to camp, began to run along the shore, back to his father, but Sven told him to stop.

The whales humped smoothly from the dark water in front of the ice blocks among which Simon had hidden. A shot sounded, followed by his hideous cursing. Two whales sounded immediately; the third thrashed its long white tusk from side-to-side and dove.

Uneasily, Sven said, "He missed."

A second later a whale breached thirty yards from us. The sound of its explosive breath was so loud we jumped. Again it breached, twenty yards away, its back glistening and spotted, the water molten along its flanks. It dove without leaving a ripple.

And then it rose in front of us, spouting so strongly that I sucked in my breath and shuddered as two shots crashed next to my ear. One missed, striking feet in front of the whale, the other . . . the narwhal sounded quickly, without leaving a splash. Sven and Karl stood with their rifles at their shoulders. As immobile as they had been for hours, Lars and Otto waited. A few minutes later a whale surfaced several hundred yards off and continued out to the bay.

Dejected, Simon walked into camp. Shaking his head, he held his rifle toward us as if it might be defective. Lars got out of his kayak and came into the tent while Otto paddled off to the north. As the three men brewed coffee, Karl shouted from outside. Another narwhal was swimming toward camp. The four hunters grabbed their rifles, ran along the ice edge and waited . . . waited . . . waited. The whale never reappeared.

They returned to the tent. Simon and Lars lit cigarettes. At last coffee was made. Lars said nothing, just drank his coffee without removing his green anorak or dark glasses, his sharp face expressionless.

Standing outside, I could still hear the distant splashing and calling of the whales. Finally, they vanished.

Sven brought out his cup, sat on his sled, and watched the water. Not a seal could be seen now. He lit his pipe.

"Did you hit it?" I asked, sitting down beside him. "Or did Karl?"

"I believe I hit her in the meat. She surprised me and I shot too fast. We did not do this well."

"How do you mean?"

"Simon should have let Otto harpoon the narwhal. But then Simon would have only gotten some meat, not the tusk." He shrugged. "I think he is afraid to use the kayak."

"You didn't want to use it either."

"But he is the hunter."

"Do you think Otto is angry?"

"Oh, no. He has gone off because he is hunting. He will stay out here until he gets one. He is a great hunter."

Within the hour a strong wind began to blow from the southwest, filling the sky with thick dark clouds. By noon it was snowing, and low, flat barges of ice moved by the ice edge, pushed by the wind and heading north. We cased the guns and, without eating, loaded the sleds with the skinned and greasy carcasses, which by evening would be dogs and people.

A few moments later the coast disappeared from sight and we sledded into the white-out. After a few hours Simon turned left, motioning to the wind and then to his cheek to show me how he was steering. After several more hours of travel he brought the dogs sharply around a ghostly berg, saying that we were now abreast of the village. Berg to berg, as if following road signs, he led us back to Kullorsuaq, which couldn't be seen until we were a kilometer from its pinnacle.

———>><<———

Contrary to what Sven had predicted, Otto and Lars did not stay at the ice edge until they got a narwhal. The wind grew so strong that they returned the next day. But the storm didn't last. Within a day it blew itself out, and I ventured to the KNI for supplies.

There, Simon's wife, Lea, a thin shrewd woman who had been to business school in Copenhagen and who spoke a smattering of English, took me to the rear of the store she managed. Alongside the nearly empty dairy cabinet stood a new narwhal tusk.

"I bought from Timotheus," she said. This was Edvard's uncle. "He got when you and Simon were at *imaq*."

"Near us?"

"Ten kilometers. Peter Aronsen, he lost one too."

I picked up the tusk. It was about six and a half feet long, its bottom third slightly crooked. The raised portion of its spirals was the color of wheat and rough to the touch. The grooves were satiny cool and stained faintly with brown algae. It wore a tag marked with its weight in kilograms and its price in kroner. It came to 12.1 pounds and $923, almost a 60 percent markup from the $577 Lea had paid Timotheus. She mentioned that a tourist on one of the summer ships might buy it.

I continued to hold the tusk in my hand, remembering the narwhal Simon had shot at and how it had frothed the dark sea with its horn. As I ran my hand up the length of the tusk it revolved in my palm. Then I held its hollow base to my ear, as one might listen to a seashell, but I couldn't hear the sea, nor any cetacean songs. Since it was spring, and the freezer of the KNI was full, Lea had been unable to buy any of the meat or the *mattak*. Both had been shared among Timotheus's family and friends.

Walking back to my shack, I met Edvard on the path, strolling with his wife, who had on a denim jacket, her auburn hair tied back with a blue ribbon. Between them, hand-in-hand, they had a young girl.

"*Qanorippit?*" I said. How are you?

"You can REALLY pronounce that!" he exclaimed.

I gave him a gossamer inclination of my head, the one he liked to affect—Hey, no sweat.

"We have a daughter now," he said.

"She grew quickly. She must be two years old."

"Our friends gave her to us," he said seriously, explaining the old custom, still in force. "They had many children and we have none, and they want us to be happy."

I couldn't tell if his wife's trembling mouth was about to laugh or cry.

"How was the ice edge?" he said.

"Good. I saw many *qernertaq*s."

"Simon and Sven were hopeless in the business of the narwhal," he said, wagging his head. As always news in the village travelled fast.

"Your uncle got one."

He lifted his eyebrows, meaning "of course."

"When do you think we might go to Tutulissuaq?" I asked.

"Oh . . ." He leered. "I am a family man now. But soon . . . perhaps."

They strolled down the path toward his father-in-law's house and I walked in the opposite direction, past the spot where Peter Aronsen kept his sled and dogs. They were gone. A working hunter, he had already returned to the ice edge. Lars Olsen's team was also gone. No doubt he was hunting for *uuttoq*. Turning up the hill, I caught sight of Nicolai Jensen beckoning me into his house. I joined him on his porch, and when we went inside there was a pot of seal ribs boiling on the stove, and a plate of sugar cookies on the table.

PART II

TROPHIES

—➤><◄—

The true trophy hunter is a self-disciplined perfectionist seeking a single animal, the ancient patriarch well past his prime that is often an outcast from his own kind. This hunter is a mixture of sportsman and conservationist, testing his skills and resources against the crafty instincts and wariness of a wise old ram, hunting with the intent to kill the very animal he admires and respects. If successful, he will enshrine the trophy in a place of honor. This is a more noble and fitting end than dying on some lost and lonely ledge where the scavengers will pick his bones, and his magnificent horns will weather away and be lost forever.

—ELGIN GATES,
Trophy Hunter in Asia

—➤><◄—

➤➤◄◄

WHEN BOB KUBICK SHOWS THE SIZE OF THE SHEEP HE WOULD LIKE TO kill in Siberia, he sweeps his clenched fists backwards from the crown of his head, back as far as he can take them, then down across his shoulders and far out before his face. With a conductorlike flourish, he draws the imaginary horns sharply over his head and again over his shoulders—a curl and a half. As he completes the demonstration his face becomes illuminated. The stress lines disappear. The under-eye pouches recede. His cheeks blush and he wears the expression of those looking at Michelangelo's *David.* He's visualizing what's physically attainable in the genus *Ovis.* Of middle height and middle age, of uncommon good cheer and well-fed frame, Kubick's heading to the other side of the world again, to the trophy fields, making memories with his rifle.

It's early evening in Anchorage and we're standing by the pool table in the middle of Kubick's trophy room—"forty-two feet long and thirty-four feet wide," as he's told me. He wears a grey pinstripe shirt, a pastel yellow tie, and lovely golden suspenders, giving him the air of a Victorian gentleman relaxing at home. His slacks are the ruddy brown of the deer on the walls, his moustache and barbered hair a bit lighter.

"One like that," he says jokingly, tossing a hand toward the argalis, the wild sheep of central Asia with fantastic spiralling horns. Vertical rows of their heads climb to the ceiling where several zebra skins stretch between the heavy wood beams. The opposite wall, "thirty-three feet high," carries the heads of African antelope and North American caribou. Because ultraviolet light bleaches the colors in mounted animals, there are no windows in this shrine. There are hidden fans, though, cleaning the dust from the air, and the walls are double Sheetrock in case of fire.

Once a medical student, then a high school science teacher, now a construction and real estate magnate, Kubick has been habitually exact about the dimensions and design of the room. When it comes to the number of species he's collected, or how many records he has listed in the *Safari Club International Record Book of Trophy Animals* (which lies on the pool table and bulges with plastic index tabs, marking his entries), he becomes less precise: "Oh, about two hundred seventy species, and I guess two hundred fifty records . . . or something like that."

Nearly all these animals can be seen hanging on the surrounding walls, rearing in the corners, and stalking across a chest-high platform, which occupies the far side of the room, opposite the entry—a pair of baronial doors with enormous brass handles. The platform is inclined at a slight angle toward the middle of the room, giving the impression that the animals upon it are walking off a hill toward you. They are a motley bestiary: wolves and cougars . . . snarling lions . . . bears. In their midst stands a bongo, a spiral-horned antelope living in equatorial Africa—a secretive and nocturnal creature, weighing about five hundred pounds, one of the world's most handsome ungulates. Its trim white forelegs end in dapper hooves reminiscent of spats; eleven ivory stripes—from spine to belly—cross its reddish-brown flanks; another creamy strap saddles the top of its muzzle; and its horns are two feet long and pointed like rapiers. To its right walks a bontebok, a southern African antelope with a purplish-brown coat. By its side looms a barren ground grizzly bear, silver and moody as a rain cloud, taken by Kubick when he was a young man, hunting alone in the arctic. Slightly behind them stands another of Africa's rarely seen antelope, a yellow-backed duiker from the Sudan, also mounted life-size, and upon the wall to the rear of this assembly hang the heads of diminutive Asian deer, arranged like florets around larger and more notable mounts from that continent: the world-record Mongolian elk; the largest whitetail ever taken in the South Pacific; and a banteng, the Asian wild ox. Guarding the corner of this remarkable platform towers a polar bear, fully ten feet tall on its hind legs. Its claws, dripping rich fur, angrily cuff the air. On its elbows the individual strands are six inches long and wispy as egret feathers.

From his perch among the ice blocks, Kubick had watched this male bear hunting a female with three cubs. The sow disappeared among the jumbled ice and the male followed. The sow and her cubs emerged, and

Kubick prepared to shoot at the spot where he believed the male bear would appear. Suddenly the polar bear roared behind him. Kubick turned and fired, at the same time sliding down among the broken ice, where he crouched for several terrified minutes, waiting for the bear to attack. When he finally peeked over the ice blocks, he found the bear dead, shot luckily through the neck.

At the opposite corner of the platform stands a Marco Polo sheep. First described by the Venetian explorer during his twelfth-century journey to China, it wasn't actually seen by a European until the 1800s. It lives between fifteen thousand and nineteen thousand feet in elevation, in the mountains where the frontiers of Afghanistan, Pakistan, China, and Tajikistan converge, and has the most spectacular horns of any sheep on the planet (the longest on record are a little over six feet measured around the curl). Kubick took this specimen in Afghanistan before the Soviet invasion, and it bears fifty-one-inch horns, placing it thirteenth in the record book. Its body is covered with greyish-brown hair, oddly short for an animal that lives at such altitudes; it's frame is light boned and seemingly too frail to support its enormous headgear.

Kubick continues to point out other exotic wildlife about which most laypeople, and even those who consider themselves amateur naturalists, have little knowledge. Standing on the burgundy carpet next to the polar bear is a markhor from Pakistan, which, according to Kubick, is "the king of the mountain—the toughest, the wariest—far and away a more difficult animal to hunt than any sheep." It's beautiful as well—a tightly muscled, grey goat with a soft and luxuriant coat, a flowing beard, and brown, spiralling horns a little over three feet long, twisted three times around their longitudinal axis. Kubick mentions that this one stands sixth in "the book."

Above its thoughtful face hangs the head of a mountain nyala from Ethiopia, an antelope with horns like an hourglass and a wariness so great that some hunters, says Kubick, have hunted for three months without seeing the creature.

"How did you get one?" I ask.

He shrugs and says, "Luck."

Next to the nyala hangs a sitatunga, a smaller antelope adapted to swamp living—its hooves are elongated, enabling it to walk upon marshy terrain. The rest of the wall is a kaleidoscope of horns, muzzles, dewlaps, and staring eyes: kudu, sable, oryx, wildebeest, hartebeest, impala, springbok, eland, lechwe (it's hard to keep track of where Kubick has been in Africa), but, oddly, no *male* eland, a common African ungulate. About the omission, Kubick says, "I hunted them sixty-nine days. And giant eland is one of the purest forms of hunting there is. You have to track them. I wore a pedometer and the least I ever walked in a day was fifteen miles and the most was thirty-six. And I never ever quit and I never ever stopped and I never ever got one."

Luck.

He had none.

Also missing are elephant tusks. Kubick tells me that they're in his home in Texas and that he's only shot two. "The biggest was eighty pounds, and though I've had lots of opportunities to shoot thirty and forty pounders, I just didn't see the need."

We walk beneath more heads—antelope . . . caribou . . . a walrus, all of whom Kubick passes over without mention until he reaches the diminutive head of a Taruca deer from the Andes, which seems out of place among the great branching antlers, swept-backed horns, and giant tusks, but which Kubick points to with pride, saying that he took it at "seventeen thousand, eight hundred feet above sea level."

To the left of the Peruvian deer hang the heads of its cervine relatives: Coues, mule, and Sitka deer; hog deer and chital. Circling behind the bar and over the fireplace the genus continues: musk deer, muntjac, and sambar, and those largest members of the Cervidae, the moose—the Alaska-Yukon variety, the Shiras from Wyoming, and a subspecies from Asia, all looking down their pendulous noses at us.

Mixed among these specimens are Cape buffaloes, black and white rhinos, musk oxen, the monstrous and wooly heads of New and Old World bison as well as a life-size mountain lion. Slipping behind the wet bar to fix us a drink, Kubick mentions that he's collected thirty-four different species of deer, more than anyone else in the world, and that his Siberian moose happens to be number one in "the book."

I take one of the padded bar stools, which face a plush couch and the large fireplace. Maasai bracelets, woven baskets, and Tibetan boots adorn the mantle, and in lit glass cases, fossils, rocks, and ostrich eggs are displayed. On the bar itself sit several ursine skulls, including that of an ancient cave bear. But all this is window dressing for the wall that faces the bar and which is densely clustered with the heads of sheep—wildly, improbably horned sheep. It's the achievement of which Kubick seems most proud. The wall contains his and his wife's Grand Slams (all four species of North American sheep) and his *two* Super Slams (twelve species of the world's sheep).

All in all, about two hundred sixty animals fill the room ("another three dozen are still at the taxidermist")—a collection put together by someone who, when he got to Alaska shortly after the earthquake of 1964, had shot nothing more than deer and antelope in his home state of Oregon. The twenty-three-year-old Kubick was also low on hard assets when he arrived in the last frontier, looking for adventure and more "magnificent" animals to hunt. On leave from med school, he had about fifty dollars in cash and a pickup bought on credit from his wife's teacher's union. Like many who came to the new state, though, he had more than a bit of bluff and what's probably necessary in all successful entrepreneurs: a pathological amount of ambition.

Looking for scarce housing, he was asked by the owner of a trailer court if he was any good with tools. "Oh, my GOD!" said Kubick. (When Kubick says the word *God,* he nearly always puts it in caps and follows it with an exclamation point.) "TOOLS are my middle name."

He leans across the bar and confides, "Honest, I didn't know what a crescent wrench was."

From maintaining the trailer court for free rent (he and Sharon lived in a tiny house with only one heater in the living room), Kubick went on to carving ashtrays from caribou hooves and operating candy-vending machines. When money was low, he taught high school chemistry and biology. But teaching wasn't a challenge, he maintains. In fact, he felt as if he were "vastly underachieving."

While driving south from the trailer court in Anchorage to glass the high peaks around Turnagain Arm and the Kenai Peninsula, he had a completely different feeling. Spotting a mountain goat or black bear, he'd climb up glaciers with ice ax and crampons—thousands of feet in a single morning. He snowshoed, he Ski-Dooed, he flew. He crisscrossed the state after moose and caribou and sheep.

"Challenge," he says.

Then he adds, "To this day I can draw *G*'s and *B*'s on a map for you." (He means goats and bears.) "I went every weekend in the fall and when trapping season started I trapped every weekend. The only void in my life was about the time trapping season stopped and spring bear season hadn't started, so we went skiing every weekend. And then once the bear season started I was bear hunting and once the bear season closed, I went ptarmigan hunting. After the first year or so, I made a mission out of getting a Boone and Crockett Dall sheep, so I hunted damn near every weekend for two years before I finally found where all the genetically big sheep were."

Like many trophy hunters, Kubick doesn't say a "record book sheep," or a "trophy sheep"; he uses the name of the club Theodore Roosevelt founded in 1887 as an adjective to imply both. Though Boone and Crockett did back the formation of a National Collection of Heads and Horns during Roosevelt's day, for scientific purposes, its original charter stipulated that it was a broad-based conservation organization, active in calling for the setting aside of forest reserves, demanding limited hunting seasons, and promulgating the rules of "fair chase," for example, not hunting animals in deep snow or at night with lights. The club didn't actually start keeping trophy records until 1932. In the ensuing years many sportsmen felt that the Boone and Crockett scoring system placed undue emphasis on an antler's symmetry and spread. Consequently, in 1977, the founder of Safari Club International (universally called SCI), C. J. McElroy, devised his own, less rigorous scoring system, which allowed more individuals to enter their trophies, and of course their names, in "the book"—the one that lies on Kubick's pool table. In addition, SCI covered all the continents, whereas Boone and Crockett listed only North American species. Though Kubick doesn't display a copy of Boone and Crockett's *Records of North American Big Game* in his trophy room, he nonetheless entered his Dall sheep in the club's archives, where it's listed as 126th. Without the slightest pause for recollection, he can name the number of points it received, "one hundred seventy-three and four-eighths," which, when I later checked, was exactly correct. The same sheep, taken on the Chitina Glacier in the Wrangell Mountains in 1967, is ranked far higher in the SCI volume—forty-eighth. Therefore to see who really has collected the biggest animal of a particular species one must consult both volumes.

Is all this arcane?

Absolutely.

And it's the guts of Kubick's life.

"I think what happened," he says, nodding to the Dall sheep on the far wall, "is that I got to Alaska and realized that my drive, which is the same as ambition, wasn't going to let me stay happy with just getting a goat, or a sheep, or a moose. It would soon mean nothing. How many rams was I going to kill? I know a guy that I hunted with a lot when I first started here. And he's probably the toughest son-of-a-bitch in the mountains that I know of. He hunted these Dall sheep down where the big ones were, and he just kept shooting them. He's now got six or seven of them in his house. Well, I think it's terrible. I've never told him that.

But I cannot believe that one person felt they had the right to kill six or seven of those great big rams."

Looking directly at me, he says, "I didn't need that many. So the only way to make a contest out of hunting was to make it more challenging. That's why I became more interested in Boone and Crockett. I don't think it was recognition . . . yeah, we all want to be recognized. Sure, there was a little bit of that for me—I'll admit it—but it was something else. The first year I really hunted Dall sheep, I bet I climbed twenty different mountains. I bet I was within fifty to one hundred fifty yards of two hundred rams greater than full curl. And I passed them all up. What would it have been? *Bang!*" He claps his hands together. "Nothing. The modern rifle has made it so easy to kill 'em. Any fool can see that it isn't that difficult, the shooting that is. So I decided not to shoot another Dall sheep until it was a Boone and Crockett one. When I shot it, I never shot another—never even wanted to until a friend called this fall and said, 'Bob, I've seen the biggest Dall sheep I've seen in twenty-five years. It'll go between forty-four and forty-eight inches.' Well I couldn't sleep for two nights!" His huge grin says, See, I'm human.

Then he turns serious and says, "What also happened with my career was that, after a while, I realized that either I had to go back to medical school, or I had to find something else that was a challenge."

Carving ashtrays from reindeer hooves and collecting coins from vending machines wasn't. Kubick took up commercial fishing, though he had almost no experience on the water. In fact, going from his new boat to the landing, he managed to fall out of his skiff right in front of an old Norwegian fisherman who asked him if he knew what he was doing. The dunking made Kubick play it straight for once and he said not totally. The Norwegian said, "When I put out, follow me." He showed Kubick where and when to lay nets, and when to pick them up. The seas being calm, he didn't show him how to handle thirty-five-foot swells, which often swept across the Gulf of Alaska. Kubick managed to outlast his first storm, returning to port with salt caked in his armpits. Soon he was commercial sealing and the owner of four vessels, his little fleet bringing in $150,000 each year.

His bankers advised him to try construction. He built a fourplex and "made money." Then he built tract houses and "made more money." He built condos and "made still more money." Starting in 1970, growing through the boom days of the Trans-Alaska Pipeline, and on into the 1980s, Kubick's enterprises built Anchorage subdivisions called Campbell Woods and Oceanview North, housing projects named Independence Park, Kempton Hills, and Strawberry Meadows. He built Resolution Plaza downtown. And he discovered that in addition to magnificent animals, Alaska had given him the other thing he'd come looking for.

"The construction-development business was challenging." There's that word again. Now he elaborates on it, keeping time with his left hand like a conductor. "The rewards were big enough. The power was great enough. The prestige was great enough, and the freedom I could create for myself was there. I said, 'This is it. I love it.' " His face—scant eyebrows, round cheeks, pale moustache, knob of a chin—beams. And there's the grin again, expansive, self-assured—Kubick.

Ten million, 20 million, 30 million . . . his net worth eventually reached 60 million dollars. He went to British Honduras to hunt jaguar. In eastern and southern Africa, he shot the big five—cape buffalo, rhino, elephant, lion, and leopard. He crossed the Sahara and Gobi deserts, starting to complete his Super Slams. His companies had a gross value of two thirds of a billion dollars. His MBAs managed them, and he hunted 180 days each year, coining the motto he still strives to enjoy: "True wealth is total freedom."

Now Kubick's forty-nine, a rich man despite a 70 percent reduction of his fortune during the recessions of the late 1980s. Even with the setbacks, his remaining wealth has continued to buy him more than freedom. By allowing him to hunt around the world, it has indirectly bought him the recognition he tends to dismiss. For his age he's the world's most honored trophy hunter, having won virtually all the major hunting awards, standards of achievement most individuals don't win until they're in their sixties. Under the eyes of the creatures whose collection they represent, the awards stand around the room.

Largest is the three-and-a-half-foot-tall Weatherby Big Game Trophy, a skyscraperlike award made from walnut and flanked by gold argalis. Its pedestal is topped by a cup on which perches an antelope head, the earth between its straight horns. Upon the globe stands a winged goddess. Each year since 1956 the award has been given by the California rifle-making company to the "individual who has made the greatest lifetime achievements in the world of big game hunting . . . a person who has contributed greatly to conservation and hunting education, and one whose character and sportsmanship are beyond reproach."

Past recipients of the Weatherby have included the gun writers Jack O'Connor and Warren Page (1957 and 1958), His Royal Highness

Prince Abdorreza Pahlavi of Iran (1962), the founder of Safari Club International C. J. McElroy (1969), and James R. Mellon II (1972). Like the Nobel Prize, the Weatherby can't be won in a match. Prospective recipients are nominated and selected by a committee.

Also in the room are the Hunter's Hall of Fame Trophy, given by Safari Club International, and the J. J. Malek Award, the Australian–South Pacific Grand Slam for all fifteen species of South Pacific animals. Kubick was the first to win it, and it's one of his fondest memories—taking up the Australian restaurateur's challenge on a few hours' notice, flying to the other side of the world with only his rifle, a duffel bag, and fifty thousand dollars in cash, hunting for days on end without sleep, having "spies" keep track of his prime competitor Gordon Alford of Sydney, and finally collecting the fifteenth animal, a whitetail deer in New Zealand, and telexing "old J.J." that he had revenged Australia's winning of the America's Cup.

"So the Malek's the best one?"

Kubick has a large glass of Coke in his hand and waves it toward the hearth where SCI's Traditional North American 27 Big Game Award rests. "Well, that trophy down there, when you've got it, you've really got something. You've hunted all the deserts of North America, you've hunted the jungles. You've hunted with the Labrador people, with the Newfies. You've been to Alberta, British Columbia, the Yukon, Alaska, New Mexico. I mean when you've got that, you've seen the wilderness of North America." Looking at it, he seems to be the boy in Oregon, dreaming.

"How about your two Super Slams?"

"Come over here." He leads me to the wall of sheep trophies and says, "For a long time I should have had the number sixth- or seventh-ranked Super Slam."

This award was created by some prominent SCI members who, in 1977, had formed the International Sheep Hunters Association (ISHA). The idea came from an article published by Jay Mellon in *Outdoor Life*, "The Thirteenth Ram: Super Slam in Wild Sheep," which was an international takeoff on an earlier essay written by Grancel Fitz, an avid big-game hunter who helped develop the trophy scoring system of the Boone and Crockett Club. Published in 1948, Fitz's article about collecting all four varieties of North American sheep, called "A Grand Slam in Rams," began a craze that hasn't stopped.

Jack O'Connor—then shooting editor of *Outdoor Life* and whom Fitz listed as the fifth man to collect a Grand Slam (he claimed Charles Sheldon, the naturalist, to be the first)—took the slam's innovator to task. Fitz "knew not what he wrought," wrote O'Connor. "[The achievement] struck hundreds of hunters as being the most prestigious caper a big-game hunter could pull off. . . . It became the Holy Grail of American hunting, and dozens of people started working toward it. . . . The term 'Grand Slam' and the attendant publicity have made the mountain sheep the most prestigious North American trophy."

Imagine a hunter's prestige after taking a *dozen* of the *world's* sheep, thought the men of ISHA. Imagine the *profits,* thought the booking agents, when hunters began travelling to other continents. O'Connor wasn't as sanguine about slams. "All this whoopla is a very sad thing," he said. "I wish Grancel Fitz hadn't started it all. The old-timers hunted sheep because they loved sheep, because they loved to be up on those high windswept ridges where they shared the sheep pastures with the sheep, the grizzly, the hoary marmot, the soaring eagle. When they brought back a ram trophy, they were not seeking honor and prestige— they were bringing back memories of icy winds fragrant with fir and balsam, of the smell of sheep beds and arctic willow, of tiny, perfect alpine flowers, gray slide rock, velvet sheep pastures. The old-timers had sheep and sheep country in their blood."

Not so with today's hunters, O'Connor went on to write. "They're after glory . . . and the sooner they can get the tiresome business over with and slap those ram heads on the wall, the better they like it." One man collected his Grand Slam in thirty days; one had collected ten Grand Slams. Some men were so desperate to accomplish the feat that their collection had "not a single head that was a trophy—all little rams from five to seven years old that when they were knocked off had useful lives before them." Worse. O'Connor alleged that the desire to complete a Grand Slam had created a "tremendous amount of lying, poaching, and cheating."

No one has ever accused the sage of *Outdoor Life* of being soft when it came to shooting animals. (Though lamenting the extirpation of the wolf in the Lower Forty-eight and Mexico, he shot all but one he saw.) Yet he was one of the few who was willing to call his fellow hunters unscrupulous: "In the days when hunters packed into wilderness areas, climbed, sweated, looked over enough sheep to get outstanding rams, shot their own, I thought it the greatest field sport in the world. It is still a great sport but the Instant Sheep Hunters out for prestige and the crooked outfitters out for the fast buck are making it stink pretty bad around the edges!"

Kubick points to the head of an aoudad, commonly called a Barbary sheep. Its horns fall like half moons toward its jaw and grey beard. "If you go into anyone else's trophy room," he says, "and see this animal, you will *never EVER* see a specimen so small. It's horns are nineteen and a half inches long. I'm sure some of the people you've talked to have aoudads of twenty-nine to thirty-five inches. This one was shot in the Nubian desert. Theirs were shot in Texas or New Mexico, on a ranch, behind a fence. Anyone who comes in here, and knows anything about sheep, says, 'Holy Christ! Look at that.' Because they know where it came from. I will *never* go shoot one of those thirty-five inchers in Texas because I know what it took to do this. Like I said, I should have had the number sixth- or seventh-ranked Super Slam. But unless I could get all of mine in the wild, I didn't want it."

I put my hand into the aoudad's beard, softer than the Marco Polo's hair, not quite as warm or thick as the markhor's. The tactile comparison is what no photograph can render. Beneath the hair, all the mounts feel the same—light, hard, fiberglass.

At this moment Bob's wife, Sharon, walks into the trophy room and announces dinner. Slim, dressed in a brown turtleneck and grey slacks, she's obviously what Bob has claimed her to be twenty years ago—the prettiest woman he had ever seen. Her blond hair is teased on her forehead and curls onto her shoulders; a silver dolphin hangs around her neck; she has enormous blue eyes.

As we walk through the foyer, where silken strands of water fall from the cathedral ceiling to a rock pool, she admits to having been a "Bambi lover," but changed her mind about hunting after she met Bob. "I was either going to join him or leave him," she says, "and I wasn't going to leave him, so I joined him."

A hallway lined with photographs leads to the den and the kitchen. Bob points out photos of Sharon kneeling above sheep in Iran, Afghanistan, and Nevada, and he mentions again, pride in his voice, that one of the Grand Slams and part of a third Super Slam in the trophy room are hers. The wall leads us on for a dozen feet of photos: brown bear; elk; Sitka deer; caribou; a bearded man in hip boots and a watch cap hoists a brace of enormous salmon into the air. He looks like anyone's northwesterner, an outdoorsy, rugged, young fisherman from someplace between Oregon and Alaska. He could be advertising outboard motors, tackle, a resort. He's not advertising himself. His smile and his eyes are full of warm delight with his catch.

"Is that you?"

He nods.

"He used to wear a beard all the time," says Sharon. "I made him."

"But it got so damn grey, I had to get rid of it. I could only afford so much Grecian formula."

In the den a marlin leaps across the wall; ducks fly around it. "I love to shoot ducks," says Bob. "These are some of the ones I get at Homer, where we have another house. And then see," he points to the window, "typically our floatplane is parked right there." This must be the turbo Beaver he's mentioned, his bush chariot that has carried him and friends across Alaska.

In a dining alcove between the kitchen and den, we sit down to dinner. Sharon, who has already eaten and has been serving us wine, shows me some photographs of their son's recent Wyoming sheep hunt. Michael lifts the sheep's head, a look of satisfaction and a little arrogance on his fifteen-year-old face. Father Kubick is in the background, enormously pleased with his brood; mother Sharon, to his left, smiles one of those smiles that sees her accomplishment slipping away from her; and sister Kim, a clone of her mother, a very pretty, eighteen-year-old girl, looks into the camera with an air of slight separation. She's the only one in the family who doesn't hunt.

"I have hunted bighorns so many times," says Kubick, pointing his knife at one of the photos. "and I have *never* shot one that big. I have never even *seen* one that big alive in the hunting field. And he went up there and shot it an hour and a half after we started. His first sheep! A hell of a sheep! And we did it together."

Kubick is right. There are many men who have hunted a lifetime and never shot, much less seen, a bighorn so fine. Michael has also gone to New Zealand and Africa with his dad. Kubick's wealthy friends in Mexico have secured coveted desert sheep permits for Sharon. Kubick's taken a cameraman around the world with him to video his hunts. He's owned seven cars, three planes, and half a dozen houses. What's it like now going through a recession, the $325,000 Beaver sold off to reduce overhead?

"I don't think my life-style has changed, but I've gone through a lot of mental agony," he says matter-of-factly. "I wouldn't really call it self-doubt, maybe embarrassment. The first time I had to go to a banker and say, 'You're not gonna get paid,' that hurt. It hurt more than he'll ever know."

He gives me a look that seems to say, "Believe me." Then, as if to give me a better insight into how he views his wealth, he adds, "Unless you're a wild-ass spender, when you have a basic net worth of four to five million, how much of a life-style can anyone want but that? Christ, I still drive my 1981 Jeep Wagoneer!"

He smiles, thinking about something that it appears he will keep private. But he shares it: "When you're really wealthy for the first time you don't even know it. And when it happens, it happens so quickly you don't even feel it. In fact, you don't even think you're wealthy. Then you go through a little period where you're guilty and ashamed of it. And then you go through a period where you're proud as hell of it." He laughs.

"Naturally, people get jealous. There was even a letter to an editor about me in a national magazine after I won the Weatherby Award. The hunter said, 'Isn't it terrible that these guys go all over the world hunting these trophies and here I take my son out and we get a deer, and that's what hunting is really about.' Yeah, that *is* what hunting is *partially* about. But if you're really going to hunt a lot, shooting a deer for yourself is a very easy thing to do if you're very skillful. So is that it? For the rest of your life, deer?

"Now that doesn't mean I'm minimizing deer hunting or hunting with your son. One of the greatest thrills in my life was when my son shot his first deer and fortunately, and you may say why would you say *fortunately, FORTUNATELY* it was a doe, and the reason it was fortunate was he was only nine years old and he still had something to look forward to. It was certainly a thrill for me and it was a hell of a thrill for him. And before we gutted out that deer we sat there and talked about that deer for about an hour, and the hunting experience that went with it, and I had him touch it and feel it. Yes, that *is* a part of hunting and that's a very important part. But, Christ, I live in the greatest hunting country in the *world* and what am I going to do? Bang away at a caribou and have a hunk of meat and that's it?"

Kubick's left hand has been conducting again. He pauses, finishes a bite of his steak that's getting cold, then adds, "So that's another way of explaining what led me to trophy hunting. I said to myself, 'I'm a young energetic fellow and I'm going to do everything there is to do here in Alaska and I'm going to get it done within a couple of years and yeah *some* of it I'm going to want to repeat.' But, my GOD! There's a whole world out there."

Ever since Kubick pointed out his Weatherby Award, and I saw the inscription on its side that, in addition to mentioning the number of species he had collected, praised "his accomplishments in game conservation," I've wanted to ask him what these were. After all, hunters, and especially trophy hunters, claim that they are the world's best conservationists. So I say, "What have you done for wildlife?"

He lays down his fork and knife and says, "That's a pretty good question and I guess if I was completely honest, I would have to say that I haven't done much. Just basic things. I've contributed. It's very easy to contribute. I've also tried to become a member of some groups like the Boone and Crockett Club. I was just at the stage where I might have become more involved when I was suddenly fighting for my economic life. So my contributions to conservation have been miniscule and embarrassing."

We stroll back to the trophy room. Its doors, viewed from the foyer, give the impression that a large coat closet lies behind them. Kubick opens the doors and turns on the lights. Six continents of animals stare at us. He makes us some after-dinner drinks, and we wander over to the sheep heads. Looking up, it occurs to me that such a collection isn't something you bequeath to the uninterested. "Where's it all going?" I ask, "when . . ."

"It's already in the Kubick Wildlife Foundation," he says. "I don't legally own it. It's a corporation in Texas and to give it more value I'm trying to have some other hunters add their collections to mine. If a foundation had six or seven hundred animals then somebody might do something with it educationally. The trouble is—and it's something that some other hunters are absolutely right about—there's nothing like having life-sized animals, especially for kids. Just these heads don't do it. But one person has his reason for putting together a trophy room and I have mine."

He stares at the wall of African antelopes with a thoughtful expression. Turning to me, he says, "*Many* guests come into my home and never see this room. The doors are always closed." His voice, so enthusiastically instructive, has softened. "But every morning, before I go to work, I come in here and sit for five or ten minutes like somebody else meditating or opening their Bible or reading Dale Carnegie. I pick out one animal, always a different one. Sometimes it's a great big thing that's growling like shit," he gestures to the polar bear, "and sometimes it's a little bitty thing that looks like you could go like that and kill it." He slaps the air with the back of his hand toward a dik-dik, a terrier-sized antelope above the bar. "And I dwell on that animal. And believe me I can tell you where every one of these animals was shot and exactly the circumstance. It's a memory jogger and gives me such a lift for the day."

Kubick's face has become illuminated—but not as it was when he mimed the horns of the sheep he would like to take in Siberia. The eagerness is there and most of the amazement, but there's also a peace, perhaps the one he experiences when he sits in here each morning alone. I know guides who have hunted with Kubick and claim him to be overly competitive; one called him "nothing more than a killer" and that he "got his animals at all costs." I wonder if his memories ever get stale and that's why he has to make more of them. I wonder if memories of the hunt are the best ones.

"Will the collection ever be complete?"

Kubick looks across the room as if he might be searching for more space among the tightly spaced antelope heads. Turning to me, he says, "There'll always be something else. It would be a sad day if you had 'em all. And it would be an even sadder day if you had 'em all and you had all the biggest. Because then you just have to give up."

I see an illustration growing behind his eyes. "There was a point in '84 or '85 where I totally lost interest in making money. It had become so easy to make that I have to laugh now." Remembering, he actually does laugh out loud. "I used to play a game with myself while driving to work in the morning to get enthused. I'd say, 'Okay, today you have *nothing.* But you have all the contacts and this big staff. What's the quickest way to make another million dollars?' And I would figure out some way that I could go make a million dollars, and I'd put it into play and the next thing I'd know, three or four months later, I'd have another million dollars.

"Shortly after that I looked at myself in the mirror while I was shaving and I said, 'You know, I think you're a hell of a guy. I like you. You're pretty smart, you have a nice-looking wife. You have plenty of money and travel all over. Not only that, but you're a pretty *nice* guy.' It was the first time I ever said that to myself."

His hands have grown quiet. He looks at his drink, then at me. "Maybe at one time I needed to prove more by bringing the animal back, that beyond the memories and all the good experiences the trophies enhanced my self-image." He pauses, as if weighing something he hasn't thought of before. "But the things that may have been important six and eight years ago may not be so important now. When I looked in the mirror and said, 'I really like you for a change,' I knew I would never be quite as aggressive . . . that I was finished."

Of course, he's not . . . not completely. He's going deer hunting with his family at their cabin on Kodiak Island over Thanksgiving. He says he might just take a crack at that big Dall sheep that left him sleepless. He'll be shooting doves in Mexico this winter. And in the fall he'll be off to Asia.

It's the first days of Glasnost and the Soviet Union has opened an area of northeastern Siberia to foreign hunters. There in the Verkhoyanskiy Range, spanning the arctic circle, lives the snow sheep of northern Asia, *Ovis nivicola*. Because of the inaccessible terrain it inhabits, and the prohibitions on travel to the region that have existed, almost no one except native reindeer herders has ever seen the creature. Only two American hunters, the Carlsberg brothers, have collected it, in the 1970s while doing business in the Soviet Union. Their five specimens are displayed in Moscow's natural history museum, in Los Angeles, and at Brooks Lake Lodge, near Togwotee Pass, Wyoming. Thus, not because of its scarcity in the wild, but because of its rarity in trophy rooms, *Ovis nivicola* has become the most coveted of wild sheep trophies.

Of course, Kubick wants to be among the first to hunt snow sheep and have a specimen for his trophy room. If he kills one, and if it wears horns that sweep back and down and out and up and back again—a curl and a quarter—he'll mount *Ovis nivicola* as he saw it in Siberia, life-size.

T W O

—→>·<←—

IN 1926, WILLIAM MORDEN, AGE FORTY AND A FIELD ASSOCIATE IN the department of mammals at the American Museum of Natural History, set out across the western Himalayas to collect sheep. Like many naturalists of the day he was intrigued by the great animal diaspora that had brought Asian species, including humans, to North America. In the early 1920s Dr. Roy Chapman Andrews, the director of the museum, an ardent explorer, and Morden's boss, had collected extensively in northern and central Asia. It became Morden's hope that by assembling a collection from the southwestern end of the continent he would complement Andrew's work. The museum would then have a series of mammalian life-forms stretching from Persia to Alaska, and from these collections the theory describing animal migrations from the Old to the New World might be refined.

Morden, an avid hunter who had shot in Africa, India, and North America, was also troubled by reports from the Chinese Pamirs of decreasing numbers of Marco Polo sheep. He suggested that *Ovis poli* wasn't nearing extinction but, harried by local hunters in China, had found refuge farther west in the Russian Pamirs. Thus another goal of his expedition became to discover if the mythical *poli* were still hanging on.

Taking the museum's assistant director and taxidermist, James L. Clark, Morden set sail for Bombay with the intention of rendezvousing with Andrews in Chinese Turkestan half a year later. The director of the museum had embarked for Peking and planned to continue his collecting work in the Gobi Desert.

Andrews, though, had bad luck. Arriving in Peking, he found a war in progress and never got underway. Morden and Clark crossed the Karakoram Range by yak, entered the Russian Pamirs, found sheep in profusion, and continued north into the Chinese Tian Shan mountains where they also collected ibex and other forms of argali. To avoid the war in eastern China, to allow Clark to see the country in which Andrews had previously collected, and to make sketches for the habitat dioramas he would have to create back in New York, they elected to travel by camel across Mongolia. Carrying only Russian and Chinese visas, they were arrested by the Mongols and tortured before eventually being released. They then made their way north to the Trans-Siberian Railway and, nine months and eight thousand miles after they had begun their journey on the Indian Ocean, reached Peking with their specimens intact.

The book that Morden published a year later, *Across Asia's Snows and Deserts,* is illustrated with black-and-white photographs that document a world of desolate magnificence. He and Clark ride yaks, plod through knee-deep snow, and cross passes of over fifteen thousand feet in elevation while icy peaks soar yet another mile above their heads. And, of course, there are those *poli,* horns curving back and down and out and up and back again—and again!—Morden by their side with two months of beard on his face. His rifle leans against his shoulder, his socks are rolled over the tops of his L.L. Bean boots, and a soft little smile plays across his face, mirroring nicely the last line of his book, "Through our labors and difficulties, we had attained the ends that we had sought."

Morden was not an expansive writer when it came to describing his inner landscapes. Perhaps he didn't have to be. His photographs and simple prose were enough to inspire several generations of hunters to follow in his footsteps as if on a crusade. Those who wanted a richer description of the emotions he may have felt upon the roof of the world, staring through his spotting scope at creatures seemingly as rare as the unicorn, found no shortage of books from authors who, like Morden, had been captured by sheep and sheep hunting, but who also analyzed their fetish.

Charles Sheldon was one. He graduated Yale in 1890 and went on to do field studies for the U.S. Bureau of Biological Survey, collecting over many years in Alaska and the Yukon, and making what remain some of the more thorough observations of North America's sheep. Unlike Morden, he often reflected on his moments of unity with mountain scenery, what psychologists would later call "the peak experience."

"Sitting on the rock," he wrote, "I rested and smoked my pipe. Three hard-earned trophies were before me. Under such circumstances, among mountain-crests, when the pulse bounds and the whole being is exhilarated by the intensely vitalizing air, while the senses, stimulated by the vigorous exercise of a dangerous climb and the sustained excitement of the stalk, are attuned to the highest pitch of appreciation of the Alpine panorama, there is no state of exaltation more sublime than that immediately following the climax of a day's successful hunt for the noble mountain ram."

Morden's partner, James Clark, was likewise taken with the high country and in a book of his own speculated that wild sheep live in a great arc stretching from the Middle East, across China and Siberia, across the Bering Strait and down into the Rocky Mountains, an arc that, coincidentally enough, mimed the shape of their horns. Those who followed sheep through these tectonically restless mountains stayed young and vibrant.

The present day's most well known researcher of exotic wildlife, the biologist George B. Schaller, has agreed—"the high altitudes are a special world"—and has offered an explanation as to how the qualities of this unique environment have been incorporated into its sheep. "Born of the Pleistocene," he says, "at home among pulsating glaciers and wind-flayed rocks, the animals have survived and thrived, the harshness of the environment breeding a strength and resilience which the lowland animals often lack."

John Muir, too, admired wild sheep, saying that they were "possessed of keen sight, immovable nerve, and strong limbs," and maintained "a brave life" amid "foaming torrents . . . slopes of frozen snow," and the "wildest storms." His friend, Theodore Roosevelt, also found the sheep of North America worthy of admiration. He claimed chasing bighorns in steep country to be "the noblest form of sport."

It seems that everyone who has observed wild sheep has respected them. And with good reason. As the critic-turned-naturalist Joseph Wood Krutch observed, wild rams are "Homeric" and have "the strength, the courage, and the muscular skills of the hero." If anything his estimation of them fell short.

Sheep live higher than any other ungulate, peering down from their lofty beds with the imperturbable and sagacious expression of Olympian gods. Like their mythic counterparts, they are also hierarchical and sexually freewheeling: souls who begin their combat early, establishing dominance through their horn size; who won't bond to a single female or even collect a harem; who, during the rut, seem more concerned with posturing, threatening, and doing battle than breeding. With horns that grow perennially, they have the good fortune to stay regal into senectitude.

To reach them, the hunter must journey both into the wilderness (for sheep prefer the sort of rough country that has thwarted settlement), and upwards, beyond tree line and through alpine terrain that tests both physical stamina and coolness of mind (sheep will run across cliffs that the average person is unable to climb). Little wonder that collecting them has become the perfect metaphor for a courageous wresting of the unattainable, the ultimate trophy for those who aspire to succeed in an androcentric world, and what Aldo Leopold more precisely named a *certificate* (his italics), attesting that its owner had "been somewhere and done something—that he has exercised skill, persistence, or discrimination in the age-old feat of overcoming, outwitting, or reducing-to-possession."

Yet not every male sheep will do. Few hunters will shoot an animal with less than full-curl horns even though such individuals live just as high as those males with more developed headgear, run as hard, and climb equally precipitous mountain faces. They have all the desiderata, but lack the crucial symbol: horns that complete a circle, stating without apology that their owner is at the top of his band.

Such serpentine horns also make an aesthetic statement, their shape expressing one of nature's elemental patterns, also seen in the spirals of the chambered nautilus, the helix of DNA, and the sweeping arms of galaxies. Growing from a still point, they are attached to first principles and primal forms, leading the would-be hero back through great difficulties to the source.

O N A BLACK, COLD, RAINY OCTOBER MORNING WE LEAVE MOSCOW
in a jet and fly east as snow begins to cover the Ural Mountains. Before
we land in Yakutsk, the capital of north-central Siberia, six hours later,
night has fallen and we are almost back to where we started in Alaska.
But it's colder. Men and women wear long fur coats and crowd amongst
us as we try to find our luggage in the airport's rundown lobby. When
we exit, our combined breaths turn into an ice fog that follows us to the
waiting truck.

In the morning we board a twin-engine plane, which holds about
forty people, and fly northeast over endless black spruce trees and frozen
ponds—no roads. At a snowy rectangle cut from the forest, a town at its
far edge, we land and wait for two hours, stomping our feet in the cold
as a small biplane is readied. Along with six Mongols dressed in furs, we
crowd behind the pilots and sit on two facing benches, our legs stretched
on piled boxes. The plane fills with the clouds of our breath; we taxi and
bounce down the runway; overloaded, we finally rise above the trees and
drone north along a wide, frozen river, flowing out of a distant mountain
range. Within a half hour, as the sun sets to the south behind us, we're
over larch-covered hills; a few minutes later our shadow undulates across
white peaks, stretching as far north as we can see. A second hour passes.
The sky turns hazy. Banking, we drop into a valley of black spruce and
fly up another frozen river as the ceiling lowers. Suddenly, on an alluvial
bench hemmed in by forest, clings the village of Topolinyy, a collection
of squat wood buildings and tendrils of smoke bleak as a line from Dos-
toyevsky. A thermometer on the airstrip's fuel shed reads twenty-eight
below.

For this hunt Kubick is paying sixteen thousand dollars, Moscow to Moscow, two weeks inclusive. He's not alone. In the plane with us is Ali Üstay, the head of a large construction company in Istanbul, and awaiting us at the lodge are Vance Corrigan, an *Encyclopaedia Britannica* distributor from southern California; Paul Asper, a retired Arctic Cat snowmobile dealer from Haneyville, Pennsylvania; and Don Cox, the president of Specialty Steel Treating, which is located in Michigan and produces, among other high-tech, aeronautical equipment, heat-treated components for NASA's space shuttle. All the hunters are members of Safari Club International.

But they're not there.

Our interpreter, Nicolai Igorevich, tells us that they're scouting the country in the helicopter that will eventually carry us another two hundred kilometers north to the hunting camp on the Barayi River. Nicolai wears a thick beige sweater and an open green army coat with a fur collar. A fair-skinned Russian from Moscow, with a black moustache and dark suspicious eyes, he seems ill at ease among the swarthy hunters in great wolf hats who carry our baggage through the double entry of the lodge.

Coats and trousers hang by the inner door, and mukluks, the knee-high boots of the north, lie in a pile beneath them. All are sewn from reindeer hides. The rest of the lodge resembles a European hostel. We pass a kitchen where two fat women smoke cigarettes over a samovar. We pass the dining room, the table set with dishes of pickled vegetables and meat. Beyond it is a hallway, the doors of the small bedrooms standing open, revealing the hunters' travelling effects: sleeping bags, shaving kits, rifle cases. On Paul Asper's bed is a worn, leather-bound copy of *Walden*.

Bob Kubick and his videoman, Buckey Winkley, toss their gear in the one empty bedroom. Buckey, when he's not videoing Kubick's trips, is a hunting guide in Alaska, a slightly built man with a leather Stetson, piercing blue eyes, and fierce moustache. When events don't turn out as he expects he becomes brash. Once again, he begins to complain to Kubick that his video camera won't work at these temperatures and that their plans for the first-ever footage of Siberian snow sheep will be ruined.

In the meantime Nicolai asks Ali if he minds sleeping in the guide's lodge down the hill. When Ali says that he doesn't mind, Nicolai tries to sort out these arrangements in Russian with Constantine, a short plump man with thick glasses who has flown up from Yakutsk, and who is to act as Nicolai's interpreter. Constantine speaks Yakutia to some of the kitchen help who shrug their shoulders at him, then Evenk, the language of the local hunters, to the guides who are still bringing in Ali's gear, which now must be taken back outside.

Bob turns his back upon this slow translation. Also ignoring Buckey's harangue about the video, he vents his own frustrations on Ali, a good-natured Turk with dark brimming eyes and the tyro in this hunters' pecking order.

Telling him that the snow is too deep, and the wind too harsh, for anyone to climb up several thousand feet to the mountaintops and glass for decent trophies, Kubick goes on to say that Lloyd Zeman, the booking agent from Safari Outfitters in Wyoming, must be held personally responsible for scheduling a Siberian sheep hunt this late in the year.

Ice several inches thick coats the triple-paned windows of the dining room, and Ali looks from them and back to Kubick with the expression of a sky diver who has leaped and just realized he's left his chute behind. His thin gloves and natty down jacket are marginal at best.

Constantine, by profession an economist in Yakutsk and drafted for this mission because of his linguistic skills, has been sniffling through Kubick's monologue and now starts to sneeze. Wrapping his great reindeer coat more tightly about his shoulders, he says, "Yes, this is the coldest spot in the northern hemisphere."

Kubick gives him a damning look and declaims to the room what he's been telling Nick ever since we left Moscow: "If you people could just get rid of socialism you'd be the greatest country on earth!"

At this affable juncture of Soviet-American relations a truck pulls up to the entry, and Asper, Corrigan, and Cox—steam pouring off their white parkas, their cheeks frozen the color of beets, their eyes wild—stomp into the hall. In a mixture of triumph and embarrassment, they announce that they've killed a sheep.

We file outside to see. In the light of our flashlights, the young ram lies on its side, its pelage dusky, its horns modest and shallowly curved. We discover that it's Don Cox who has collected the animal. The guides begin to skin it, and we return to the dining room where Corrigan, a tall, greying man with a quiet voice precise as a jeweler's, tells Kubick that the bands of sheep they've seen today all have small horns that hardly go below the line of their jaws. Silently, Asper goes to his room.

Meanwhile, Cox is shaking hands with the guides who have remained at the lodge, accepting their congratulations, and laughing continuously in his high-pitched voice. A gangly fellow in his late sixties, a Norman Rockwell caricature of the general-store proprietor, complete with bobbing head and avuncular smile, he's given the trophy-hunting world a legacy of determination in the face of bad odds. Diagnosed with life-threatening heart disease, he was advised to have quadruple bypass surgery, which would have terminated his expeditions. Instead he went to California's Weimar Clinic and adopted a fat-free diet and a regimen of exercise. He eventually returned to hunting, in fact crossing the Tibetan Plateau at sixteen thousand feet. Then back problems incapacitated him. Surgery and physical therapy allowed him to return to the field. In 1988 he was inducted into SCI's Hunter's Hall of Fame, and is now one of the leading contenders for the Weatherby Award. When I first met him at that SCI annual convention in Reno, he was busy accepting congratulations, having his photo taken, and booking hunts, walking from booth to booth with the brochures of outfitters in his hand and a mental list of the animals he thought he needed to win the Weatherby. He expressed the hope that one more year's hunting, and the collecting of a Siberian snow sheep, would put him over the top for the coveted trophy. When I finally cornered him for a cup of coffee, he said I could best understand him by going hunting with him. He invited me to Yugoslavia, Tanzania, and Siberia. I said I could probably make the last trip but, if I were unable to go, might I ask him, SCI's man of the year, one question right now: Why did he hunt?

"I end up having something no one else has," he said without hesitation. "And I'm saving animals."

How?

The money he left in developing countries, he said, transformed herders, subsistence hunters, and poachers into game protectors and spared rare creatures such as markhor and ibex from going into the village pot. Of course, he and his fellow SCI members could then shoot a few of these animals for their trophy rooms.

Suddenly Kubick's voice drowns out Corrigan's. Nicolai begins to talk Russian to Constantine, and Buckey, who has his own version of many words, cries, "What a fiasacle!"

The upshot is that Don, Paul, and Vance were not only scouting with the helicopter, they were also hunting from it. It landed Don near the sheep and then, as they attempted to escape, hazed them back to him. Kubick says, "I told Zeman that under *no* circumstances would I use a helicopter for hunting these sheep."

"Wait until you get out there," says Corrigan.

"We should go home and demand that Zeman send us back next year, earlier in the fall. This is ridiculous!"

Corrigan says that Bob has no right to be "holier than thou" since back in the days when they were hunting polar bears off Barrow with Super Cubs, he took one of his bears by hazing. Kubick calls him a "goddamn liar" and stalks off to his room. Before Buckey joins him, he turns to me and says, "They've been fighting for years."

Cox has gone to his room as well. I knock on the door. He sits on a narrow bed, taking off his boots. His rifle—black synthetic stock, stainless steel barrel, telescopic sight—stands in the corner. Insulated jackets and bibs fill a chair under the frosted window. The fixture on the ceiling casts forty watts of light.

We talk about the flight from Yakutsk, the vastness of the country, and the cold. Then, in the awkward silence that descends between us, he says that it wasn't an ideal situation. They had flown tents to the camp that we'll occupy tomorrow, and had gone on to a village of reindeer herders where they took on board several of the local men. Flying over the ridges for a half hour, they finally spotted three groups of rams and approached them with the helicopter.

"They looked like something in the thirty-inch range," he says, "maybe between thirty and thirty-five inches."

Like most trophy hunters, Don is looking for a sheep whose horns, "taped" around the curl, measure forty inches. In the trophy-hunting world, collecting such an animal is about the equivalent of running a sub-four-minute mile.

"And the guides asked me, 'Is that good? Do you want to land and we'll chase them?' " He pauses, just as he probably paused in the helicopter, wondering what he should do. "Just then, higher up, we spotted another bunch, about maybe another half dozen. So we flew past them and I still couldn't make up my mind, and Vance was looking out, and Paul was looking for a moose so he wasn't paying too much attention. Well anyway, we found still another band, maybe about eight. And the guides were still asking me if they were big enough. Well, my eyes aren't that good. I'm looking out of the cockpit of the helicopter. It's going like crazy. The sheep are going like crazy. I see horns and they look like, again, in the thirty-two- to thirty-five-inch range. I have a license for two. And I thought that the hunt was not getting off to a good start, with all the cold and snow—maybe if I could take one it would be a start and we could get things rolling. I asked Vance if he was interested in one and he said, 'Well, I don't think so.' So I said, 'Okay, I'll take one and we'll go from there.' He said, 'Okay, I'll help you.' They made a big circle around the rams, and I put some shells in the gun and got my clothes together.

"*Bang!* The chopper landed. They threw the door open and everyone was screaming, 'Go! Go!' Vance slid out and I jumped." Don lets out a high-pitched giggle and lifts his hand to his mouth, as if to hide it. Then, controlling himself, he says, "We landed in about a foot and a half of snow. The blades were whipping snow all around and I was almost completely blinded. I didn't know which way to go, but at least I wanted to get away from the chopper. About that time Vance's hat blew off. He was running as fast as he could, trying to catch his hat, and I was running with him because we thought the sheep were probably in that direction. It was cold and I could feel it, trying to breathe. There was a little spot with some grass, and we thought we could duck down there. The helicopter sort of herded the sheep, trying to get them back our way a little bit. I dropped the bipod on my gun and it went clear to the barrel in the snow. So I flipped it back up and rested off my knees. Vance had these little binoculars, and when the sheep ran past he said, 'The third one.' I wasn't settled and I missed it. So I shot again and rolled it. But it wasn't completely dead. I hit it too far back. So we followed it up and Vance finished it off. It was quite a little job to get it in the helicopter because they landed it on the side of a hill, and Vance started up on the high side and he's tall and the blades were coming down, and I was screaming at him to duck." Don clears his throat and stops. "That's it."

Then in a subdued voice he adds, "It's cold out there, running, and they told us that the snow was only about four or five inches deep, and it's about two feet." He pauses, then adds another postscript, "The only thing I was thinking, coming back tonight, was that, you know, I'll take one." He clears his throat again and, when he starts to speak, finds himself in back alleys out of which he needs to reverse. "I don't really care a lot . . . I mean I have a license for a moose or . . . no I don't, I have an *okay* to shoot a moose. What I have is a license for two caribou, if I want them. And I thought, I don't particularly care . . . if they want to hunt caribou from a helicopter, and it's easier, it doesn't bother me one way or the other. The second sheep . . . I'd like to take that sheep with a stalk and with the whole thing, and my plan was that I'd get two permits and take one sheep like this, that's a mediocre sheep, and now I can look for a better one for myself, and this one I skinned out for a full mount. There's a couple of museums that would be real happy to have it." He takes a breath, mumbles something, then says, "Maybe it's right, maybe it isn't, I don't know. Maybe I'd been better off to just look for a good one. But I've done that before and you'll pass up one that's pretty good looking for a better one, and then never find one as good as the one you passed up."

When Don and I go to the dining room for dinner, we find the other hunters seated quietly around the table, crowded now with vodka and wine bottles. They look toward a stout man in a padded, blue Mao jacket, seated at its head—Kim, the director of the local reindeer co-op, who also has the heavy eyelids of Mao. Raising his glass, he says some brief words in Russian.

Nicolai Igorevich translates. "The director has complimented you on the start of a good hunt."

Don gets the place of honor next to the director and I sit between Kubick and Ali. We set into the predictable salad of beets and canned peas, the not-so-predictable boiled reindeer tongues, fresh sheep steaks, and pilaf. The wine is poor, the champagne excellent, the vodka easy to drink. Paul Asper turns red, Constantine giddy; Nick's translation becomes slow.

Seated on each side of the director, Don and Vance debate one of trophy hunting's more controversial issues: the differentiation between the similar-looking Altai argali (*Ovis ammon ammon*) and the Gobi argali (*Ovis ammon darwini*). A final geographic line should be drawn between the ranges of the two, says Vance, so those hunters who take the larger-horned *ammon* don't enter it in the record book as a *darwini,* eclipsing the records of the smaller sheep. Who would do it? asks Don, laughing. A committee, replies Vance. What about trophies taken in the past when the ranges might have been different? The director's eyes seem to be following a tennis match.

Buckey shows Nick and Constantine photographs of hunting on Kodiak Island. "This is a brown! bear," he says in his loud voice, which adds exclamation points to adjectives. "Very! large."

Asper takes the photo in hand. "Where was this?" he demands, as if with all his hunts in Alaska, he might have missed some hot spot. Arms bulging from his polo shirt, he looks like a retired wrestler.

Bob and Ali talk about Africa. "I think I met you the first time just after you started hunting," says Bob. "That was in the C.A.R. You were coming out and I was going in. You must have had a great hunt, because I didn't see a thing."

"I was charged by a lion," says Ali.

"Were you hunting with Rudi?" he asks, failing to give Ali an opening for the story of the charge.

"Yes. Didn't you do *anything* in that time?"

"Oh, I shot a couple of those buffalo," he says, the way a golf pro would say, "I shot two over par," and adds, "I shot a *big* reed buck, a very big one. In fact, remeasured, it was number one."

"Would you advise me to go there for bongo?" asks Ali, probing the master.

"I don't think Rudi's got the bongo that Fred Duckworth has or . . ." He searches for the name of another professional hunter. "Robin Hurt was very successful last year. Robin is a success-type personality and always does a first-class job. I don't think he's going to his area again because he can't provide the logistics. If Nicky Blunt is going to hunt there, that's the man to hunt with. He's probably the finest white tracker in the world. He's probably better than the Sudans."

"Where did you see him?" interjects Buckey from across the table.

"Last year in Tanzania."

"I haven't hunted with any of them," says Ali, getting back Kubick's attention. "I started only in '76. I'm not quite up to you. I've hunted on five continents with about a hundred forty heads." Ali speaks a delicately accented English, sweet as halvah.

"A hundred forty *species?*" asks Kubick.

"*Approx*imately."

"Well that's a lot. One of the current Weatherby nominees has about a hundred thirty-five."

"How many do you have?"

"I'd have to recount . . ." Bob's voice drifts off as if he is actually tallying. "About two-sixty-five, two-seventy."

"Not many people in the world have that."

"The person who has the most is Valentin de Madariaga."

"I think you come second."

"No, I'm not second. Hector Cuellar has killed quite a few, Rudolf Sand." He thinks. "Then McElroy. I come in the next group."

"Have you read the book of this Spanish fellow, Ortega y Gasset?" Ali asks.

"Ricardo?"

"Or-Te-Ga. *Meditations on Hunting.* You've haven't? Please *do* read that book," he says, "because you are so interested in hunting."

"I'd love to read it."

"He catches the essence of it. It is unbelievable. And he never hunted."

"It's simple! why we hunt," says Buckey from across the table. "We did it fifteen million years ago."

"To me it's the same as business," says Kubick. "It's goal seeking, it's thrilling, and it gives an extreme sense of self-reliance, self-accomplishment, overcoming almost any difficulty, because the hunter has to go across the river and up the mountain." Now he's paraphrasing his Weatherby acceptance speech, several copies of which he's brought to Siberia, along with eight-by-ten photos of his receiving the trophy, and copies of the menu/program for the evening. All three are included in the type of advertising folder handed out by publicists.

"Difficult as getting to Siberia!" Buckey laughs.

"Please read *Meditations on Hunting*," Ali says again.

"It never ceases to amaze me," says Kubick, now talking for my benefit rather than Ali's, "that there is so much criticism by some hunters of the trophy hunter. What's the difference? You're going to eat the animal anyway. Most people in the United States do not go *hunting*. They go killing. They're killers. I've been with those Texans. They drive you out, and a guy spreads half a sack of corn on one field and half a sack on another, and they put you in a thing that looks like an outhouse—"

"And they take a case of beer too," says Buckey, who hasn't touched a drop all evening.

"And the automatic feeder goes off, and a deer comes up, and you shoot it. That's not hunting. That's an exercise in marksmanship. It has nothing to do with the essence of the hunt, of stalking along with a young son, looking over, and saying, 'That's a pretty good one, and we could shoot it, but let's just let that one go and look for another.'

" 'But we might not get another, Dad.' "

Kubick has entered his favorite instructional mode, the interior dialogue, his voice soft and intimate.

" 'That's okay,' " he tells Ali, the imaginary son, and me. " 'We're not here proving ourselves by killing *anything*. We're here to have a sport, to have a challenge.' If you're just going to go out and shoot something . . . that's not where it's at. Trophy hunting allows you more days in the field. You want to be out there, having those *days* in the field."

"I hate the word *killing*," says Ali, echoing the word Bob has used several times but not directly criticizing him. "Some hunters tell you that they've *killed* that ram, *killed* that antelope, *killed* that zebra. Why do they use the word *killing*? I never use it. I'm hunting." Ali is both angry and distressed.

"The success of the hunt," says Bob, finishing his vodka and taking up Ali's argument, "shouldn't *ever* be measured in poundage. And it should *not* be measured by *getting* something. Of course, to finally take that animal adds a lot to it. But it's a shame when you go out the first day and get what you came for. Like here it would be *terrible* to shoot the ram on the first day." He pauses significantly. "I mean what kind of experience is that? Even if it was a great ram, it would be a shame. The ultimate would be to get the great ram on the last day."

Ali gives Bob a clap on the shoulder and refills his glass while Buckey says, "That doesn't mean Bob won't shoot a forty-inch ram tomorrow!"

When Ali and I follow Nicolai outside, we find the sky partially cleared. Two bands of green aurora stream across the hills. Between them lies the Dipper. The North Star is overhead. We follow a trodden path in the snow, down through a copse of birch, a half moon lighting our way.

Ali and I share a tiny room on the second floor of the guide's lodge. Only a few feet separate our beds, covered with enormous down comforters. After we wash up and get into bed, Ali says, "If you ever have a chance, please, I kindly ask you, write something about this term, *killing*. We're not killing. We're hunting. A slaughterhouse kills, a hunter hunts."

This is obviously a subject that has disturbed him greatly. I turn on my side and face him. His hair is curly, his eyes brimming. He has a large black moustache. I listen to him as he describes how some hunters, usually the ones who use the word *killing* so lightly, have come to the point where they don't even know who they are or what they are doing. "They will say, 'My hunter was in such and such district. My hunter told me to shoot and I shot.' Who was the hunter? *They* were! *I* am! But since one doesn't always know the terrain, the country, the logistics, of course it's normal to have someone to help you out. Why not call them guides and hunters as you do in America, or host hunters and guest hunters instead of professional hunters and clients? These are warm words, not cold ones. And hunting is a warm relationship between two hunters."

Ali's voice is mellifluous, yet full of sharp inflections revealing his anger. "Let me tell you a story," he says. "In Africa, in Chad, we were sitting around the fire and the professional hunter began to talk about hunters and clients, and I thought *I* was the hunter he was talking about, and someone else was going to come and buy something, an elephant tusk perhaps, or something. I never realized that I was the client he was speaking about. Because I was so *green* and so happy that I was being addressed as the hunter!" He almost whispers these words. "But they were talking about me, the *client*."

Then his voice rises. "I hate to be addressed as a *client*. A client is somebody who goes out and *buys* something from someone who doesn't know him. Fine. But we are not doing that. Of course, I realize I must pay because my P.H. has overhead. And he has to make some profit. But we're going out there to share something . . . to be part of something. I remember all my professional hunters and all of them remember me. You share the camp fires, the camp food, the camp jokes, the talk, the history. So I think I deserve to be called some other term, not *client*. It can be sport hunter, guest hunter, or just hunter, or friend, or guy that has been here. Even just asshole, but not *client* for God's sake. *Client* I can't stand. That's a murderous term. Like *killing*. It ruins everything."

"What word would you use instead of killing?"

"Hunting," he says softly and precisely. "A hunter hunts. A killer kills. I'm not a killer. I'm a hunter and killing, unfortunately, is part of hunting. It is such a part of hunting that it cannot be torn out of it. If that would be possible without ruining hunting I would have done it long ago. But it is not possible. Therefore hunting includes killing, like sex includes orgasm. Killing is the orgasm of hunting." He says this as if explaining a sad truth. "But like in making love—talking and touching and, you know, looking in the eyes, and just smelling—the long story is the real lovemaking, and orgasm is the inevitable end of it. That is the killing of hunting, but only one part of it. We are not killers—we are hunters, and therefore I do not want to be called a killer."

—➤✦◄—

WE FLY NORTH INTO A SKY BLUE AS A ROBIN'S EGG, HARD AS STEEL. IT seems as if the arctic wind has frothed the land into whitecaps. For an hour, range after range of snow-covered peaks break beneath us. As we descend, we begin to spy the meandering trails of sheep on the ridges. The trails end in high bowls where the sheep have pawed out beds. Soon we see the animals themselves, dusky white and black, running from the helicopter. As we cross a forested valley four specks—lit gold by the sun—fly over the trees: ptarmigan.

We land on one channel of the braided and frozen Barayi River. On the banks, just visible in the birch trees, stand four wall tents, their chimney stacks sending cozy smoke into the air. We pull the gear from the back of the huge helicopter and, as we carry our bags to the camp, it takes off, lashing us with ice crystals. Its pulsing noise recedes down the valley, and a pure, lovely crack—ax on wood—greets us.

Don and Ali have remained in Topolinyy to hunt moose and caribou for three days, while Vance Corrigan, Paul Asper, Bob Kubick, and Buckey Winkley look for sheep on foot, and by reindeer-drawn sleds, when and if the sleds arrive from a village downriver. Vance and Paul take one tent; Kubick, Buckey, and I another; Constantine and Nicolai a third with the guides. The fourth is the domain of the cook.

By midday each of the hunters has been assigned a local Evenk man by Nicolai. There are twelve hundred of the seminomadic herders in the region, tending reindeer for their hides, meat, and milk. Organized into a local co-op, the herders can't individually own any of the domesticated caribou—they are paid two hundred rubles per month for their work. Nicolai has quickly let the Americans know that their pay scale is a sore point among the Evenk. Whether they're herding reindeer or guiding foreign hunters, they get the same two hundred rubles. Perhaps Gorbachev will remedy this in the near future, says Nicolai Igorevich with a nod toward our arch capitalist, Kubick, but in the meantime a handsome tip would be appreciated.

Bob's guide, Ghanya, makes no pretense at enthusiasm. A dour man with a flat face and broad nose, he wears an enormous wolf-skin hat, a white anorak, and knee-high felt boots. A military carbine is slung across his back. As we don insulated suits and white overalls, he waits outside our tent, immobile as a tree.

He leads us downriver, walking on the frozen channels when we can, on round river rocks where the ice is too thin. We climb a steep bank and enter an old stand of birch, their branches glittering like prisms in the low sun, which sheds not a calorie of warmth.

Soon the birch give way to black cliffs that climb into denuded larch. Unlike most conifers, larch lose their needles in winter, giving the impression that the slopes they occupy have been sprinkled with cinnamon. Above them, bowls of snow rise to wind-blown summits. The river is at about three thousand feet in elevation, tree line is at forty-five hundred, the peaks top out at seven thousand. At the first side valley, a narrow canyon with steep black walls, we find a barnyard's worth of sheep prints—sharp, small, cloven hooves, all ewes and lambs. We turn left and go upstream.

Every few minutes Ghanya pauses, raises his binoculars, and glasses the cliffs, the larch, the upper slopes, heavy with snow. Bob also glasses with his binoculars while Buckey plops in a drift and cradles his video camera on his lap.

He's disgusted with Ghanya's hunting methods, saying that we should get high, sit, take out the spotting scope that Bob carries in his small backpack, and glass for a couple of hours. Bob counsels patience, saying that maybe the Evenk knows something about his own country.

We climb for most of the afternoon, following tracks in the snow that dusts the stream ice. At the junction of another tributary we stop. Ghanya, who has not said one word since we met him, surveys the new stream, the dim sky. He glances at his watch and nods his head back the way we came.

Buckey, who has been filming Bob and the guide, suddenly cries, "Oh, no!" He shakes his camera, puts it to his ear, looks up and says, "We're finished."

Kubick suggests warming it in the tent, and begins to follow Ghanya, who has already departed. Two hours later, near the mouth of the canyon, Ghanya kneels in the luminous twilight and chips a hole in the frozen stream. Water seeps out like blood from a wound and he puts his mouth to the hole and drinks. Standing, he extends a hand to the fountain as if offering us a gift.

Outside the tent our thermometer reads thirty-three below zero Fahrenheit. Inside, around the woodstove, it's eighty-five. The rime, which has frozen on our brows and lashes, runs down our faces like tears. When we walk through the trees and enter the cook tent, we find Paul Asper leaning across the table and shouting in his Pennsylvania Dutch accent, "If I didn't have my earflaps down, I would not be hearing you talk to me because the guide started shooting with the muzzle by my head. By my head!" Brawny, in his mid-fifties, smooth shaven and with black hair, he's doing all he can not to pound the table.

Constantine and Nick, looking trapped, sit across from Vance and Paul. Two candles illuminate the blue-and-white tablecloth, set with bowls of reindeer stew and piles of brown bread. At the stove, the cook stirs a large, bubbling pot. We take our places on the benches and Paul retells his story for us.

"We went very far, at least twelve kilometers. My guide found four rams down in this ravine. So he drew one thousand meters in the snow. And we said, no, we wouldn't shoot that far. I drew three hundred meters in the snow. Then he drew one hundred meters. So we took it that he could get us to within one hundred meters of these sheep. Vance and I were together, but the original understanding was that we were all going to hunt separately." Turning to Bob, he says, "We've cleared that up now. In any case, the closest they got us was maybe three hundred yards, but one young ram spotted us and they began to run. There was one full-curl, shootable ram. It was ridiculous. First they made me sit down. Then they grabbed me by the shoulder and had me stand up. Then they were very confused because Vance would not shoot. In the meantime the rams are getting further and further away. Then one guide grabbed me and I think he said stand up. So I stood up and shot offhand. The ram was probably three hundred fifty yards and running."

"Did you hit him?" I ask.

Paul looks at the table and gives his head a small disconsolate twist. "I don't know. One shot sounded very good. *THOOMP!* But they all went up the mountain. And then both guides started shooting. They shot twenty shots! I could see fire from the barrel as he shot by my ear!"

"Why are the guides carrying guns in the first place?" asks Kubick. "If my guide fires one shot . . ." he raises a finger, "that's it. I won't take the sheep."

"Oh, I told them," says Paul, "if the guide would have killed a ram it's not my sheep."

"Why do the guides need guns?" Kubick asks again.

"Bob, they have licenses for *fifteen* sheep! They wanted us to kill all of them. Vance and I just had this discussion in the tent with Nicolai and Constantine."

"May I have the Tang, please?" asks Vance.

"Oh, yes, excuse me." Paul hands Vance the bottle he's brought from the States. "Anyway, I count myself fortunate, and also Vance fortunate, that neither one of us got a sheep because it would have been one or two in the morning until we got back. No time for skinning. Maybe we could have pulled the guts out and thrown a piece of clothing over the carcasses to keep the wolves off. But it was nearly an impossible scenario."

"It was a different experience," says Vance, trying to throw some levity into Paul's description.

"It was a real circus."

Nick begins to explain. "The guides have permission to shoot fifteen sheeps for meat."

"But not while we're here," says Kubick.

"Therefore we must decide one thing," says Nick, holding up a finger and parodying Kubick's gesture of a minute ago. "When these Evenk people are going with you can they shoot after you or, just in any case, cannot they shoot at all?"

"No. They cannot shoot at all," says Kubick, now the spokesperson for the group. "We've travelled eight thousand miles to come here and hunt, and we're not going to have someone else blasting at the sheep. Their season opens the day we leave."

"This is also dangerous hunting," says Paul. "There were places in this ravine where the ice had frozen, and just when you think it would hold you, you'd crash through. If you had been leaning forward you could have broken your leg very easily. And the guides kept walking."

"Do you want some soup, Paul?" asks Constantine, trying to be solicitous.

"No, thank-you," says Paul, finally calming down. "What kind of meat is that?" He nods to a plate piled with fatty chunks.

Vance says, "Salt pork."

"Is that what it is? That's bound to stir up a most tremendous thirst."
He samples a piece anyway, then says, "Zeman should be taken to task
for sending us at this time of year. The cameras don't work. The binoculars fog up. It's difficult and I'm sad, very sad. I look at this as a once-in-a-
lifetime experience, and I have three cameras with me and I haven't taken
a single picture. It's a goddamn crime. I'm sure my movie camera
wouldn't work either. I haven't even bothered to try."

"Tell me about it!" says Buckey. "Mine's thawing in the tent. Bob's
idea is that we put a canteen of boiling water in my pack and wrap it close
to the video."

Kubick takes another helping of stew and reminds everyone of what
he proposed in the lodge. "We should have left immediately and told
Zeman we'd come back next year."

Sitting huddled in his reindeer coat, its collar turned up to meet the
flaps of his fur hat, Constantine says, "You do realize that this is the
coldest part of the northern hemisphere—what we call the Cold Pole—
and it is already October."

Kubick, sitting catercorner from the little interpreter, looks at him
with disdain. "Constantine," he says, "cold weather and adversity show
a man what he's made of. They tell him if he's strong or not." He makes
a fist over the table and waits three seconds, giving us all time to decide
if he is, indeed, a colossal asshole. Then he says, "Certainly, I'm not. I'm
as weak as they come." He lets his arm collapse.

Even Vance, seated at the far end of the table from his old adversary,
chuckles. Then Kubick adds, "And I don't like to carry my own pack. I'll
give any man a hundred dollars to carry it tomorrow."

Lighting a cigarette and leaning back on the bench, Nicolai Igorevich
says, "I will go tomorrow and carry your pack for nothing."

He does, all meager ten pounds of it, walking barehanded, smoking a
cigarette, several days of beard on his face, his long green coat open, a
black fur hat on his head. Along the way he points out sable tracks
crossing our trail of the previous evening. At the side canyon we ascended, sheep have also walked over our footprints. We continue down
the Barayi, which becomes wider, tall peaks rising from each of its banks.

The temperature has climbed to fifteen below zero, but on the open
river a strong wind, skimming snow along the ice, drops the effective
temperature to about minus forty. We walk; we glass; Kubick carries
only his rifle, a nine-pound .300 Weatherby Magnum with a 20X scope
that Buckey calls "the instrument." When I asked Kubick why he car-

ried the extra weight of a twenty-power sight, when most hunters used scopes of four to eight power, he answered that whereas most hunters aim at an object the size of a quarter at three hundred yards, he looks at an area the size of a pie plate. He never wanted to make the shooting part of a hunt a sporting venture, he explained. He wanted to kill animals with one perfect shot.

We walk into the shadowed side of the valley and head toward the mouth of a canyon. The wind becomes so intense that we're forced, for a few minutes, to shuffle backwards, hands over our faces. Buckey points out that Kubick's cheeks have begun to turn white with frost-bite. Bob tries to put on his face mask and gets it cockeyed over his balaclava. His hands, which he's exposed for an instant, become useless. He balls them into his gloves and leans over at the waist as if someone has hit him in the gut. Agony in his voice, he says, "This isn't even a challenge."

Buckey, swinging his arms to restore their circulation, suggests going back to the sunny side of the river bottom and building a fire. His moustache is a curtain of ice. Nick, who at last has put his hands in his pockets, says that while we are warming ourselves he will make a reconnaissance up the canyon before us to see if he can locate some "sheeps." Like the silent Ghanya he seems unaffected by the cold.

We find a little peninsula of larch and birch jutting into the river, and on its leeward side Ghanya and Buckey build a fire. Here there is virtually no wind. We stand around the small flames as the punky wood burns quietly. The sun hangs over the peaks, and shortly we hear the sound of faint sleigh bells. In a few minutes a half-dozen reindeer teams, pulling wood sleds, whisk by along the river. On the sleds mothers hold small children who wear perfectly tailored reindeer parkas and pants. Litters of puppies shiver behind them, dogs trot alongside. The men, riding saddled reindeer, wave to us. Then they vanish in a swirl of snow.

Kubick has his hands spread over the fire. We have downed several cups of tea from a thermos, he's straightened his balaclava, and the pinched, beaten look is gone from his face. Staring after the sleds, he says, "Hey, we're cussing this out, but this is a hell of a deal. We're right here in the middle of Siberia."

Ghanya, who has been looking worriedly toward the canyon into which Nick disappeared, motions across the river, indicating that he's going to look for the Russian. As he leaves, Buckey heads up into the larch to collect more wood. Kubick pulls a log toward the fire, settles himself on it, and rubs his hands in satisfaction. The likelihood of our seeing sheep this afternoon is small, but his relaxed posture seems to say, "Here we are around the fire, hunters all, doing what we love best."

I ask, "What's been your favorite hunt, Bob?"

Amused by the question, he says, "People are always asking me, 'What's your favorite animal? What's your favorite hunt?' They all are. I can have just as much fun shooting doves in old Mexico as I do getting a Marco Polo sheep. I might talk more about the sheep, but I have just as much fun."

In reality, he's spent more time describing his Mexican dove and duck hunts—his gun barrel so hot he couldn't touch it, his shoulder black-and-blue after shooting several hundred birds in a day.

"As far as one of my favorite places," he says, "that was in northern Australia, hunting banteng. We would take the skiff back to the boat each night, and it would leave two lines of phosphorescence behind it. And the fish, coming up to the surface, would leave glowing trails. Coming out of my stand, and walking back along the beach, I'd see these wet drag marks with tracks on each side of them—saltwater crocodiles, sixteen, eighteen feet long. It's the only time that I've ever carried my rifle with a shell in the barrel, the safety off, and my finger just in front of the trigger. I never saw a croc, but I heard them go in the water ahead of me."

Reaching for his pack, he makes a cushion out of it against the backrest of the log. "My son, Michael, and I would troll in a skiff with these little pack rods we'd brought, and we'd hook a fish and get the giggles because we'd start pulling and never get them in. They were so huge! Sometimes we'd catch a couple of little tuna to eat. But the phosphorescence was just beautiful with the fish coming up around us."

He thinks a moment then says, "Another place a person ought to go is Central African Republic, or the Cameroons. They have some of the purest forms of hunting in the world. All tracking. You select the track of the animal you want—eland, elephant—and just follow him. And most of it's in his favor."

"So it's not hunting out of a Land Rover?"

"Oh, GOD! I don't do THAT! I don't even do that in the other parts of Africa. I won't even shoot a *zebra* out of a Land Rover. That's ridiculous."

"Did you hunt from a Land Rover the first time you went to Africa?"

He doesn't backpedal. "Yes. The first time I did. And I shot anything and everything. I remember leaning across the driver—with his permission—and shooting out the side window. I was thirty-two years old, and I came back and the full impact of how great a trip I had didn't hit me until half a year later. Then guess which animals I really remembered— the ones I wanted to think of when I put myself to sleep at night and the ones I meditated on in my trophy room? . . . You bet. It was the few I walked after. That made a believer out of me. The very next safari I went on—in fact, Buckey went on it, to South Africa—I said, 'We will hunt only by walking.' They said, 'It's impossible to get a Cape hartebeest by walking.' I said, 'Maybe it is but we're going to try.' We got it, by walking across ridge after ridge after ridge, and even the guy who took us said it was the most fun he'd ever had. And he had some special Austrian four-wheel drive, something with a big pad on the front so people could shoot from it."

"A Unimog," says Buckey, who has returned with more wood and has been listening.

"If you could just see the way those Africans track," he now adds, "you'd never want to do anything else. In 1978 we went to the Sudan and it's a rain forest. You can have fifteen elephants standing thirty yards away and you can't even see them the brush is so thick. Huge leaves and vines. They'd call us about four o'clock in the morning, we'd have a light breakfast, get in the car, and they had these trails cut through the forest. You might drive three or four miles just at daylight, and the Africans would look for tracks that the elephants had made across the road during the night. Then they'd pick out the bull tracks, and you start tracking that particular elephant. You might still be on the track at seven, eight o'clock, when it got dark, and never have seen the elephant. You might walk twenty-five or thirty miles."

"Sometimes you'd camp on 'em," says Bob, continuing Buckey's story. "You'd lay down, start a fire, and put ashes all over you so the bugs wouldn't eat you. But sometimes you'd go back and start the next day. Sometimes the tracks would cross another Land Rover track so the guide could bring up the car."

"We did that for eighteen days," says Buckey, "of a twenty-one-day hunt. Bob had plenty of opportunities to shoot, but none of them were big enough."

"Even the Sudan's still not as pure a tracking as you get in the C.A.R. or the Cameroons," Bob goes on. "There's just a track and many days you see nothing. I mean you see *nothing*. You don't expect to go to Africa and see *nothing.* And some days you'll see something, but rarely the animal you want to shoot at. I enjoy that. That's a real challenge. You have to walk and take your time. Throw another log on the fire, will you Buckey?"

Kubick puts his hands back to the warmth, gives his shoulders a little involuntary twitch, then says, "Like here, the longer it takes us to get a sheep, despite the conditions, the better the experience will be. We don't want to do something life-threatening or Christ," he motions up to the peaks, "get ourselves killed in these mountains. Still, I'll do my best, given these conditions, to get a big sheep, but I'm a realist, and you have to be a realist when you're on these sort of trips. One of the bad things about trophy hunting and record books is a person comes all this way and they don't get something big enough to qualify and then they're un-happy. I have seen circumstances like this that are the most tragic things. I have been with guys and we've all viewed the animal. 'Great, great. Great size,' we've said. Even the guy shooting, we ask him, 'What do you think?' 'Oh my God, I'd love to have that,' he's said. 'It's beautiful, magnificent.'

"*Boom!* He shoots it and we walk up to it. All of us right up to it. 'Great, lovely.' He's standing there, stroking it. It's perfect until he takes out the tape and measures the horns. It doesn't score high enough, it's three inches too small, and he doesn't want it. *That poor son-of-a-bitch is lost.* He's lost the *essence* of it right there."

Less intensely, he adds, "Once I've shot, I gear my mind to the fact that the animal is going to be wonderful. And when I go up to the animal—well sure, Christ, I'm a human being. I'd like to run faster than I can, or climb harder, do everything a little better. Always I strive to be better. But there it is. It's the hunt. *That's it.* You can't change it. When I get to the animal I'm happy. And ninety-nine percent of the time I really am happy. I made the decision to shoot and it's terrific. Measuring it means nothing to me. Yeah, if all of sudden I shot one of the biggest ones, that's kind of neat. But you don't have to have the biggest. That's not the *essence* of it. I look at the sheep Madariaga took here in August," he mimes the giant sweeping horns by the side of his head, "and I think there's probably one chance in a hundred that I'll get one like that. I'd *love* to get one like that. But I'm not jealous of Madariaga and I don't covet his sheep. I'm happy for him. Plus it shows me what may be possi-ble. To me, that's one of the great things about the Safari Club Record Book. Here are all these different animals, some of which I didn't even know existed, each one of them a new adventure. If I live long enough, I can go and find them. And yes, it's nice to have your name in there."

Kubick is in a particularly good mood now, so I ask, "Why hunting, Bob? Why not golf, why not mountain climbing, why not skiing? Why the hunt? I mean you don't even have to hunt animals anymore to eat."

He looks at me, laughter in his blue eyes, and says, "I guess for me there has to be something tangible at the end—good or bad. You know, we all have different personalities. I think if I was here in Siberia and I wanted to climb that peak," he points to the white mountain across the valley, turning the color of peaches as the sun sinks toward the horizon, "I would not think of climbing it for fun. But if there was a sheep on it, I'd get to the top. For me, I just don't get the same . . ." he pauses, "intensity of thrill from any other sport."

"Fishing," interjects Buckey.

"Well, I meant fishing and hunting. I scuba dive, for instance, and I love it. But it doesn't have the same *ZING!* to it." He punches a fist through the air. "It's not that I have this gathering instinct, that I gotta collect *everything*. In fact, most of the fish I catch these days, I release. And these days, I don't ever shoot an animal that I wouldn't mount. Now a lot of people will say, 'Why not take pictures instead?' Well, I answer them in a couple of ways. Number one, I don't even see the most avid amateur picture taker spending fifty-five days trying to photograph a bongo with the spiders falling on him, half on his knees part of the time. Now the person who gets that photo, or a photo of a Siberian snow sheep, I'll take my hat off to him. Have I ever stopped and taken pictures in the national parks when I was in East Africa? Yes, I have. Did I enjoy it? Yes, I did. But it didn't have the same essence as hunting. Photos just don't give the same *ZIIIIIING!* to life that hunting does." Again, the fist punched through the air accompanied by the delighted twist of the head.

"What gives you the *zing,* Bob?" I reproduce his punch through the air. "The trophy you take home or the act of killing?"

He stares at me. "This is kind of getting down to the basics, isn't it?" I shrug.

"Okay. It's all those things. I'm a fairly sensitive human being. I don't like to see the death of anything. You know, you drag a big salmon up out the water and there's this beautiful thing. It's almost a shame to kill it. But you do. It's like, personally, I could never shoot another mountain lion from a tree. It's the most helpless son-of-a-gun. Yet, there's the chase with the dogs and that's terribly exciting. But it ends up with this *magnificent* beast in a tree, helpless, and I take a 30-30 and blow it away. 'My God!,' you have to say, 'That's a pretty neat thing to be running around wild in this day and age.' But in most other circumstances, I guess to take only a picture is . . . too . . . too artificial. If we saw a snow sheep over on that cliff, we could look at it through the binoculars and we'd have a memory. Or you could take a picture and you wouldn't know until you got home if the picture was exactly right. But you raise that rifle, shoot, and you *know* right away. You've proved that you could take it."

"How about the pain you cause animals for the proof?"

Kubick pushes himself onto his feet and crouches by the fire. Picking up a branch, he churns the embers. "There's been a study done in Africa showing that when a kudu eats on a plant that plant generates a bitter-tasting compound so the kudu won't eat it anymore. But what is really fascinating is that the plants within a twenty-foot radius, sympatheti-cally, produce the same compound so *they* won't be eaten. Now we finally know why kudu browse selectively, taking a bite of a plant and then moving about thirty feet before taking another bite. So what this means is that plants, too, can feel pain, that they don't like being eaten. We're an animal; we were born an animal; we were born a gatherer; we were born a hunter. I don't want to see anything suffer either. . . ." A tiny breeze blows smoke in his face and he shifts around the fire. "When I was a kid I had to put fryers on the chopping block. That stuff means nothing to me." He shrugs. It just means *nothing.* Most of the time I try not to get in these discussions because it isn't going to do any good. I think we should be working on the nonhunters and the antihunters so they realize that one of the most useful tools for the preservation of game animals, particularly endangered species, is hunting."

"You're in front of my warmth, Bob," says Buckey.

Kubick moves over slightly and says, "The Afghan government did it perfect. As the human population increased the herders started grazing their domestic sheep higher and higher in the mountains until they were grazing them in the winter range of the Marco Polo sheep. They also started to shoot the Marco Polos. The government bought the herders' domestic sheep, hired the herders as game wardens, and the Marco Polos increased. But the money was generated through hunting. That's some of the good things SCI and the record book have done. The same thing could happen here and you wouldn't have the Evenk blasting away at these sheep."

"What happens when the record book pushes people into blasting sheep from helicopters?"

"I don't think the record book does it," he says flatly, "so much as the thought of the money you've paid, and that you've got to take something home. The record book is like anything. It's like the Democratic and Republican parties. There's some really good things about it and some things that aren't. Yeah, I think occasionally the record book causes some people to lose the essence of hunting. Some! Some!" he emphasizes. "In every group of people there's some who do it one way and some another way."

He takes a deep breath as if entering ground that he'd really rather not get into, but he will. "On this hunt, for example, I think there are people who feel so compelled to get a specimen, and who also think that they won't come back, that they'll do anything. To them I don't think it's a hunt. When you have taken as many big game animals as they have, as I have, some of these trips are not *hunts,* they're *collecting.* For instance, if you're going to hunt a bontebok, you'll find them in only about three places in South Africa, on ranches. And I've taken one—walking—but they're about as wild as these tame reindeer. It was brutal. But I wanted a complete collection, not from an ego standpoint, but to have most of the animals of the world. So I shot it. . . . I elected to *immortalize* that animal." He laughs heartily, letting me know he's said this tongue in cheek. But he does add, "And in truth that animal *is* immortalized because I sent it to a museum, life-sized. But those aren't the good memories from the trophy room."

He studies the fire, rubs his hands, and puts his gloves on. "We are ambassadors with these people," he says at last. "Why not come here with a little more style? You know Don Cox would feel better if he went on a little bit of a hunt and got his sheep, instead of the way he did it, because there's no essence of the hunt in the way he did it. In his case, he's striving for the Weatherby Award, which is the ultimate. So I think he may be in that stage where he wants it so bad that he'll do things without thinking. He wanted to be sure he had that extra species."

"Surely if anyone found out what he did, he'd be disqualified."

"Probably there's a good chance that some of the judges may find out."

"How would they do that?"

"Now, I don't know." He laughs.

"Do you think other Weatherby Award winners have hunted that way?"

"Well . . . it depends . . . I don't . . . it's hard." He stops. "The answer is absolutely yes. *Absolutely yes.* But I don't know if it's an indiscretion. It's kind of like saying, Americans eat bread and Mexicans eat tortillas. But when you're in Mexico they're only serving tortillas. Are you going to eat tortillas or not? Here, it's the method of hunting."

"By helicopter?"

"It appears to me it could be. Like sitting up in one of those big towers in Europe for deer. That's the method they hunt by. Now who's to judge whether that's wrong? Because it's not our standard is it really wrong? Here's another example. If I thought I could only get a Jentink's duiker at night with a light, would I get it with a light? Absolutely. Is that traditional? Well for Jentink's duiker, I think the natives netted them or they dug pits. So I don't think we can say, 'This is the way we hunt in North America so we'll hunt the same way in Liberia.' "

His voice has been confident, but now his eyes lose some of their certainty. "So if Don Cox comes over to Siberia and shoots a sheep with the help of a helicopter, is it really wrong? Is it? Well, it bothers *me* the way he did it. It bothers me that the Russians hazed it back to him, and then an Evenk guide got out of the chopper and started spraying it with submachine gun fire, and the other hunter, Corrigan, shot it too. I don't know why they didn't just drop a bomb on the little son-of-a-gun right off the bat."

I look at him.

"Yes, that's what really happened. And I went to all those guys the first night we were here, after you and Ali went down to the lodge, and said again, 'Let's load up and go home right now. Because we can't properly hunt trophy sheep in this kind of weather. My idea of sheep hunting would be every day you'd pick a different mountain range and walk up and glass all day long, and you'd get a feel for the size of the animals. And we know we can't do that, guys. We know it's going to be tempting as hell the last day or two to go home with something so you can put a head on the wall. If we all go back now, we'll force Zeman to send us again.' But they didn't want to do it, nope, not at all. They said that at the last resort they'd shoot one from the helicopter."

"So if it comes down to the last couple of days will you hunt from the helicopter?"

Kubick laughs enormously, right from his belly. "As I stand here today, I would say I don't think so. I think I would go back to Lloyd Zeman and say, 'Lloyd, you made a mistake in sending us at this time.' But even so I have to tell you that when I first came to Alaska, the accepted method for shooting caribou, particularly meat caribou, was to take our Super Cubs out, find the caribou, land, and shoot 'em. And I found it pretty exciting and I did it. I never felt there was anything bad about it and I never had anyone haze them to me. Would I go out, land, walk over, and shoot a caribou here? Maybe. What's the difference between that and a sheep? It's still an animal. These questions don't have simple answers." He looks at the canyon up which both Nick and Ghanya have disappeared and says, "Maybe we should start walking."

IN THE MORNING THE PROMISED REINDEER COME UP THE RIVER, bells tinkling, their drivers yelling. Nick, limping about the camp, matches hunters with drivers and sleds. Arriving with Ghanya long after we had finished dinner, he had set to his bowl of pasta and caribou, and only when pressed did he explain his gimpy leg. Following three ewes, he had slipped on some steep ground and "damaged a little bit my left foot, which was just a bit unpleasant." Cutting a staff, he had "one by one come down the mountains," and met Ghanya searching for him. He declared his sprained ankle "a little nothing for a hunter," and went to bed.

Kubick, who has complained about Ghanya's "walk 'em up" style of hunting, is assigned a new guide, Stephan Romanovich, a small, good-natured man with a light step and a big smile. He arranges our gear on his sleds with energy and care. Patiently, the tame caribou wait in their harnesses, steam coming from their hair-covered nostrils. Some of the animals are brown, some grey, some pure white. As we pass by them, they nuzzle our arms and lick a palm if it's extended to them. A few of the more feisty bulls twitch their antlers sharply and try to hook a pass-erby. Some of the more aggressive bulls have had their antlers sawed off at the pedicel.

With Paul and Vance ahead of them, Kubick and Buckey head upriver. Two reindeer pull each sled, which are constructed of lashed-together willow and alder. Stephan kneels behind the first team. Kubick, who has put on enormous mittens and his bulbous, vapor-barrier footwear, called Mickey Mouse boots in Alaska, lies on the last sled, flat on his back, dozing. Buckey and I sit crowded on the middle one. Occasionally, Kubick's two reindeer catch our sled and trot alongside of us, pink tongues out, brown eyes curious, their breath hot in our faces. The one on the right pushes our shoulders with its muzzle, as if we're not going fast enough. The one on the left bangs its antlers into our heads and we have to cuff it away. Their anklebones, like caribou the world over, click as they trot.

After an hour Paul and Vance turn into a side canyon. We continue upstream, sometimes on snow, often on smooth river ice over which the caribou slip and skate. Forty-five minutes farther along, we pull into a narrow gorge, deep in shadow, full of snow, silent and obscure. Stephan tethers the reindeer to some willow bushes and they immediately set to pawing the snow to find the moss on which they feed.

Crossing the tracks of lynx, musk deer, and ptarmigan, soon sheep, we walk slowly up the defile, which widens into two forks above tree line. In knee-deep snow, we stalk up the right branch, glassing ahead of us. A couple of hours pass, the sky grows dusky, and we enter a bowl above tree line. In the dark rocks on its far side stand eight ewes. Greyish-brown, they're well camouflaged and also looking directly at us. They turn and climb effortlessly over a pass, which appears to be at least an hour away.

With sign language, Stephan communicates that we can follow them or return to the sled. Buckey has put his camera in its makeshift hot-water jacket and says, "I'm game." Kubick looks at the climb and nods downvalley. As we trudge through the snow, a current of bitterly cold air follows us and he says, "That helicopter is looking better and better." He turns around and grins.

In the last light we reach the reindeer, harness them, and sled down-river. The western sky is lit deep blue. A reindeer comes up to my side and nuzzles my face. Touching his shoulder, I feel the muscles working under his hair, which is moist with frost. The lashings of the sleds creak; the reindeer pants; ahead Stephan's whip hisses. A star comes out, the only one for a long time—and the hooves of the deer click, click, click, lulling. We pass several ridges before spying the cook tent, shedding candlelight on the river ice.

Eager for hot tea, we bound up the bank and open the tent flap. At the table sit Don Cox and Ali Üstay. They've shot moose and caribou with the assistance of the helicopter, which has also brought them into camp and returned to Topolinyy. Ali recounts how they've scouted thousands of square kilometers of terrain, seeing only four caribou. "You could not hunt this country any other way than by flying," he says definitively.

In addition to their sets of antlers, they bring a legion of complaints.

Ali's guide has refused to work on his animals. With the air of a movie star who has found himself forced to take the subway, he says, "I hate skinning my own trophies!" Don points out that there are hardly enough candles for the cook tent, the sugar is nearly gone, and the pounds of coffee they originally flew into the camp have mysteriously disappeared. Furthermore, he and Ali were to have been left off at a separate location from Bob, Paul, and Vance, but the Russians couldn't locate enough tents or reindeer to supply another camp. Hence, they're here. He can say no more.

The tent flap jerks open and Paul comes in with Nicolai in tow, followed by Vance. After only the briefest of hellos to Don and Ali, he tells us that the Evenk guides have once again broken their agreement and shot at sheep. His guide Victor had spotted a pair of rams late in the afternoon. "He climbed up a ridge toward them," says Paul, his voice breaking, "and instead of waiting for me, he shoots both of them!" Unable to control himself, he pounds the table, making the plates jump.

"Paul," says Constantine, holding his glasses over a candle to defog them, "you are getting worked up."

It seems that Asper—wearing a great down parka and green wool pants—will grind up the little economist from Yakutsk with his bare hands. But he sits down and says, "Don, Ali . . . I am very discouraged."

Vance's guide, also named Stephan, spotted sheep as well, small rams, and when Vance thought them unsuitable for trophies Stephan asked him to shoot one for meat, which he did. Vance is quick to point out that this isn't a sheep he will include on his licence. Then he reminds us that the real problem with which we're dealing is socialism itself. Look at the severe quotas these people live under—1.5 kilos of meat per person per month—and it's no wonder they'll shoot sheep for some extra protein.

At this point, led by Ali, who is eager to see the rams, we go outside. They lie on the river ice, grey animals with black bands crossing the tops of their creamy muzzles, giving them a curiously wise look. Their pelage is long and thick. A hand thrust into their hair disappears up to the wrist. None of them have the grand horns the hunters are looking for. As we walk back to the cook tent, we pass the antlers of Don and Ali's moose and caribou, lying in the snow. "Have you seen my trophies?" asks Ali.

"Oh yes, very nice," says Paul, glancing at the walnut-colored antlers.

"A very nice moose," says Vance.

"Thank-you," says Ali, pleased.

In the cook tent, seated once again around the table, Paul brings Don and Ali up to date, and they agree that they won't hunt with guides who are carrying weapons. He then browbeats Nicolai with suggestions and threats until the Russian agrees, once again, to talk with the guides about leaving their rifles in camp. In the meantime Vance has been telling the newcomers how dangerous it is to come down these ravines in the dark. He wonders if a hunter who broke his leg could survive the night until the guides got help in the morning.

"Don," says Paul, "I will tell you that sometimes I feared for my life here. I have honestly thought I might not be going home."

Since Kubick's guide, Stephan Romanovich, has carried no gun today, Bob has elected to stay out of the conversation. At last the cook, a quiet man with a week-old beard and sorrowful eyes, puts the nightly reindeer stew on the table, accompanied by piles of bread and gouts of frozen butter. Ali recounts how they flew for two days and how, when they finally spotted caribou, landed, and got out of the helicopter, his eyes were so stung by the icy wind created by the blades that he almost couldn't shoot. Again Paul tells of the guide's rifle going off by his ear, and Vance wonders if anyone will shoot a ram with horns larger than forty inches.

Paul and Vance are seated across the table from me, and when I ask Vance if he has shot many rams that large, he says, "All the rams in my Grand Slam are over forty inches." He has big hunched shoulders, a greying widow's peak, and a long grizzled face, weary with cold. In a soft voice he recites their measurements down to the eighth of an inch, then qualifies his résumé by saying that as a kid in college he put seven animals in the Boone and Crockett book and has never entered anything else. "Today getting the biggest Grand Slam is nothing more than an award for who's spent the most money."

"I agree," says Paul. "It's a disgrace."

The cook serves the second course—reindeer tongue and pasta. Slowly, the food warms the hunters. They become less cynical, even cheery. Don fetches a photo album from his duffel and shows Nicolai and Constantine a snapshot autobiography of his hunting career, page after page of him posing behind dead animals.

Paul leaves and returns with several color brochures of his Fin, Fur and Feather Wildlife Museum, located in his hometown of Hanneyville, Pennsylvania. He hands one to Nicolai and one to me. The cover shows a photo of Paul and his wife, Carole, standing by a life-size bongo, with antelope grazing at their feet, and the foliage of equatorial Africa behind them—just a small sample of the 270 full-size mounts that Paul has collected and displayed within reproductions of their natural habitats. Inside the brochure a line of text explains that Paul was inspired to create the museum "by a deep concern for the wildlife of the world and the rapidly diminishing environment necessary to support it."

Exchanging a copy of "Fin, Fur and Feather" for Don's photo album, Paul says that he's becoming ever more worried about the quickening rate of worldwide animal extinctions. He says that Kenya's human population is growing faster than any other nation's—"four percent a year!"—and no one has any idea of how to stop it. And that's only one country. He wipes the back of his hand across his brow and flicks away an imaginary bit of sweat.

Don repeats the adage that it's the hunter alone who is the best conservationist. At the homily Paul's face becomes pensive—Don's totally missed his point about population growth. Closing the older man's photo album, he gives his head a little downward twist, repeating the same fatalistic expression he wore when, the previous evening, he described the sound of his bullet hitting the distant sheep. He catches me looking at him, and completely out of the blue says this line from Thoreau, "There are a thousand hacking at the branches of evil to one who is striking at the root."

As the rest of the hunters make small talk I turn to the last page of Paul's brochure. There, beneath a photo of three mounted raccoons on a tree, are printed these closing words from the naturalist Henry Beston, written while he lived on Cape Cod during the 1920s: "We patronize them for their incompleteness, for their tragic fate of having taken form so far below ourselves. And therein we err, and greatly err. For the animal shall not be measured by man. In a world older and more complete than ours they move finished and complete, gifted with extensions of the senses we have lost or never attained, living by voices we shall never hear. They are not brethren, they are not underlings; they are other nations, caught with ourselves in the net of life and time, fellow prisoners of the splendour and travail of the earth."

I'm surprised. Even though the remarkable passage is now quoted in at least two popular books of natural history and graces the calendar of an environmental organization, it is not widely known and I wonder if Paul, a student of Thoreau, is also one of Beston. I also wonder because his brochure omits the paragraph's two introductory sentences. When I ask him where he found the quote, he says, "On a plaque in the Zambia air terminal," adding that the passage remains the most wonderful thing he has ever seen about animals and that he has never been able to discover who the writer was.

I mention what I know of Beston's life, and he asks if any of his works are still in print. I tell him that I have two copies of *The Outermost House,* in which the quoted passage appears, and offer to send him one. With a sincerity all the more touching because of his innate gruffness, he says that this would mean a great deal to him, "for such authors are few and far between." I hand him back his brochure and he tells me to keep it. Then he rises with a "we have a big day ahead of us" and leaves for his tent.

Shortly, I go to mine. Pausing above the riverbank, I listen to a birch crack in the cold and the subtle electrical vibration of the green aurora, shimmering at the end of the valley. Just beneath the bank the reindeer lie on the ice—snug, content, and thinking their reindeer thoughts, whatever they might be. Despite our attempts at radio tracking, first-hand observation, and empathy, they remain, as Beston said, unmeasurable and perhaps unknowable. Writing during the same years in which Werner Heisenberg formulated his uncertainty principle for subatomic particles, Beston came to a similar conclusion about the limits of human knowledge. Heisenberg's principle states that the interaction between a measurer's instruments and the object being measured always results in a slight disturbance to the object, limiting the accuracy of the measurement. Beston made a similar leap of intuition, and began his passage about the intermingled destinies of animals and people with these words: "We need another and a wiser and perhaps a more mystical concept of animals. Remote from universal nature, and living by complicated artifice, man in civilization surveys the creature through the glass of his knowledge and sees thereby a feather magnified and the whole image in distortion."

It was these two sentences that the Zambians omitted from their plaque, and Paul from his brochure.

SIX

→>×<←

SLIGHTLY AFTER SUNRISE WE BEGIN SLEDDING ALONG THE BARAYI. Stephan Romanovich has chosen to reexplore the canyon that we scouted with Ghanya on the first day of hunting. He whips the reindeer far beyond our previous high point, then we walk through a forest of thigh-deep snow until we reach tree line. Before us rises an immense alpine basin. Windblown clouds curve over the jagged summits; snow devils whirl on the ridges; the sun has left this north-facing valley weeks ago. Glassing the slopes, we finally spot a single ewe and her lamb. When we lower our binoculars the two animals disappear, and the black objects we first thought were sheep take on their true dimensions—boulders the size of houses. It is about as inhospitable a place as one can imagine, and as we stand shivering in our sweaty clothes night falls. The canyon we easily ascended now seems crisscrossed with blown-down trees. We stumble around them like drunken men and break through the ice of the stream, which fortunately has gone dry.

When we arrive at camp, five hours later, we find that Ali has taken a sheep. Measured by the annular rings of its horns, it's eleven years old. But its horns are thin and describe barely three-quarters of a curl. Though none of the other hunters show any excitement over his trophy, Ali is ecstatic. He has taken a specimen of *Ovis nivicola* after one day of hunting and with barely a mile of climbing. The gentle-mannered Turk can now relax in camp.

Both Paul and Vance have seen large rams far up the Barayi, but were unable to stalk them. They look tired, as do Don and Bob. Their eyes are swollen, and their cheeks are raw and covered with several days growth of beard. The thermometer has hung between fifteen and thirty-five below since we arrived in camp.

In the morning it takes the herders several hours to round up the reindeer, who have been let loose to graze through the night. At eleven o'clock, the sky promising snow, the hunters begin to sled upriver as if going to work.

The temperature climbs to zero; the wind begins to blow. After an hour Paul's team turns up a side canyon. Vance's team, and Bob and Buckey's, continue upriver, making for a canyon Vance hunted the day before and about which he's said, "It has a few sheep." The two guides, both dressed in reindeer parkas and black velvet hats trimmed with wolf fur, stand on their sleds, snapping their whips and showing off.

Kubick's guide, who has been distinguished as "Old Stephan," though he is only thirty-five, rocks steadily with the bumps. Vance's guide—"Young Stephan"—trips lightly over the crosspieces, a slim man with a boyish face. All this bypasses Kubick who has gone to sleep on his sled, looking like a beached whale in his many layers of clothing. Vance sits upright, wearing a fox hat and a down parka. Alert, he grips the side rails of his sled and scans the riverbanks.

At one o'clock we reach the vertical walls of shadowed canyon, its mouth perhaps thirty yards across. A stand of larch grows on its rim and for a few minutes weak sunlight angles across the treetops. Suddenly Young Stephan yells and points. Along the cliffs a trio of rams gallop away. Gripping their rifles, Vance and Bob lumber through the snow; but it's no use. The sheep are gone.

Irritated, Vance tells Bob that they should split up, to which Bob cagily responds that he'll leave such a decision to the guides. Neither, of course, speaks English and Vance doesn't speak Evenk so nothing comes of Vance's haranguing them. It's obvious, though, that both Stephans don't want to understand Vance's wish to separate the parties. They prefer to hunt together.

The teams continue upstream; a thin haze obscures the sun; the larch end. Here the valley broadens, flanked on each side by massive snow peaks that recede several miles to join in a great cirque of rock and ice. The guides stop and the hunters glass. Soon they spy two half-curl rams lying on a pingo that rises from the valley floor a half mile ahead. Chewing their cuds, hair blowing in the wind, the sheep stare back at us. On a steep slope beyond them, five ewes and lambs climb, playing follow the leader and switchbacking. Still farther up the valley a solitary, full-curl ram disappears into a hanging basin.

It's clear why Vance wanted Bob to turn back. This is the sheep cache of the Barayi. Bob breaks out his spotting scope and glasses the two young rams while Vance says that this is exactly where he was yesterday, and that at the head of the valley he spotted a very large ram. He reminds Bob that both Nicolai and Constantine have promised them that each hunter would go his separate way.

Bob says, "Well, we're both here now."

While Bob and Vance continue to argue, Buckey takes his video camera from his pack to film the sheep. As he unwraps it from the down parka, he gives an anguished cry—horror-struck, despairing, final. The water bottles have opened, and he holds up the dripping machine like a massacred child. When he turns the video on, a green light glows for an instant; a red light flickers; then the camera stops; the water on it instantly freezes. Buckey drops the camera in his lap and says, "What a fiasacle!"

Bob suggests drying it off. Furious, Buckey yells that it's totally soaked, and he pulls out the wet video cartridge and shows it to Bob. "Ruined," he says.

Old Stephan points to his wrist, indicating that time is flying. Then he motions up the valley and curls his hands by the side of his head, meaning "big sheep."

"Yes," says Bob, "let's go."

In disgust Buckey jams the video into his pack and the two guides whip the reindeer into a trot. We cross overflows of hummocky ice, which tilt the sleds on one runner and force us to throw our weight on their high sides. Once, not responding quickly enough, Buckey and I are tossed off our sled, which turns over and is dragged upside down by the enthusiastic reindeer for fifty yards before the teams stop. No one is hurt.

For another half hour we sled at a fast clip, passing beneath the two young rams atop their lookout. Then we cross a steep sidevalley and a corniced ridge, both to our left. A hanging amphitheater appears. Even without glasses, we can see a half-dozen rams bedded within it. The Stephans halt the caravan, and Bob sets his tripod on one of the sleds and mounts the telescope. Two of the sheep have full curls. One sheep stands from the herd, paws through the snow, and crops some grass. His massive horns spiral back and down and out and up . . . and almost back again—a little more than full curl. Vance says, "That's the sheep I saw yesterday."

Bob shrugs and says, "The other ones are good too."

The Stephans have been collaborating. With gestures and a sketch in the snow, they now lay out this plan: Old Stephan will stay with the sleds while Young Stephan will lead the hunters back to the sidevalley we have just passed, up which they'll stalk, shielded by the intervening, corniced ridge. The wind, blowing downvalley, will be in Vance and Bob's favor when they sneak over the top and shoot the sheep. Pleased with themselves, the guides smile broadly.

The reindeer have already agreed with the plan. They have lain down with their legs curled under them. Young Stephan leads us down the ice of the stream. Soon we enter a thicket of willow where he cuts several stout staffs for us to use on the climb. Buckey, still hopefully carrying his video, refuses the aid.

The tributary, a creek no more than a dozen feet wide, rises in frozen steps of ice and rock. Stephan takes off at a trot but within seconds must slow his pace. Vance—fifty-six and not in the best of shape—has fallen behind and is catching his breath. Soon he is stopping every hundred feet to lean on his staff. Sweating heavily, he unzips his parka. Kubick, in his pebble camouflage suit, the only one of us not wearing white coveralls, stays zipped-up, wearing the inexorable expression of a man with unlimited patience.

Slowly, for almost an hour, Stephan climbs, and it becomes clear that this sidevalley will curve upwards and to the right, ending at a col from where Vance and Bob can look down at the unsuspecting sheep. However, as we step around a protruding snow slope, we see a bedded sheep on a ridge higher than the col. He watches the country below. Stephan motions us back until the slope hides us from the ram's sight. He thinks a moment before motioning us straight up the hill to our right. Without waiting to see if anyone will follow him, he begins kicking steps toward the sky.

Slick moss and miniature willow lie beneath the snow, and Stephan, in his mukluks, has to hold on to his staff to keep from sliding backwards. Vance places his feet in the steps of the guide, but the small platforms Stephan has kicked break away beneath his large boots and he's forced to support himself with his staff. By the time Kubick and Buckey step into the tracks they're on slick snow mixed with trampled vegetation. Every other step one of them slips backwards. With crushing slowness the entire party zigzags up the slope, the men pulling themselves over little benches of rock and pausing every other minute so Vance can catch his breath.

A bunting arcs from the sky and lands ten feet away. Whistling once, it flutters back into the air and is gone—the only sound except the men's breathing and the soft crunch of the snow. The valley begins to drop away; far below, the stream becomes a winding grey thread; above, the slope finally lays back. Hunched over to stay out of sight, the hunters approach the crest of the ridge as a fine, stinging curtain of ice crystals blows in their faces.

They peek over the knoll. To the right the ridge falls into space and down to the distant valley. Beyond it, mountains rise to the north— range after range of hazy white peaks curving over the horizon. To the left the ridge climbs, bending around to form the rear of the small cirque in which the sheep are bedded. It's now late afternoon. Bands of ragged yellow cloud swirl across the top of the cirque, indicating where the sun has set. In the pale, shifting light we spy the sheep, grazing six hundred yards away.

Stephan motions up the ridge. Dropping into its lee, he leads through pockets of deep snow and chest-deep cornices. The slope below grows ever steeper, an easy seven hundred feet drop to the streambed we abandoned. Some of the snow pockets are thirty yards across, perfect starting zones for an avalanche. Oblivious to or ignoring the danger, Stephan kicks steps across them, and the hunters, oblivious as well, or absolutely determined, follow. At one point Vance seems to falter and shoves his staff deep into the cornice by his right hip to keep himself from peeling out into space. Is he remembering the story he told at dinner several nights ago, of the former Weatherby Award winner, Arthur Carlsberg? Descending from a tahr hunt in the Himalayas, Carlsberg grabbed the branch of a small tree to steady himself on a steep slope. It broke and he fell to his death. This seems a perfect end for a sheep hunter. But not today.

Stephan wades back to the crest of the ridge, crawls on his belly, peeks over the top, waves us forward. The rams are within four hundred yards and Kubick wants to shoot, but Stephan shakes his head. In the meantime the sky is losing light. The peaks to the north have turned lilac.

Breaking trail, Stephan descends slightly, cuts his way through another cornice, traverses another unsafe pocket of snow, and scrambles upward through a steep boulder field. At last he reaches the near end of the col for which he was aiming when we were turned out of the streambed by the sentinel ram, who is now nowhere to be seen. Vance and Bob catch their breath, pull back their hoods, check their rifles, and creep up to the very last rim of rock overlooking the saddle. They nod to each other and ease their heads over the lip. The rams are gone. The two hunters visibly deflate. Limp and sweating, they sit in the rocks.

"Hurry, hurry," gestures Stephan with his arm, jerking his head toward the saddle. Vance looks exhausted but he follows on the guide's heels, carving a trench for Bob and Buckey. All keeping close together, they cross the col and continue into the bowl beyond. There they find snow scuffed from the grass, a half-dozen kidney-shaped beds, and a trail of meandering prints leading into the very valley where the sleds wait—an ironic turn. Will the sheep walk back to Old Stephan?

Keeping a fast pace, Young Stephan follows the tracks, which drop over a knoll and head down the fall line of much steeper terrain. He motions for everyone to sit on their butts. Quietly, we slide down several hundred feet until the slope becomes more precipitous. A stone, set rolling wouldn't stop. A tiny frozen creek runs in the narrow gorge below us. Stephan holds up his hand, points. Across the gorge a single ram browses. A hundred yards from him nine others paw the snow. In the dusky light they're difficult to see, so well do their dark-and-white coats mix with the rock and snow. They seem about a quarter mile away.

Bob acts the gentleman. In a whisper he says to Vance, "Which one do you want?"

Bob is left, Vance right—both are seated, steadying their elbows on their knees and looking through their binoculars. Buckey and Stephan crouch behind them. Vance says that he'll take one out of the group of nine and Bob says fine, since he's on the left he'll take the single ram to the left. He asks Buckey to sit in front of him. When Buckey's in position, Bob rests his rifle, "the instrument," on his shoulder.

Unaware, the sheep continue to feed. Chunky and powerful, the single ram paws the ground, clearing the snow so he can shove his great horned head into the drifts and browse.

Stephan motions "no" to Kubick. Standing, he waves to Old Stephan who, far below us, whips the reindeer and sleds into the mouth of the gorge. For a moment, the hunters don't understand what the guides can be up to. It's Buckey who says, "They're driving them."

Outfitted with military carbines, effective only at short range, the Evenk have evolved the same strategy humans have used for as long as they've hunted big animals—herd them close. However, running targets are the last thing Bob and Vance want.

Bob says, "Let's shoot. Count of three?"

Vance has settled himself into a sitting position and studies the sheep through his scope.

"They're looking up," says Buckey. As if the sheep were one animal instead of ten, they simultaneously turn and stare downvalley at the distant sleds.

"Ready?" says Bob.

The nine rams turn and run toward the tenth, who stands motionless, looking.

There is a boom and an ear-splitting crash. A millisecond later the single ram rolls down the slope, like a child playing in the snow—over and over—and comes to rest as if sleeping on the bank of the creek.

Vance doesn't shoot. He tracks the running herd for a long time as they head up the gorge. At last his rifle goes off, seeming to make hardly any noise compared to Bob's. The sheep continue to flee across the slope, toward the crest of the ridge, and safety. He fires again. Still they run. They seem very far away. Vance fires a third time and a second later one of the rams falls behind and turns downhill, making a sweeping turn and dragging his right leg. Vance shoots again and misses—the ram begins to climb. Surprising everyone, he turns to Bob and says, "If you want to shoot, go ahead."

Bob rests the rifle on Buckey's shoulder, sights for what seems an age, and again there's the boom instantly followed by that heart-piercing crash. The sheep, dragging his leg, continues to run. Stephan shouts at Bob to stop shooting, for it will drive the sheep over the ridge and into the next valley. The rest of the herd has already gone over the top. After a few minutes of hard going, the wounded sheep slows, stops, stands, and finally lies down, curling his legs beneath him. Across the gorge from us, he rests alone on the great snow slope.

Stephan begins sliding and tripping toward the creek with Vance hobbling behind. Bob and Buckey follow more carefully, trying to keep their footing in the last of the light. It's a long way down, much farther than it originally appeared. Stephan and Vance cross the creek and start up the other side.

Bob and Buckey angle upstream and find the sheep lying on his side with his eyes open. They're amber, profound, and not yet glazed over. There's blood on his white muzzle and grass still in his lips. His body is the color of slate, his horns that of autumn wheat, spiralling just a little bit more than one full curl.

"Well, there it is," says Kubick. He shakes Buckey's hand.

Far above us the bedded ram turns his head over his shoulder and stares at Stephan and Vance, climbing after him. Though they're still a half mile off, he stands. Dragging his leg, he disappears over the top of the ridge. Before Stephan and Vance can return, it's dark.

We take some flash pictures of Bob kneeling alongside the sheep, and Buckey says it's a crying shame that his video wasn't working, for this stalk would have been one of the greatest hunting films ever made. Bob gives him a tired look. "I'm not complaining," says Buckey. "This has been one of the best experiences of my life."

Bob asks him how far he thought the ram was when he shot. Buckey says 425 yards. Bob says he thinks it was closer to 350.

Old Stephan comes up with the sleds, and when Vance and Young Stephan join us the latter indicates that tomorrow he will come back to get the ram, who will bed down on the opposite side of the ridge and not go far. As we secure the sheep to the last sled in line, Buckey says that if we can hurry, getting the ram back to camp before he freezes, and if we can keep him warm until tomorrow so he'll look good, and if he can get his camera working, he may be able to get some footage of Bob posing with the ram, which may salvage his video.

Avoiding rocks, the guides keep the reindeer at a slow walk down the sidevalley. When we reach the larger stream, where Old Stephan waited, the reindeer increase their speed. Slamming into hummocks and snowbanks, the teams careen through the dark. Suddenly, the sled on which Buckey and I ride crashes to a stop, pitching us headlong across the ice. The front of one runner has wedged under a block of ice and broken. While the two Stephans take a half hour to lash it together, Vance sits somberly on his sled and Kubick, just as silently, sits on his. The stars disappear behind cloud cover and the night grows very dark.

Upon reaching the Barayi, Old Stephan's sled strikes another hummock and its prow shatters. The guides spend another forty-five minutes in repairs while Buckey and Bob jog along the sled track, windmilling their arms to keep warm. They've eaten no more than a piece of bread and a swallow of tea since breakfast. By the crackle of the cilia in his nostrils, Buckey declares it to be twenty below. Vance doesn't move from his sled. Hunched over, he remains buried in his thoughts, his hands cradled in his lap.

At about ten-thirty we see the faint light of the cook tent, and the two Stephans raise a call. The cook, the guides, and the other three hunters meet us at the riverbank. Don has been unsuccessful; Paul has killed two rams; and for a minute everyone mills around telling their stories. Then Paul takes a steel measuring tape from his pocket, walks to the sled, and lays it around the horns of the ram Kubick has killed. Disgusted, Kubick walks away.

Constantine tries to make a show of having a celebratory dinner but fails. The tips of Vance's thumbs have been frostbitten, and he's silent with pain and disappointment. His injury might be considered the cost of a great ram, but the animal lies in the mountains tonight. Immediately after eating, Kubick leaves, and within a few minutes Paul too heads for his tent.

I follow and find the museum owner sitting on a well-worn, brown steamer trunk. A candle burns by his side as he works on the horns and cape of one of his trophies. I ask if he minds if I watch. He says no and adds, "Skinning is part of the adventure. I enjoy it." He wears a plaid wool shirt and a ram's-head belt buckle.

When I ask him about how he took his sheep he doesn't tell a long story. He and Victor sledded three miles up a side canyon and hunted another three miles on foot. He had decided that he wanted two sheep for his museum and although he knew that a second license would cost him another fifty-eight hundred dollars when he got to Moscow, he shot the pair.

Mentioning the price of the second license makes him think of something. He sets aside the cape and opens the trunk. A drawer in its top contains leather pouches and a small movie camera. Paul lifts out the drawer. Extra clothes are folded neatly below it. He removes a manila folder, closes the trunk, and gestures for me to sit by his side.

Opening the folder, he shows me a typewritten list that describes his Super Slam. The common and taxonomic names of the twelve sheep he's taken are listed in the left-hand column, the cost of each hunt is on the right. He turns to the second page and points to the total, $185,000. He bows his head slightly in his usual manner of expressing an unpleasant but unavoidable truth.

The agents who book these international hunts, he says, have become like the hair-splitting taxonomists of the 1800s, who named dozens of subspecies of bear, sheep, and elk. By advertising hunts for many species, which in reality are no more than color variations of the same animal, the agents can make huge profits. Yes, he will come back for a Kamchatka bighorn, but he'll be damned if he'll give Lloyd Zeman another seventy thousand dollars to collect four more, nearly identical snow sheep. He's happy with his *Ovis nivicola borealis.*

The name he uses, *borealis,* surprises me. This subspecies of snow sheep is listed as endangered in the Russian Red Book. It can't be legally hunted. When I mention that Lloyd Zeman, who has taken one of these sheep on his exploratory hunt to the region last year, claims them to be *Ovis nivicola lydekkeri* in all his published literature, and legal to hunt, Paul cites the map in James L. Clark's *The Great Arc of the Wild Sheep.* According to it, says Paul, we're right in the middle of *borealis*'s range. However, Clark compiled his map in the United States, from museum samples whose actual points of collection still hadn't been verified. On the other hand, the Russian scientist, L. M. Baskin, has more recently classified the sheep in the Yakutia region, in the very center of which we're camped, as *Ovis nivicola lydekkeri*, giving their population as a quite healthy forty-four to fifty-five thousand animals. Does Paul really believe that the sheep he's hunted are the endangered *borealis*? He doesn't answer, but gives his head that little downward nod, as if indicating that he's caught in a web too profound for him to change.

Attached to his accounting sheet is an anatomical drawing of a ram seen in profile, accompanied by instructions on how to dismember the animal's skeleton so that it can be brought home to a museum. Paul mentions that he's contributed several skeletons of Asian sheep to the Denver Museum of Natural History and that if international hunters were only willing to educate themselves, and spend a little more time in the field preparing their trophies, science's knowledge of these little-known animals could be increased.

Taking the leather pouch from the drawer at our feet, he empties its contents, showing me a kit of small knives, screwdrivers, and a piece of deer antler, the last used to turn ears. "Where I grew up," he says, "there was only one other family in the mountains. I had my dog, my guns, and my traps, and that was my life. I started trapping at five years old, and skinned everything—skunks, raccoons, foxes, everything. The first time I was in Mongolia, in 1975, I shot a big Siberian elk, a seven by seven. And the guide started splitting the ears. I mean he was cutting them open! It would have been kaput. I chased him away. Even in Africa, where some of the blacks are great skinners, I supervise the work closely. Often, they'll miss rubbing salt into the ball sack, or they won't rub it right out to the edges of the hide." Going on to extol the virtues of salt, he says that it has saved his skins even in the rain forest. "Tomorrow I'm going to work on these sheep all day, rub in plenty of salt, and scrape the skulls. Once they're skinned some people will boil the skulls, and we

could do that here, easily, but it leaves an unsightly ring on the horns."
Holding up a small sharp knife, he says, "Better to scrape."

I find Kubick in our tent, sitting on his enormous sleeping bag, boots
off, stockinged feet stretched toward the glowing sheet-metal stove.
He's tossed his camouflage coveralls behind him and wears only his plaid
wool shirt and khaki pants held up by a ram's-head belt buckle just like
Paul's. In the opposite corner lies the snow sheep, hooves also pointing
to the warmth. The ram looks as if he might have walked in and lain
down. When I stretch out on my sleeping bag Bob asks me where I've
been.

"Talking with Asper."

"I wish there was more comradery in this camp," he says tiredly.

"How did you feel when you got the sheep today?" I ask.

"*We.*"

I don't understand him and say, "We?"

"We all did it. I just happened to be the guy who pulled the trigger.
Buckey could have shot it. You could have."

I look at the sheep. Even in death his shoulders retain their blocky
strength, and I remember him pawing through the snow with certainty
and power. His horns curl toward the peak of the tent like half moons,
like eternal question marks.

"How would you like to be remembered, Bob?"

He stares at the pulsing red spot on the side of the stove. Without
looking up, he says, "As a good father."

In the middle of the night I wake to find the tent lit by an unusual
orange glow. Wanting cooler sleeping, Bob and I have let the fire die
each night and the tent has approached the outside temperature. This
drove Buckey into tirades and then into the guides' tent. When I poke
my head out of my sleeping bag to see if, perhaps, we're on fire, I see Bob
crouched before the open door of the wood stove. He's in his long underwear and grey balaclava, rolled up as a stocking hat on top of his head.
Breaking twigs, he puts them on the embers of the old fire. Leaning
close, he blows on them until they ignite. He's trying to keep the dead
sheep warm so it will look lifelike for Buckey's video in the morning. But
when morning comes Buckey's video is as dead as the ram.

After breakfast Don sleds up the Barayi with his guide. Vance stands
on the riverbank, watching him depart, followed by the two Stephans,
who tow a pair of empty sleds. He's elected not to accompany them as
they search for his wounded sheep. He can't hold onto a sled with his
frozen hands, and he looks exhausted.

Bob, with Ali assisting, begins to skin his trophy. "You know," he says to the Turk who is gingerly holding back the hide on the ram's belly, "you ought to work on your skin when you get to Moscow. Turn it out, dry it, rub in more salt."

"No need," says Ali breezily, "I'll have it in Istanbul, at my taxidermist, in three days."

Kubick pauses in his skinning. "You are such an aristocrat," he says good-naturedly. "If you come to Alaska and we go crabbing, that'll be real work."

"I won't mind," says Ali, "if I'm prepared and expecting it."

On the other side of camp and without letup, Paul cleans his trophies. Inside the dining tent Constantine and Nicolai talk Russian while Vance and Buckey trade yarns. Outside, the cook bucks and splits wood.

"I've seen him three times," says Buckey. "The biggest Dall sheep in Alaska." He makes the sweeping sign language of horns by the side of his head, bringing the tips back upon themselves to complete a curl and a half. "Just like an argali. Bob may go after him next year."

"Where did you say you saw him?" asks Vance.

"Oh . . . in the Alaska Range."

In Bob's tent, the skinning done, he and Ali lounge on sleeping bags like pashas.

"*BOOM, BOOM, BOOM!*" cries Bob, rapidly working the action of an imaginary rifle. "And the lion kept coming! Buckey has this little twenty-two-magnum. *Ping, ping, ping!* And in his excitement he pulls out the bolt!" Kubick slaps his leg and laughs uproariously.

Ali meets this story with the tale of his lion charge—he had to shoot four times because he had inadvertently loaded with solids instead of expanding bullets. "All the time he rrrrroared!" says the Turk, closing his eyes and giving an involuntary shiver. "What a sound!"

Bob raises him a tale of elephant tracking, and Ali offers an escapade with a brown bear. Bob, of course, has had more experience with the animal and reenacts another charge. "*Ba-boom!*" he cries. "And I'm down to my last shell. It's toward evening, so when I shoot from the hip I can see fire burn all the way to the bear. That's how close he was. *BOOM!* And he didn't get up. I sent a tooth into Fish and Game—that bear was twenty-six years old. Huge. Eight days later, the salted hide squared ten-foot-eight."

On and on.

Late in the afternoon Don comes in with two sheep. They're smaller than both Bob and Paul's rams, what the collector calls "representative specimens." No one lingers by the sleds an instant longer than necessary—it's twenty below. Following Don to his tent, I ask him where he got them. He mentions a side canyon all of us have passed. He pats his rifle, saying he was glad that he had his custom magnum because the shots were very long, and he doubts that he could have walked closer, the snow being deep and the sled ride having hurt his back. His mouth is stiff with cold, his face wizened, and his eyes wear something more than exhaustion. He's like a soldier in that place between battle and welcome home, knowing clearest the costs. "I'm glad I got them with the sled," he says before ducking into his tent. "It takes the smell away from the other one."

At his tent Paul shows me the mandible of his sheep, clean and white, the teeth stained brown. Turning it over in his hand, he says, "Look at this jaw, the teeth are in super shape, sharp for a fourteen-and-a-half-year-old ram. Our sheep in North America live ten years and they die of disease or predation. Why do they live so long here?" He hands me the jaw. "Isn't it beautiful? What I have in my museum, things like this by the hundreds. And it was so easy to do."

After dinner the two Stephans arrive with Vance's sheep, who is the grandfather of them all. In the beams of our flashlights his horns sweep back and down and out and up . . . and almost back again. They are massive and perfectly formed—they look like the horns of the ram on the hunters' belt buckles, a hope fulfilled, a chord completed. Vance beams, more so when he puts his steel tape to the ram. "Thirty-nine and a half inches," he says, standing up, "by *forty* and a half."

Bob's sheep, measured by Paul, taped thirty-four inches, and as we walk back to our tent Kubick seems in a sullen mood, head down, shoulders hunched. Just before we go inside, he says, "In a competitive world you like to come out on top."

We step into the candlelight and warmth, and he glances at me, sorry that I've seen him miffed. Sitting on his sleeping bag, he begins to unlace his left boot. He tosses it aside and his smile begins to grow. He unlaces the right boot, looks up, and his smile turns into a laugh—expansive, self-assured, unapologetic. Kubick.

"At least," he says, "I have the biggest snow sheep in Alaska."

SEVEN

—>><<—

THE FIRST BILLBOARD APPEARS AT THE JUNCTION OF INTERSTATE 180 and Route 44, where the road climbs up Pine Creek toward Waterville—a deer and an otter announce FIN, FUR AND FEATHER MUSEUM, OUT OF THE ORDINARY. Log letters, old-timey.

Beyond the sign the road curls into white pines, eastern hardwoods. The Susquehanna drops behind. Winks of misty blue sky. Mostly clouds . . . shades of grey. Pennsylvania. "The biggest wilderness between New York and Chicago," says Paul Asper, native son, adding, "It's the best country in the world."

Alleghenies. Appalachians. Red barns. Geriatric telephone poles. Rhododendron. Mountain laurel. Rusting bridges. Roadcuts through igneous rock, ice hanging on the north sides. Smoke goes straight up from a chimney—a red frame house on Pine Creek bottom. The tang of wood smoke. In the front yard a gutted deer hangs by its antlers from an oak, above a turned-over bicycle with trainer wheels. So many deer in these mountains. Black bear. Ghosts of Indians, who thought the meat of these animals medicine.

It's the second weekend of deer season in Pennsylvania. The shelves are heavy in general stores: camouflage parkas; blaze orange caps and gloves; green-and-yellow boxes of cartridges—30-30 Winchester, 300 Savage, 35 Remington, names like prayers. A pickup truck, packed door-to-door with three orange-capped men, turns off the pavement, crosses a rill, puts clean tracks in the skiff of snow . . . underneath, mulched leaves, shades of brown. The last view: three rifles slung across the back window.

A smaller road diverges, climbs steeply. Upper Pine Bottom Creek. "Brown trout over twenty inches in there," says Asper. "You have to wait for a dry spell and a night of hard rain. Then you drop whatever you're doing. It's unbelievable." He wipes the back of his hand across his brow and flicks away imaginary sweat.

The road crosses and recrosses the stream, climbing. Pool and drop. Pool and drop. A tannin pool and a silver drop. Maple, hemlock, and ash. Furniture and ax handles. Oak, sycamore, and pine. Once a squirrel could walk from the Atlantic to the Mississippi without ever setting paw to ground, they said. Has the ring of truth, here along Upper Pine Bottom Creek.

The road levels onto a ridge, still thick with forest. A junction. South 664 and North 44. Choices. Lock Haven or Coudersport. And signs: WELCOME TO THE MOUNTAINTOP INN, HANNEYVILLE BAPTIST CHURCH. Just down the road another billboard: duelling bucks, a black bear, moose antlers, FIN, FUR AND FEATHER TRADING POST. A log building painted leather brown.

First the roadside store: magazines, tourist art, fur hats, polished rocks, bookends, candy bars, apples, Styrofoam cups of coffee. Behind it a supermarketlike building: high ceilings, carpeted aisles of fishing tackle, camping equipment, clothing for the woodsman. A partition runs the length of this enormous room and an unprepossessing door leads through it to an equally large art gallery put together by an omnivorous collector: pen-and-ink sketches of Dall sheep; calendars done in the faded colors of *The Saturday Evening Post;* charts, using Noah's Ark as a motif, disgorge the snakes of Pennsylvania and the salmonids of North America; Smokey the Bear, shovel in hand, says, THANKS FOLKS FOR BEING CAREFUL. On it goes—prints of sharp-eyed loons, venerable bucks, storm-bound geese, sagacious grouse, mallard decoys, the entire sporting hagiography culminated by a wall of posters from Paul's travels—lions from South Africa, Ethiopians in feathers. A door opens upon a paved yard. Twenty yards away stands the museum itself.

Glass entrance doors. A foyer with twenty-foot ceilings. The pensive quote by Henry Beston—"We patronize them for their incompleteness. . . ." The heads of caribou, moose, sheep, high overhead. One gallery leads right—Europe and the South Pacific. Two lead straight on— North America, Asia, and Africa. In either direction the menagerie stands in cliffs, jungles, and grasslands.

But one can't proceed without passing the touch-and-feel exhibition, antlers, horn, and patches of fur (red fox, opossum, raccoon, grey fox, skunk), and passing, one has to touch, noting their decreasing silkiness. Elephant foot, rhino foot, hippo foot, giraffe hoof, varying textures and in order of decreasing size. An elephant tooth, six inches long and two and a half pounds in weight. Rhino skin, an inch and a half thick. Mountain goat fur—deep white warmth. Somewhere, at some time, entire cultures knew these creatures seasonally, perennially, intimately—knew how long it would take to skin an elephant and how many people it would feed.

At the entrance to the American, Asian, and African halls hangs a plaque with a few words from *Walden*—"We need the tonic of wildness. . . ." Directly beneath it is a photograph of a Paul . . . a lean Paul with less concern in his face. He wears a pale-green down jacket and kneels by a Dall sheep, white and fluffy as a cumulus cloud. He holds up its golden horns, a look of tender compassion filling his face.

"There's an early bird!" booms Paul from the front door. He has on the same style of wool pants and plaid shirt he wore in Siberia . . . the ram's-head belt buckle. His black hair is combed back wet from a shower. He smells of soap. Beaming, he shakes hands.

"I got a call from Lou Hoffman last night," he says, mentioning a friend, his voice rising in that diaphanous mix of German, Dutch, and country inflections, a little vinegar and clove—a sharp, sweet brew. "Is he ever on cloud nine! He got a nice eight-point buck. Seventeen-inch spread and eight-inch tines. It's the only good rack he's ever taken."

As we walk into the main hall I pause again in front of the photo of him with the Dall sheep. From behind me he says, "When I walked up to that ram my guide told me, 'We'll bury it.' He thought I was hunting for the biggest one on the mountain and he was disappointed at its size. But this was a wonderful sheep! Thirty-eight inches. 'Hell no,' I told him. 'I'm keeping it.' " He wags his head. "That's what the book does to some people."

The gallery before us is a hundred feet long by fifty feet wide. We walk along its left side where artificial vegetation and a background mural depict the natural communities of North America: beaver ponds give to hardwoods and muskeg to conifers; mountains rise to the arctic and fall to the Sonoran desert. In the beaver ponds ducks fly through dead snags; pheasants and turkeys scratch among scrub; raccoons peer from hollow trees. Blacktail, whitetail, Sitka, Coues, and mule deer stand in their native forests, inviting comparison; coyotes sing, black bear amble, wolverine sniff, lynx crouch, elk and pronghorn stare regally; bison and moose tower over us; a grey wolf pads along on oversize paws; a barren ground grizzly lurks by caribou; bighorns look down from their crags; Dall and Stone sheep clamber over the papier-mâché outcrops; a mountain goat stands on the edge of a precipice.

A glass case, long as the gallery itself, separates us from the animals. It's filled with explanatory texts about the animals as well as photographs from Paul's hunts: pack trips; floats in canoes; bush planes. In the middle of the room, splitting the North American from the Asian side, stands another row of glass cases, holding traps, skulls, and old cartridges.

"I started taking a couple of number-two fox traps with me," says Paul, pointing to the display case, "to add variety to the collection. That's how I got these Indian civets and mongoose." He sweeps an arm to the far side of the hall.

We walk on, Paul explaining that besides tourists his biggest customers are schoolchildren, senior citizens, and people from institutions for the old, the blind, and the retarded. He mentions how a group of blind schoolchildren recently spent several hours in the museum, feeling the animals, returning often to the ten-foot-high moose.

He leads me past a polar bear and walrus, resting on ice floes, and into the African hall where we stand in front of a mountain nyala, which to my surprise is as large as a five-hundred-pound elk. Bob Kubick's nyala head, hanging in his Anchorage trophy room, never hinted at the size of the rest of the animal.

When I mention this to Paul, he says, "Once I had a couple of animals mounted life-size I was ruined completely. You can't really appreciate them any other way." He pauses, then adds, "I think this will be the largest life-size collection in the world when it's done. And you know, I couldn't have done it any other way. I couldn't have justified my trophy hunting without making it a public service."

Rain forest, acacia trees, and savannahs move us along. A painted backdrop of Mt. Kilimanjaro stands over nearly the whole of Africa's large fauna. The giraffe and elephant, however, are given only head mounts. Tragically, says Paul, the hair on the giraffe's hide slipped, even though he took it to Nairobi within twenty-four hours. About the elephant head, he opens his hands as if to say, "There are limits to everything."

Back in the Asian hall, we stroll by a magnificent *Ovis ammon ammon,* its dark, weathered horns thick and spiralling one and three quarter times. "The grandfather of all the wild mountain sheep," Paul says. Flanking it is a large Siberian wapiti, which held first place in the book for half a dozen years before being pushed into second, third, and now fourth place by three higher-scoring entries, including Bob Kubick's number one.

"I knew it when I saw his antlers in our hotel in Ulan Bator," he says of Kubick's wapiti. "It was going to fly right into first place. And then I saw the moose he had taken. 'Holy Christ,' I said. 'Bob, do you know what you have done? You have two number ones!' " He wipes his brow with the back of his hand and shakes his head in wonder at the man's luck.

Taking a few steps toward a tiger, he says, "Now look at this. This is one of my unique exhibits." But he's not talking about the cat, its shoulders high as our waists. He points to a giant Nepalese flying squirrel, soaring off the wall. "It's a female and still thirty-four inches long. A male would have been even bigger. I'm really proud of it."

When I ask him where in India he shot his tiger, he says, "It's from a zoo. I was too late to hunt in India. They closed it down. But look here."

He leads me on to a sloth bear. "Stick your finger in his mouth," he urges. I say that it feels like the hose of a vacuum cleaner and Paul nods. "He'll put that in a termite hole and suck them right out."

It takes us another hour to get to the South Pacific wing where we linger before a glass case filled with aboriginal clubs used for killing small animals such as wallaby. Behind the case fly two stunning rufous ducks. Their heads are shiny black, their necks cinnamon and circled by an ivory band; their wings are green with white leading edges.

"I saw these mountain ducks and fell in love with them," says Paul, the tone of his voice matching the expression he wears in the photo with the Dall sheep—one of most tender regard for something precious. "I just had to have a pair of them."

The tour done, he suggests going to his home, where we'll be more comfortable and get a bite to eat. As we walk by the front of the trading post a station wagon pulls away. On its roof lies a dead whitetail buck, tiny forked horns sprouting from its head. Paul raises an ambiguous hand to the departing deer and the two hunters in the car: too small . . . why didn't you have more patience . . . what a waste . . . can anything else be expected when thousands are in the woods? The gesture tries to say it all.

We drive past the junction of Upper Pine Bottom Creek and go over a hill where the snow gets deeper. A trio of orange-coated hunters heads into the woods from a parked Suburban. We coast down into a long clearing and turn into a stone gate. A sign says: POSTED AND PA-TROLLED GAME PRESERVE. ALL PERSONS ARE WARNED AGAINST HUNT-ING, FISHING, OR TRAPPING. TRESPASSING FOR ANY REASON FORBIDDEN. VIOLATORS WILL BE PROSECUTED. FIN, FUR AND FEATHER ESTATE.

A tarmac road goes past an old barn. On its door hangs a dial ther-mometer that goes to thirty below zero. Beyond the barn are evergreens . . . an orchard of Chinese chestnuts . . . apple trees. A score of whitetail deer bed to the right of the road, looking at us as we drive by. To the left lie big meadows of vetch, brown with autumn, where more deer browse. On the far side of the meadows stands a mute forest of red-and-white oak . . . maple . . . a few birches whitening the edges. The stone and wood house appears, sitting majestically over the fields. When we step from the cars we can see down the sweep of meadowland, over the forest, and across the rolling, greyish-green hills of the Alleghenies. Behind the house a few does feed around a corn crib.

"Everything we do here," says Paul, motioning to the deer "is with an eye for game. The vetch produces a lot of insect life—grasshoppers—and we always have three or four flocks of turkeys in the summer. The squir-rels take the corn out of the feeder, carry it up in the trees, eat the heart out of the corn, and the deer eat the droppings."

A buck limps among the does. "He was hit by a car last week," Paul mentions. "Broke his right rear leg." He opens his hands. "What should I do? We don't need the meat."

We walk into an elegant country farmhouse: high ceilings, exposed beams, the warm sofas imprinted with quail and grouse, the coffee tables full of picture books. Whitetail deer heads gaze dreamily from the walls; a double-barrel shotgun leans by the hearth, another stands in the hall leading to the kitchen. A brick hearth between the two rooms contains an oven. One entire side of the house looks over the deck, down to the fields where another herd of deer scampers by, white tails flying.

Gazing at the deer, Paul says, "There's probably close to four million acres left in the area. We owe a big debt of gratitude to those old game commissioners who had the foresight back in the twenties, thirties, and forties to take our license money and buy up this land."

He says this with a bit of nostalgic pride. After growing up at Hanneyville junction with six other children, raised by parents who had emigrated from the Swiss-German border, he spent five years with the Pennsylvania Game Commission, going through their Ross Leffler School of Conservation and becoming a district game protector. "But it killed me," he says, "to be out there patrolling when I wanted to be hunting or beaver trapping myself." He left law enforcement and went to work for Piper aircraft, then the Hammermill Paper Company before conceiving of the trading post. "It was needed in the area—a place where people could get gas and kerosene, groceries, and odds and ends." He and his wife, Carole, lived in a one-room cabin while he added wings on to the trading post. Then, in the early sixties, he began to see ads for snowmobile dealerships. He liked the name Arctic Cat and in the first year of his dealership he sold two machines. Then in 1965 he sold twenty. "The next year a hundred nine. And then four hundred. And then sixteen hundred. Then thirty-two hundred. And then seven thousand, ten thousand. Just unbelievable!" He wipes his forehead with the back of his hand. "For a country boy, you know, without any college or training . . . We even won the President's Award, and Hubert Humphrey, the vice president of the United States, gave it to us, in person."

More deer bound across the field, kicking their rear legs high. Paul, making coffee at the kitchen counter, says, "Look at them coming out now! They're just playing and happy. You get the feeling that they know the pressure's off and they're safe in here. We have three days of doe season coming up and that's what I fear the most. It's when I have trouble. . . . Meat hunters." He fills the word with accusation, like a social worker saying, "Child molester!" "All they're looking for is hamburger. They see deer and shoot from the road. I usually have one other person helping me patrol."

Wondering how Carole came by the venison she'll be serving for dinner, I ask Paul how he gets his annual deer.

"This year," he says, "I hunted in Texas, in February and March, and I shot that barasingha deer and that good mouflon sheep that you saw up in the museum, and a dama gazelle from Africa. And I brought all the hindquarters and loins home so our freezer was full. I'm not saying . . ." He lets his voice drift off to the unstated. "I do carry my two-seventy in the jeep. If I saw a big trophy buck that I never saw before . . . I might be tempted. Last year I took a little eight point on the adjacent farm because we needed the meat. Then the second week of the season, Thursday, I saw a trophy buck and it was really tempting. I looked at him and he was with a doe, following her, out of his territory. And I thought, 'Well, you made it to the second week. Two more weeks and there'll be no more hunters in the woods. You'll be bigger next year.'

"But both these bucks were strange deer," he emphasizes. "On the bordering farm. We couldn't shoot the deer we see here, all the time." His face becomes somber. "I made a mistake one year. It was just daylight over there and I shot this buck that looked bigger, different than I remembered, and it turned out to be one I knew from here. I just took the entrails out of him and brought him to my tenant. I couldn't eat him, I felt so bad."

Carrying our mugs, we descend the wide staircase to the "basement," an L-shaped room with fourteen-foot ceilings. A fire burns in the hearth. On the long side of the L is a wet bar opposite an entire wall of windows, again facing the fields.

A great flying turkey—red wattle, blue crown—soars along the stairs. Sheep, deer, caribou, eland, oryx, and zebra heads decorate the walls. A map of the world, pins stuck on every continent except Antarctica, traces Paul's hunts. On one side of the fireplace is a giant toothed trap, now illegal, on the other side a smaller one without teeth.

"When I built this house I didn't have the museum in mind," Paul explains about the elegant basement. "So I said to my wife, if I want to hang an elephant head, we're going to have ceilings high enough to do it. This was to be my trophy room."

Catching me looking at the traps, Paul says, "The Newhouse is really a wolf and coyote trap." He kneels by the smaller one he has pointed to and opens its jaws. "Last year I caught a seventy-five-pound bear cub with it, right here on top of my farm. And I came home and told Carole, 'Call Sid and Johnny. I got to figure out a way to let this bear go.' We put a barrel over him and set him free. Took off like a streak." Paul slaps one hand against the other.

"We got a bear now that I'll show you later. He comes down every night. The other evening I took some corn up there and he ran within fifty feet of me, sat down, and watched me put it out. Before I got back in the Jeep he was eating."

Picking up a rusty spike from the mantle, he touches it to the pan of the Newhouse. It snaps shut with a wicked clack. It's one of those noises that makes a person think.

He frees the spike from the trap, puts it back on the mantle, and then straightens the trap on the hearth. "When you catch a small beaver," he says, "a six- or seven-pound one, in a leghold trap like this one, you can actually release him. The Conibear, though, what they call a *humane* trap, whatever you catch in it, it's dead. In fact, that trap's been responsible for the near extermination of muskrat and beaver in Pennsylvania because you have to set it underwater so as not to catch domestic pets. You block off a channel and it becomes suicide for the beaver. But with the leghold trap, he can get away. I've caught beaver—big old grandfathers . . . trophy beavers—with two feet missing completely. Toes missing on the other two feet as well. They had twisted out of steel traps. But when they came out with the Conibear, there was just no more escape."

A stock-taking look crosses his face, not unhappy or disappointed with himself, just counting up the pluses and minuses. "I thought when I got home from Russia that I'd be boiling and setting traps. But you know when you come back from one of those trips you have a pile of mail and other business problems. . . ." His voice trails off and for some reason he looks suddenly troubled, but he dismisses it by saying, "Well anyway I didn't make opening day and maybe it was a good thing because we had so much rain and frozen ground. Come here. I'll show you something."

We set down our mugs and walk through the door of an attached workshop. On the floor stand dozens of buckets, traps hanging in some of them, others filled with sand. Paul shows me how he cleans his traps by using a wire brush on them. Then he puts a small nail between the jaws so that when he boils them the entire trap becomes odor free. He hands me a board on which he stretches pelts and explains how he sets his traps.

"Last year," he says, "the big challenge for me was a coyote. And I got him using coyote urine and coyote gland scent. Forty-nine pounds, on the next farm. But when you use coyote scents you'll never catch fox, 'cause they're afraid they'll get the crap knocked out of them."

Like a curator, he points to more traps hanging on the wall. "Some of these older traps are antiques and I'm going to have a section for them in the museum. Here's my number two fox trap from when I was in high school." He takes it down and hands it to me, not the way a priest handles a chalice but close. "For a couple of years I made a living trapping four dollars bounty. I had a brand-new Jeep, which was nineteen hundred seventy-five dollars. I wasn't married and I had one Jeep payment and paid my mother and dad fifteen dollars a week room and board, and that's all the problems I had."

He laughs, thinking of those simple times, then he takes a breath. If he were a bit freer with his emotions, it would be called a sigh. "I don't like to admit it, I like to be an optimist, but these days I think the antifur people have just about won the battle. Already women are sneaking out the back door with their fur coats. . . . What are we going to do?" He hangs his number two fox trap back on its nail and gestures to the buckets. "I'm always gonna trap, especially as long as I own Fin, Fur and Feather, because I get my pelts made into fur coats, ear muffs, and hats. As far as the humaneness of it goes. . . ." He lets a hand drift into the air. "You have to check your traps every day in this state. There are people that don't. But there are slobs behind the wheel of an auto-mo-bile, and in every walk of life. You always have those kind. I myself check 'em every day, and I can't wait till morning, daybreak, to get out there."

Speaking of the trapping itself, he regains some of his enthusiasm and heartily says, "Like an old trapper friend of mine used to say, he was a justice of the peace, 'Paul, trapping's like Christmas.' 'Why do you say that, Frank?' I asked. 'Well,' he said, 'every morning you don't know what's going to be under the tree.' " Paul smiles warmly. "You know, when I was younger I couldn't sleep at night, thinking about going out the next day with my dad. He had a trap line and we'd climb the sides of these mountains. Just to tag along with him and see a fox or a live raccoon in the trap was like . . . well, at that time, it was just like a trip to Siberia for me."

We amble back to the trophy room and Paul leads me around the bar, full of antique Wild Turkey bottles and historic cartridges, and into his office. His large, paper-cluttered desk sits before the stonework of a fireplace. Glass bookcases line the adjacent side of the room. They're filled with old copies of *National Geographic, Gray's Sporting Journal,* and neat stacks of esoterica that only someone who is both deeply possessive and incurably nostalgic would keep, *Pennsylvania Game News* from December 1937, *Hunting & Fishing* from January 1936 (a nickel in price), copies of *Fur-Fish-Game,* dating to Paul's boyhood. About the last magazine he says, "This is a special one, pretty close to my heart. It was something that a Pennsylvania country boy, a farm boy, could relate to. And you can see that some of these issues were in the flood, in '72, and somehow survived." He shakes his head over the old, water-stained magazines.

"So it was *Fur-Fish-Game* that got you dreaming about hunting around the world?"

"No. Oh, no, no. I wouldn't allow myself to dream about that, ever, because I knew it was an impossibility. I didn't think I could even afford to go out West back then. What I read about was trapping muskrats and fox, and hunting coon, and turtles, hunting snapping turtles. I read about what I could relate to. But who would ever have dreamed you could go to Africa and hunt leopard or hunt Siberian snow sheep! I'd read about brook trout fishing or whatever was possible in my world. Then when I made the money in the snowmobile business, I said to one of my best friends, 'What am I going to do now, with all this money?' He said, 'Spend it, Paul.' So I started taking advantage of the good fortune and hard work. I started hunting."

He walks across the room to where a pair of elephant tusks stand in front of the bookcases and brings back the Safari Club International award brochure. Putting on his half-frame glasses, which hang from a cord around his neck, he points to lists of animals that he's checked off. It looks exactly like the back of a birder's book, except all these are big mammals whom he's collected and displayed in his museum.

"When I really started hunting," he says, "my major goal was to hopefully collect all the major game animals of the world. And I'm almost done. These award programs—the inner circles, the pinnacles of achievement, the grand slams of bear, and deer, and cats—they didn't exist then. Now McElroy . . ." he mentions the founder of SCI and the inventor of its award programs, "knew how to make a dollar." He gestures to some trophies on the shelf. "You have to buy these. They don't give them to you. If I get three more species from Europe, I'll have nineteen gold medals and a diamond one. But this would cost me sixteen thousand dollars to actually get them!"

"And what would that do for you?"

"It's given me goals to work toward."

"But would it do for you now? You know, if you paid the money and got the trophies and medals?"

He gives me the Asper look, his head twisted slightly to the side, his eyes slipping off into imponderables.

"Fame is a vapor," he says.

And he stops, not dramatically, but as if this is answer enough for anyone.

Looking over the tops of his glasses, he says, "But I love it. If it was three or four thousand dollars to get the trophies and be listed . . . How many members are there in SCI? It's a small group, only a few thousand, but in it you can be widely known."

He points to the stonework behind his desk. "If I had one glass show-case up there on the wall, just to show what I'd done, for my own satisfaction, nothing more, it would be neat. But it would cost," he goes down the list of prices in the trophy book, counting aloud, "another twenty-seven or thirty thousand dollars on top of the sixteen thousand it takes to have your name in the award book. And I have a catalogue from the Jonas studios in New York—they make these miniature animals. And I have a good friend who's a master engraver and woodworker in Williamsport. And I'm a bullheaded Dutchman. I could have these trophies made up for one third the price McElroy is charging."

The lists he's been pointing to include animals that are on the U.S. Endangered Species List. When I mention this incongruity, he says, "Sure, SCI knows they're on the endangered list. But this isn't just an American system, it's a worldwide one. Anyone from outside the U.S. can go and get these animals—legally. Say a polar bear. If you're from Mexico you can legally shoot a polar bear in Canada and bring it home to Mexico. Of if you're an American, you can hunt that polar bear, le-gally, in Canada but not bring it back to the U.S. Even though our government lists it, the Canadians think there are enough to hunt. I find no problem with that. But I do feel this way—if you kill the last of any species, another heaven and another earth would have to come to pass before it could exist again." He says this with grave sincerity.

"So who's to decide? How do you, yourself, determine which species are truly endangered and shouldn't be hunted?"

He looks off to the side and closes the award book. "You should let your conscience be your guide." The silence that follows this statement seems to ask him another question, which he answers in this way, re-phrasing what he said in the museum: "I don't think I could justify what I'm doing on a personal basis if it weren't for the museum and the educa-tional aspects of it. Even though it's a dream come true for me, the hunting, I just don't see how, as an individual, I could justify what I've done."

Behind him, outside the windows, I notice some deer bound across the fields. He follows my glance and says, "Let's jump in the Jeep and see what we can see."

In a few minutes we're driving away from the house, contouring around a hillside on a pair of overgrown ruts. Paul's .270 Winchester rifle, the same he used in Siberia, leans on the seat, muzzle to the floor. An orange vest, a license pinned to its back, lies crumpled behind the gear shift.

"When I got out of high school," he says, "I used to trap on the edge of these woods, and I'd look down at these buildings and houses and wonder who lived here. I never even let myself think I could own one square foot of it, much less all two hundred fifty acres."

He points out the white egg sacks on the bases of some of the oaks we've been passing, saying, "Gypsy moth. Killed about twenty percent of our trees ten, twelve years ago. And now it's back and I think it'll kill eighty percent of the oaks." He shakes his head. "Used to be a lot of ruffed grouse around here, too. I don't know what happened to them, whether it was DDT or some other pesticide."

He parks before a tiny stone house, covering a spring, and shows me a fourteen-inch brown trout in the pool beneath. We drive past small ponds that Paul has deepened so as to make them suitable for brook trout. As we climb another hill, he points out where he cuts his firewood as well as another feeder that he has to fill before he leaves for Austria on Sunday, to hunt chamois. "Normally," he says, "I put poles on the feeders so when the snow gets deep the turkeys can jump up."

A little farther along the two-track, he parks on a point overlooking the entire farm and shuts off the engine. We look down at the roof of his home, to the fields, the forest, the hills rolling away like their name, Allegheny. You can feel them going down to the Smokys, valley and hollow and ridge, each one of them holding some native son.

He points to the southwest where his neighbor owns 160 acres. "I called in his first turkey and I ran the first bear into him he ever shot. And he became a good turkey hunter, and a good Pennsylvania black bear hunter, and a good Pennsylvania buck hunter. And he just quit, completely, kaput! Developed Hodgkin's disease, but that wasn't the real reason, 'cause he was out hunting between his sieges. I think it was just owning his farm and seeing these bear and deer and turkey. It changes your whole outlook. It becomes harder to hunt 'em. And he also started living with this woman."

"You still hunt deer on your other farm."

"Yeah," he says, "but I'm not mad at 'em anymore."

He says this as if mentioning the time of day.

"Were you mad at them once?"

"No . . . But when you're younger I guess . . . maybe . . . I don't know if it's peer pressure or something like that, but you think you gotta get your deer and you gotta get your wild turkey, each year. You go to the store and someone asks, 'Did you get your buck?' Maybe you go out hunting a little pushed, a little mad. Now look at that. Something brought an ear of corn clear up here." He points to the road. And starts the car. And we head down. At the house a trio of small does run up to him, stretching their noses forward.

"What's a matter, girls?" he says, "You want an apple, don't you?"

When they realize that he doesn't have one, they trot off. It's getting on to dusk and we stand on the deck, watching the deer fade into the trees. Suddenly a black bear appears from the forest not a hundred feet from them. In his rolling, nonchalant gait, he pads directly to the feeder, plumps down on his rear end, grabs an ear of corn to his mouth, and begins to eat it as if nursing from a bottle. Paul gestures to the bear and says, "Now how could someone . . . ?"

We watch the bear a while then walk through the sliding doors into the house. But it's hard to leave off watching. We stand inside the warm house, the glass between us and the bear. There's no sunset. The forest seems to emanate obscurity until the bear is a blacker blob than the dusk surrounding him.

"What happened in the helicopter?"

As he turns toward me his face holds the very last light of the sky. "I disliked that very much," he says, "and I talked to Constantine about it. They dropped Don and Vance off, because Don is old and Vance was there to help him, you know, to pick out the biggest ram for him. And then they circled the rams and pushed them right back into him. And I could see the bullet. The first shot missed. And then he shot him in the back and that ram must have gone from here to where those deer went into the woods, dragging his back end. I don't know why he didn't finish him off. If he was shooting I couldn't tell. Then we landed, and Kim, the director, got out of the chopper. And the ram stood there and pawed the ground, mortally wounded, pawed the ground like he was picking a place to lie down. Then Kim opened fire with his submachine gun." Paul shakes his head. "Terrible." He looks at the bear, eating corn.

I stare at him and remember the meeting with the director after our return to Topolinyy. Kim told the hunters that they had used up their allotted flight hours, and those who still had moose and caribou permits would get a refund. Paul pounded the table, shouting that the Russians were breaking their contract and that he still had to get a Siberian moose and caribou for his museum.

"You wanted a moose and caribou, though, and were willing to collect them from the helicopter, if there had been the time."

Paul stares through the patio doors at the bear. "I don't know how I would have gotten home with a life-size moose and a life-size caribou," he says. "I had six pieces of luggage as it was." He sends a glance toward the kitchen. "How 'bout some chow?"

Carole has set the counter between the dining room and the kitchen. A tall, pleasant woman in her early fifties, with short dark hair, she seems extremely nervous. She nearly stutters a few times as we make small talk, and when she begins to pass the salad her hands shake. We set to the food. Everything is delicious, especially her homemade pickles and dried venison in cream sauce, which is full of smokey flavors. When I compliment her cooking, Paul says, "I've never had any bad game meat, if it's taken care of. But we've had tenderer than this."

"Once," says Carole, "I heard this blatting noise from the house, right there at the windows." She points to the dining room. "A coyote had killed a little fawn down in the field and I called Paul to get his rifle." She describes how Paul shot the coyote, who ran off. When they reached the fawn, they found it dead, but only its entrails had been pulled out, and Paul asked her if they should try to save the meat. "I couldn't even think about it right then," she says, touching her heart. "If you'd heard that blatting. So I said, 'If we put it in the freezer and wait a while, till I forget it was that baby deer, maybe I could." She lays down her fork and knife. "Honest to God, when we got around to it, it was just like veal. Melted in your mouth."

Telling the story and passing around more pickles and venison seems to relieve some of her jitters. As she makes coffee, Paul gets a file folder from the dining room table and when we're seated around the counter again, he says, "I shouldn't tell you this, but sometime you just have to let things out. When I got home from Siberia I knew something was wrong right away when Carole picked me up at the airport. But I'll let her tell you the rest."

She looks at him for reassurance and he nods at her. "That morning," she says, her voice breaking, "the doorbell rang. When I answered it there were six Federal Wildlife agents standing there, flashing their badges and drawn guns at me. They showed me a search warrant that claimed Paul had been involved with importing wildlife into the United States in violation of the Endangered Species Act."

Tears start to flow down her cheeks. She wipes them away with a napkin. The agents searched the house, taking papers, movies, Paul's files. In the meantime other agents were searching the museum where they confiscated six trophies, including a Jentink's duiker and a jaguar.

"They held me like a prisoner," she says. "I tell you, I felt raped in my own home."

"We'll see this through," says Paul in a calm voice. Standing, he puts an arm around her. "There was the flood, and the fire, and the burglary, and we saw them all through."

He pats her on the shoulder then opens his file and hands me a letter that claims his jaguar was donated by a game farm and the one he legally shot in Mexico has remained in a freezer in that country. About the endangered black-faced impala, which Fish and Wildlife claims he illegally imported, Paul says that it's really a "regular, old impala" on whose face he sprayed black paint so that he would have a specimen for the museum. As far as the Jentink's duiker goes, of which there are "supposedly only two hundred left in the wild and who can tell that," his attorney advised him that he could hunt it since there was some ambiguity about whether it was on Appendix I or Appendix II of the Convention on International Trade in Endangered Species (CITES) at the time when Paul was in Africa. In addition there was a foul-up in the exportation papers he was to have received in Liberia. He never obtained a valid Liberian export permit, which would have made the Jentink's duiker legal to import into the United States. Given this lack of an export permit, he is now going to try to prove that the specimen in his museum was donated to him and the one that he entered in the SCI record book, where it stands as number one, was really left in Africa. He fetches the record book and shows me the photo of him and the Jentink's duiker. Smiling and wearing a camouflage polo shirt, he kneels over the dead animal, a creature the size of husky deer, with a black head, and small sharp horns. Forest closes behind them.

"Can this be America?" says Carole. "They were like the KGB or the gestapo."

I hand him the record book. "Did you really believe that the duiker wasn't endangered when you shot it?"

Paul looks at me steadily. Then he looks down and away, as if looking into a canyon.

When they show me to my car the bear is still eating corn at the feeder. At the bottom of the long hill twenty does lie bedded under the oak, snug, safe, and chewing their cuds, waiting out the last week of deer season on Asper's preserve.

"THERE ARE FIFTY MILLION HUNTERS IN THE WORLD. SO YOU PUT UP a plateau representing them. And above that you put those hunters who have hunted outside their immediate area."

On the reverse side of a pink, "While You Were Out" memo, C. J. McElroy, the father of the organization known as Safari Club International and the founder of its record book, award program, and International Wildlife Museum in Tucson, Arizona, draws with a pen.

He has thick silver-grey hair, combed up in a wave, and his brown eyes and tan face have the energy and shine of a man three decades younger than his seventy-seven years. Seated behind his desk of polished wood, and wearing a calfskin jacket dyed silver, under which is a casual blue shirt, he resembles Ronald Reagan in the prime of his presidential years. A heavy gold watch, its band adorned with two sheep heads, circles his wrist. Behind him, recessed lighting illuminates the mounted heads.

He still has the faintest trace of a south Texas accent, which he explains in a mythological, storytelling voice that takes one down the gentle roller coaster of the years: "Well, you know when you're ten years old and you've never had anything, and you're barefooted and you're in a cotton patch, your dreams . . ."

Now forced from the helm of Safari Club International because of internal rivalries, but having organized his own Global Adventures travel company in Tucson, Mac, as he is known, continues to draw on the back of the "While You Were Out" memo, creating what appears to be a Mayan pyramid. In fact, his sketch reproduces the diagram of SCI's hierarchical award structure, which is printed in the organization's brochures.

"Then you establish another level. These are the people who have hunted in other continents besides their own. Maybe a few thousand. Then you say, 'How many people have done it all—hunted the six continents and taken at least a hundred and seventy-five different species?' Oh, now you've got it down to a hundred men. Then you come up and make a little pinnacle right here, at the very top. And you say, 'Give me the seven people who should be on the summit.' You're talking about seven people out of forty or fifty *million* hunters. That's a hell of a lot of prestige." He rests the nib of the pen atop the pinnacle. "If I don't sit there today—and I still think I do—I sat on it for many years, there's no question about it. And it was a great feeling. Any place in the world I went people knew me. And they still know me, any place I go. That's quite an accomplishment and only a few can say they've won it—the Don Coxes for instance. Don is a truly great hunter, no question about it. There are only four or five more of his caliber and then it's done. Then you're dropping down to this baby here." He points to the second plateau. "The hunters on this level don't like to admit that they haven't made it to the very top, but I could reach back here and pull out their résumés." He waves a hand to a wall of file holders behind him.

Then he lays down his pen and sighs. "But I paid for it in many ways . . . many ways. I could have made three times as much money if I had concentrated on my business. One of the guys I started out with in floor covering just sold his company for forty-three million dollars. Instead of running with him, I went off to Asia, to Australia, Africa."

Reflecting, he fiddles with his pen and looks up. "And somewheres along the way, let me tell you, I lost the great thrill of hunting. You know what it developed into? A job. Being a top professional at it. And don't get me wrong. Hunting as we know it, trophy hunting, is a great competition, one of the worst things in the world. I had to get there first, shoot the animal first, and make sure it was the biggest. And when it lay on the ground, if it wasn't within the top ten, I didn't feel the old adrenaline that I used to feel when I got something down. It had disappeared. A person gets on that glory road and God help him. He's lost the thrill of just going on a hunt for the sake of going. Christ! Once I'd go on a hunt and be gone six or seven days, climb up and down the mountains and come home with nothing and be very happy. But not anymore. I've got to go with the best possible guide I can find, the best possible place, be sure of success, and try to get the big one."

His face becomes fatherly, kind. "And I'll tell you something else.

Even though I'm still actively hunting, I don't have the old killing urge. I get more kick out of watching animals. Unless a tremendous buck shows up," he adds quickly. "Then I'll say, 'Jesus! That's a hell of a buck, I wonder where he would place?' And if I thought that he'd place five or six or eight or ten, I would want to take him. But if he were only an average buck, then I'd just enjoy watching him."

------------ >><< ------------

After spending $300,000 on his defense, Paul Asper was found guilty of violating the U.S. Endangered Species Act and the Federal Smuggling Statute for his importation of a Jentink's duiker from Liberia, a black-faced impala from Namibia, two gorals and two serows from Nepal, and two northern huemuls from Peru, all of which were exhibited in his museum. The federal prosecutor made particular note that in Asper's file cabinet were found copies of both the CITES treaty and the U.S. Endangered Species Act, predating his hunts for these species. Pertinent sections of both acts, dealing with the illegal importation of endangered wildlife, were highlighted.

Asper was sentenced to two and a half years in prison and fined $195,946 for nine felonies and seven misdemeanors. The trophy hunting world was shocked by the severity of the sentence. However, in the opinion of Judge Muir, who could have fined Paul $1,300,000 and incarcerated him for twenty-seven years, the sentence was "stiff but fair." In his sentencing statement he explained why.

Particularly aggravating was evidence that had been offered outside of the jury's presence and that Muir had excluded from the trial, believing that it would have been "devastating to Mr. Asper in the eyes of the jury." For instance, in 1976 Paul attempted to smuggle into the United States the skins of a Nile crocodile and a leopard, both hidden within the skin of an elephant. He paid a twelve-hundred-dollar administrative fine. In 1974 Paul shot a bald eagle in Canada and imported it to the United States rolled inside a mountain lion hide. He then instructed the taxidermist who mounted it to list the bird as a goose on the taxidermy bill. He was assessed a civil penalty of five thousand dollars in 1981 but the court that tried the case so long deliberated that the statute of limitations was deemed to have run out. In addition to the two gorals that he was found guilty of importing, he also shot another pair, several years later, and had them shipped by a hunting partner from London to Mexico where they were seized by customs authorities. Finally, Paul had secured a false donation letter from the same hunting companion, stating that the Jentink's duiker he had shot was killed before the date on which it was placed on the endangered list. The ink with which this letter was written wasn't produced until seven years after the letter was dated. Paul also obliterated the date on one of the transparencies showing him with an endangered northern huemul from Peru. Judge Muir concluded that "these items and numerous other items contained in the 361 Findings of Fact demonstrate beyond all possible doubt that Mr. Asper is guilty as charged."

When I wrote Paul, questioning him about his marking sections of the CITES treaty and the E.S.A., and whether he cared to comment on Judge Muir's sentencing statement, he answered me from the federal prison camp in Bradford, Pennsylvania. Someone had sent him a couple of pages of the acts, he said, and he had taken these to an "attorney friend" to determine whether the Jentink's duiker was on Appendix I or II. He said he had underlined sections of the act not as a way of targeting endangered species for collection, but as a means of determining their status. "Go and collect your trophy," his counsel had advised. Paul went to Liberia, shot a Jentink's duiker, imported it through U.S. customs, entered it in the record book, and displayed it in his museum. A year later, he told me, he realized that he had "made a mistake." As in the case of five other "mistakes," out of the approximately six hundred fifty specimens that he had collected during his life, this was a case of an unintentional violation of a hypocritical law. He had purchased legal hunting licenses in all the countries in which he had hunted, and the money he had spent for these licenses had supported those countries' wildlife protection programs—a worthwhile end. Was it right, he asked, that citizens of other countries could hunt these animals and he, a citizen of the United States, couldn't?

As to commenting on his previous illegal importations of wildlife, outlined in Judge Muir's sentencing statement, Paul made no reply.

In light of the case, and over the protest of its members outside the United States, Safari Club International removed from its record book and award programs all animals listed as endangered by the U.S. Department of Interior as well as those species, such as the polar bear and walrus, covered by the U.S. Marine Mammal Protection Act. Those animals taken before they were listed will remain in the book. Before being expelled from SCI, Paul resigned.

Having failed to obtain a Liberian export permit for the Jentink's duiker whom he had shot, Bob Kubick left his trophy in Africa. He remained immune from the prosecution that brought down another SCI member in addition to Paul. Like Asper this hunter was unable to resist bringing home to the United States this curious and little-known antelope, named after a Dutch scientist from the Leiden Museum.

Even though he had international hunts booked into the future, Kubick continued to lose sleep over the giant Dall ram whom Buckey had seen in the Alaska Range. Hunting on horseback with his son, Michael, he never found the ram; but they didn't return empty handed. Michael took a sheep of thirty-seven and a half inches, and Kubick, ever lucky, killed a ram whose horns curled back and down and out . . . it was forty-two inches—his largest.

A month after returning from Siberia, Don Cox became the thirty-third recipient of the Weatherby Award.

WEBS

No culture has yet solved the dilemma each has faced with the growth of a conscious mind: how to live a moral and compassionate existence when one is fully aware of the blood, the horror inherent in all life, when one finds darkness not only in one's own culture but within oneself. If there is a stage at which an individual life becomes truly adult, it must be when one grasps the irony in its unfolding and accepts responsibility for a life lived in the midst of such paradox. One must live in the middle of contradiction because if all contradiction were eliminated at once life would collapse. There are simply no answers to some of the great pressing questions. You continue to live them out, making your life a worthy expression of a leaning into the light.

—BARRY LOPEZ,
Arctic Dreams

ONE

——>><<——

FLYING OVER THE WIND RIVER MOUNTAINS, COMING HOME . . .
Around the peaks clouds bundle and tear away, revealing lakes still frozen and snow swirling across the sheer rock walls—Pingora, Musem-
beah, Sacajawea. I watch another summit, the great snowy hump of
Gannett, Wyoming's tallest, slip beneath the plane. Then glaciers and
forest sprawl north toward Union Pass. From this divide the watersheds
of the West begin—Columbia . . . Colorado . . . Missouri.

We bank west, climb over barren cirques, and dip our wing to a
plateau of red rock where a half-dozen bighorn sheep lie, looking over the
country. Then the wide sweep of the Gros Ventre River loops beneath
the cabin. Its roof flashes through our shadow; the aspen stand bare; the
pines blow. Suddenly the Tetons push white and jagged from a garland
of clouds and seal off the western edge of a world.

Walking to the cabin from the road, I step over bison pies, kick them
for freshness, and pause a moment, letting the prop vibration sink out of
my feet and into the ground. North the Snake River plain sprawls to the
foothills of Yellowstone; west the Tetons soar; east and south forested
ridges climb into the Gros Ventre Mountains. Stepping over some deer
pellets, I open the front door. The frig and water heater are momentarily
off and there's not even the hum of electricity to mistake for quiet.

Merle, the yellow Lab, follows me in, and when I sit on the couch, just
letting my pores feel the place again, he sits in front of me, looks at me
with his deep brown eyes, and puts a paw against my chest. I defrost and
fry an elk steak, give Merle a leg bone, and eat my meal sitting at the
table that looks north over the valley. The meat is solid, dense, and lean,

and when I cut it, looking at it at the end of my fork, I think of the moment. The grey dawn. Crawling through the frozen grass. The boom of the rifle among the hills. The rest of his herd, several dozen cows and a few bulls, moving slowly away. And the trumpet of swans flying up the river as I turned him into meat; the ravens watching; the long pack out, across streams, around ponds, through the forest. I put him in my mouth and begin to feel the land pass through my body.

Later I join Merle on the front steps. He works on his bone, and I lean against the logs and watch the crescent moon set over the Tetons. Venus comes out, and over the mountain called the Sleeping Indian the sky begins to fill with stars. From my gut the elk begins his slow combustion, the physiological sense of warmth and well-being that those who live in cold climates note and which fills me with a sense of indebtedness to him. He gives me this place, my strength, and I like to think that someday my bones will fertilize the grass that will make his grandchildren fleet. I listen to the sound of this happening, the long, stately hum of starlight, a hum deeper than silence. Tonight, among all my orbits, this seems the most complete.

T W O

————>><<————

T HE SILENCE DOESN'T LAST. IN THE MORNING, DOWN AT MY OFFICE in the village, a mile and a half by dirt road from the cabin, I'm greeted by a pile of mail, news releases, and accumulated faxes, as well as Orion, the orange-and-white cat whom I've raised from a kitten. Self-contained, half feral, coming and going as he wishes, he nonetheless has a soft spot and insists on lying on my lap and purring deeply as I sort through the bundles on my desk. I organize them in two piles: issues of land use like the depletion of wetlands, the erosion of beaches in the Grand Canyon, and oil development in the Arctic National Wildlife Refuge; and those of wildlife management, predominantly about hunting, for instance, the closing of the grizzly bear season in Montana, a proposition to end all lethal forms of wildlife management in Arizona, the successful reinstatement of a black bear hunt in California, and a paper about nonviolent alternatives to managing burgeoning deer populations in suburbia. Both piles have a similar theme—our ongoing attempt to structure the interface between nature and culture—but it is the wildlife management pile that seems the more volatile. With increasing frequency these issues center around the concept of rights.

Ever since 1215, when English barons forced King John to sign the Magna Carta, protecting some of their feudal privileges, intrinsic natural rights have been extended to an ever-wider field of those who have, accurately or not, considered themselves to be oppressed minorities. (Clearly, the English barons weren't.) In the ensuing centuries the Magna Carta was interpreted as a guarantee of trial by jury and of habeas corpus. In 1689 the British Bill of Rights acknowledged that English-

178 << TED KERASOTE

men possessed inviolable political and civil rights, and in 1776 American Colonists announced their "unalienable Rights" to "Life, Liberty and the pursuit of Happiness" in the Declaration of Independence. Black slaves then won their right to freedom under the Emancipation Proclamation and the Thirteenth Amendment to the Constitution, women the right to vote with the Nineteenth Amendment, Indians the right to citizenship in 1924, and in 1973 the United States gave "rights" to endangered species. It is hardly surprising that some wish to extend this seven-century-long tradition of granting rights to the disenfranchised to individual animals. However, the biology that runs all life on this planet doesn't work on the same principles that govern social relations between people. Elk eat grass, and grizzlies sometimes eat elk, and people can eat both without eradicating the species to which these individuals belong. The question then becomes, Can a cultural being ethically participate in these natural cycles, cycles that may entail taking the lives of individual animals, animals who are as bright, as bold, and tenderly aware of sunshine and storm as we are? Can one be both cultural and natural?

It is a question that my predecessors to this place—whose camps I can see from my windows—never knew. Their world wasn't made of cities, farms, and faxes . . . of set-aside wild places, of differentiation and reduction. It was whole and through it they went like fish in the sea.

Often, at moments like this, a pile of mail on my desk and the same sky that they saw sprawling north to Yellowstone and beyond, I can't help but wonder if we are even the same species, if we could converse if we met. Dressed in skins, constrained enormously by weather and topography, and without any idea of their ultimate destination—in other words unconstrained by maps, plans, or any notion of the idea of progress and betterment that so prejudices our every action—they *walked* from Asia to here. Over generations, they crossed the dry steppes where the Bering Sea flows today, and came south through what we call Alaska, Yukon, British Columbia, Montana, and Wyoming. Some continued to Central America, along the way becoming the Navajo people of the Southwest, and some stayed in the high valley where I live, separating the Great Plains from the Great Basin, and which is now called Jackson Hole. They left no name for themselves or this place; nor did they leave any artifacts besides the rock ovens in which they roasted plants, and the obsidian points of their projectiles, which isn't much when you've called a valley home for nine thousand years.

Like all hunter-gatherers, they didn't need many durable goods other than those that helped to keep them alive. They were free, not poor, and if one can trust the record of modern hunting-gathering societies, they worked only a few days each week to get their food, using the rest of their time to participate in activities many of us have lost: singing, dancing, telling stories, raising children, and actually communicating with the world around them. They were the original affluent society, and hunted small and large animals while following the flowering of the seasons. Bistort, hyacinth, tobacco root, bedstraw, cattails, sage, elephant's head, arnica, yarrow, berries, and blueflax were some of the plants that they ate raw and cooked, slept upon, died their clothes and salved wounds with, decocted into medicines, and twined into cordage for nets.

Their fire rings still dot the valley: Blacktail Butte where they roasted bison and munched sego lily, Cottonwood Creek where they speared spawning cutthroats, and Jackson Lake where they dug blue camas and arrowleaf balsam root. Beneath the slopes where I've shot several years of elk they drove bighorns over the ferrous cliffs of the Gros Ventre, and also stopped to collect pigment to decorate their faces, which may have given the drainage its old name—The River of Red Paint. Where the northernmost Tetons disappear over the horizon, I imagine them snowshoeing over Conant Pass, bound to the warmer and less snowy valleys of Idaho to spend the winter. In April, or what they may have called the Moon of the Melting Snow, they came back, following the greening of the plants into higher elevations as the summer progressed, lingering for a couple weeks on the redds of the cutthroat trout, and killing bison, antelope, and sheep whenever they could find them. Elk, deer, and moose, the animals I see most often and who have helped to build my bones, they hardly ate, as revealed by their middens containing virtually no remains from these ungulates.

Then, around 1600 A.D., the valley saw a Moon Of Melting Snow in which the Nameless Ones didn't return. The bighorn sheep were no longer driven into killing traps on the Gros Ventre; the blue camas wasn't dug; and generations of trout felt no spear in their back except the talons of osprey and eagle. In the entire valley no archaeological site has been found that can be dated between 1640 and the early 1800s, using either carbon-14 or obsidian hydration analysis. During this century and a half perhaps only the occasional traveller saw the Snake River eroding its channel farther west, the Teton Glacier spitting rock onto its terminal moraine, and lightning-set fires opening the coniferous forest and rebirthing the aspen.

Because they left no written records and handed down no oral history, we don't know why the Nameless Ones left this high valley never to return. One theory has it that the Shoshonean people, migrating northeastward out of the Great Basin in the 1400s, rapidly colonized the semiarid valleys around Jackson Hole, which were the winter hunting territories of the Nameless Ones. Driven off and assimilated, the Nameless Ones disappeared.

The Shoshone, relying on seed gathering and eating large mammals throughout the year, found little reason to settle in the alpine valley their predecessors had found so attractive for roots and seasonal meat. When the horse found its way to northwestern Wyoming in the late 1600s, the Shoshone had even less reason to journey to Jackson Hole. Over the next two centuries they developed a culture whose food, shelter, and symbology was based on the equestrian hunting of the plains' bison, and whose males found their status in warfare and stealing horses. Crossing from Great Basin to Great Plains, Shoshone braves sometimes travelled through the valley, naming its tallest peak, whom we now call the Grand Teton, Elder Brother, and occasionally climbing to its highest shoulder, only five hundred feet below the summit, which has been named the Enclosure for the circle of rocks that have been found there. Fasting, questing for visions, dreaming, they stared over the country for days. But when they descended, it was to other valleys that they journeyed.

Decade after decade, no one lived in Jackson Hole, not even the French, British, and American trappers who called these mountains *Les Trois Tetons*, "The Three Teats," and who first began to deplete the beaver in the winter of 1810–1811. Adventurers and financiers, the mountain men trapped a season and left. Even those who were most fond of the place, like Davey Jackson, who returned to the valley for several years and for whom it was finally named, never settled. And when the beaver were trapped out, the mountain men had little use for what the Nameless Ones appreciated and that, if anything, had grown richer. As the trapper Osborne Russell wrote in his journal, "The valley produce[s] a luxuriant growth of vegetation among which wild flax and a species of onion are abundant. . . . [And] like all other parts of the country abounds with game."

Unfortunately, Russell wasn't more specific about what sort of animals abounded in the 1830s. The records of other trappers suggest that the same species that sustained the Nameless Ones were still present—

bison, antelope, and bighorn sheep. Not until the 1870s and 1880s did those who followed the trappers notice elk and moose increasing, perhaps as a result of the slaughter that was taking place outside the valley. Like Yellowstone, which became the world's first national park in 1872, Jackson Hole had become a refuge.

In 1883, when John Carnes and John Holland built the first homesteads in the south end of the valley, elk were already wintering there in great numbers, and soon began to attack the settlers' haystacks in winter. By 1909 the state of Wyoming appropriated five thousand dollars to help feed the herds; by 1912 a National Elk Refuge was created north of the new town of Jackson; and in the 1930s the boundary was extended to what would eventually become the back fence line of my cabin. In 1950 the fence line of our village became the boundary of Grand Teton National Park.

From the turn of the century onward elk supported the valley, first as food and then as cash, outfitters guiding Eastern dudes and the aristocracy of Europe into the Gros Ventre and Two Ocean country for trophy animals. Such excursions still are one of the principle businesses of the region, hunting contributing $6 million each year to the local economy.

Our blue camas, our sego lily, our bison.

Ignoring the mail, I look north to Conant Pass, over which the Nameless Ones probably left for a last time. I think of them as the only true knowers of this place . . . the only ones who were wholly immersed in its ecology and constrained by it in a now inimitable way—moving with its greening and freeze up, eating exactly what it grew and no more. I understand them best when I eat huckleberry and thistle, rose hip and miner's lettuce, and too when I eat elk, though it wasn't their animal. But it's what this country presently grows, and so connects me to the ground the way the animals they knew connected them.

For two days snow squalls cloud the valley and when the sun returns I see the last rough-legged hawk of the season. Sitting on a bare tree, the bird watches me walking at a distance before slowly flapping toward the horizon. Breeding on the arctic tundra, it won't visit again until the fall. But its cousins, the red-taileds, soon arrive. Within another week, as I poke along the edge of sage and firs behind the cabin, I hear the keening of a courting duo. Deep in aerial erotics, they spiral overhead, clutch talons, and go into a spin. Parting, they chase each other over the treetops. Then, from deep in the trees on this northern hillside, comes the only sound of the country that resembles something from the industrial world. Sounding like a pneumatic compressor, a ruffed grouse rapidly thumps his wings on a log.

I angle down toward the river, finding a crimson splotch of snow and the hind feet of a snowshoe hare at the base of a tall Doug fir, its north side covered with lichen. The pentagonal florets of coyote paw, left in the skim of snow, tell who made this meat. Picking up the hare's feet and turning the soft wet fur in my hand, I wonder at the coyote's abandoning them. Usually, they grind up everything, leaving only turds of hair and bone chips as clues to what they've been dining upon. I put it down to one more unknown among the myriad that fill the woods and fields around the cabin. Like the day a young coyote sprang from the sage and ran alongside me, nipping at my pedal as I biked home. What could she have wanted? Was she rabid? Did she want to play? I dismounted and held out my hand to her. She sniffed and might have touched me had a car not come along and scared her away. Looking up, I see the roof of the car and the top of the cabin—perhaps coyote saw me walking home last night and, wary rather than curious, dragged its kill away.

Contouring around the hill, the grouse still drumming below me, I come to the open spot where I laid the boned-out rib cage of the elk whom I've been eating since October. I brush the duff aside, but not a scrap of him remains, and I think of other animals whom I've helped to recycle, especially the yearling moose who died nearby, in the winter of the big snow, my hand on his head as he shivered his life up to the stars. A couple of neighbors and I dragged his carcass into the sage, and when I walked out there the following July, accompanied by my two young nephews, all that remained of him was a four-foot circle of hair and a scapula. At seven years old, my nephews weren't impressed with the scavengers' efficiency. They did mark though, in the calculating way of children measuring their elders, our returning the scapula to its bed of moose hair at the end of the day.

Remembering these souls gone and present, I take a handful of needles, rub them into my nose, and inhale deeply, sensing at the very limits of my olfactory consciousness the evanescent whiff of elk—now duff . . . now coyote . . . now me. I think of his herd leaving the refuge and streaming in long ragged lines over the hillsides behind the cabin before descending to the Gros Ventre River. Gathering on the rocky shores these past evenings, the moulting elk have seemed pale and bleached among the dark trees. At sunset, when they've forded, their manes have glowed rufous and deep chocolate brown in the slanting light, some of the bulls still wearing antlers and the cows heavy, chirping among themselves like shore birds as they've gone to their birthing grounds. Four . . . six abreast they've crossed the park road at a canter, leapt the fence, and continued north across the hay fields, led by an old matriarch sure of her direction. Following them deep into that prairie, I've found grouse on their leks—the cleared spots in the sage where they mate—the males inflating their throat sacks, spreading their tail feathers, and make popping noises as the females mill about . . . their mating rite of spring.

Spring! Spring at last! Spring at home, after so many months away. It's good to lie in bed in the morning, underneath the warm elk hide, as the first pale light takes away the darkness, and listen to the deer chewing the rose hip bushes just beneath the bedroom window, while the caw of ravens floats faintly in the air.

Yesterday a larger visitor came. As I lay half asleep, I heard a heavy tread by the woodpile, then a thud that shook the walls. Naked, I slipped out of bed, crept to the couch, and peeked through the living room window. A bull bison was directly below the sill, his shoulders not more than two feet from me, his head sweeping rhythmically back and forth as he rubbed on the cabin, his horn hitting the wall—*WHONK!*

Behind me, Merle stomped his feet and whined with excitement. Over the pines Saturn shone brightly.

Slowly I cranked open the window, leaned out, and intertwined my fingers in the thick hair covering bison's head. He grunted softly, as if doubting what he was feeling; then he reared, slamming my hand with the base of his horn, and leapt over the low woodpile, skittering sideways about fifty feet before coming to a stop and snorting at the cabin. I let out a joyful whoop—my hand was wriggling to the elbow with power. Bison lowered his head and looked at the cabin suspiciously. I made no other sound, hoping that he would stay where he was, which he did, staring at me. In another minute, he began chomping grass.

Today, as I leave for the office, he stands on the path to the car, and I can see another half-dozen bison in the aspen. They have begun to move from their winter range in the Elk Refuge to Grand Teton National Park, where they spend the summer. In the spring, they visit the cabin.

"Mind if we pass?" I ask, making a wide detour around him. He stares at Merle and me, and doesn't move in the least.

In another few days he's gone off to the Warm Springs, three miles north, where, with a bunch of other, rowdy young bulls, he breaks buck-rail fences and rolls joyfully in the dust. Then the buttercups speckle the grass, and with their arrival the first human migrants of the spring appear, my friends Robin, Pam, and their daughter Kiely. For years I stayed at their home in Kathmandu while Robin was the Peace Corps' doctor, and it's now good to reciprocate so much of their hospitality during a time when they're in transit, going from Alaska to Montana to Wyoming, and looking for land, a town, and jobs. We linger over morning coffee, and then they leave me to writing while they hike, hang out, and relearn North America.

One night I defrost an elk tenderloin and we drive to String Lake, at the base of the Tetons, for a picnic. As we broil what we of Western society consider this choicest bit of meat, a small herd of cow elk, now in their summer quarters, sift among the trees and call to each other as the full moon rises. Robin, thin as a blade and with a bristle of moustache, kneels by the fire and explains to four-year-old Kiely that what's cooking for dinner is what's calling out in the fields beyond the trees. Kiely has short black hair, round cheeks, bright precocious eyes, and a little dab of a nose, a miniature version of her mom, who is of Chinese descent. Taking her parents' hands, she walks to the edge of the meadow and they look at the elk together. Then we eat our salad and this smokey piece of flesh, tender as meat can be, and full of dark, musky flavors while a pack of coyotes howls from the other side of the lake.

"It would be easier," says Robin, a Buddhist who sometimes eats meat, "if they didn't taste so good."

Which is only the half of it.

I think of this elk tossed off his feet and lying still—one of those careful and lucky stalks ending in the magic bullet, the instantaneous death from a high neck shot, the grass still in his mouth, his hooves lying sideways in the wet imprints where he had been standing, his fall so sudden that, other than making a startled jump at the crack of the rifle, the rest of the elk in his herd continued to graze. Would that they were all like that instead of the times that I've knelt by their heads, and their breath has grated and their legs have kicked and shivered, their eyes filming over—another life prematurely departed between my hands. The first elk I shot died like that, and I swore that I would never hunt again. I even thought of running away and forgetting the carcass. But I sat by her, holding her head, then finally started my penance. Slitting open her belly through the shining lineaments of muscle, my hands up to the elbows in her warm innards, I cut away windpipe, heart, and lungs, then sawed her spine in half, and in half again lengthwise, my hands . . . her haunches . . . steaming in the subzero air while the smell of pine and fat wafted around us. And as I worked, making what I knew would be most of my food for a winter, what was elk, and what had been the grass she ate, and what was the man grass and elk would become, lost their edges, as did my quick judgment about the wrong I had done. I bore her heavy quarters down through the forest, one by one, her gift at last accepted, her pain not pushed away. After all, where could her pain go? To the next county? To the next state? Or perhaps to the arctic where the oil needed to transport rice and beans to Wyoming, equivalent nutri- tionally to the meat of these yearly elk, spills and ends the lives of three otters, a half-dozen seals, and a score of common murre chicks, which is how I reckoned the costs of being a fossil fuel vegetarian.

Licking her fingers and closing her eyes, Pam, also a Buddhist who occasionally eats meat, says, almost in defeat, "This is delicious," and Kiely, her head just above the level of the picnic table, adds "Mmmm," maybe sincere, perhaps just miming her mother.

My friends have had a hard time coming back to North America—so full of companions who offer them wild flesh for dinner. Here at least the animal has already been converted to food, but in Alaska, wanting to participate in the gathering, they found themselves not only picking berries but also reeling in halibut on a friend's boat. However, like many Buddhists who are willing to eat meat if it is offered to them but who won't actually kill it themselves, Robin and Pam were unable to admin- ister the coup de grace. Their friend handled the billy. The whole busi- ness has left them uneasy despite their claim that it is better to kill large animals who will feed many individuals—a two-hundred-pound flat- fish, a five-hundred-pound elk—rather than slay a multitude of animals, shrimp for instance, to feed a few.

"Why?" I ask.

"Because each creature has a life and they're all equal," says Pam. "A Buddhist will try to do the least harm possible by taking as few lives as she can." However, both she and Robin have recognized what many do not: It is truly impossible, no matter how low one eats on the food chain, to take no lives at all. She calls this "the cruelty of vegetarianism": the countless small creatures—invertebrate, rodent, and avian—lost as the fields are plowed and harvested.

"Invertebrate?"

"Yes, invertebrate," she says, going on to explain that the ability to feel pain as mammals do, sentience, shouldn't be the criterion of how we judge worth. A life is a life is a life: elk, shrimp, human, amoeba. Like others who follow Buddha's teachings, she simply feels sorrow for the endless stream of protoplasm needed to keep the web spinning.

She stops speaking and cocks an ear to the trees. Elk call and the coyotes yip from across the lake. Are they hunting mice or elk calves, or just singing to the moon? The white glow illuminates the mountains, and looking up at the peaks, Pam thoughtfully licks the elk juice from her fingers.

T H R E E

———➤✕◄———

COLD RAIN MIXED WITH SLEET FALLS INTERMITTENTLY FOR A WEEK, which is nothing unusual for this valley when the calendar says it's spring. In fact, once while riding my bike on the summer solstice I was caught in a snowstorm. When the sun makes its first appearance through the misty clouds, I begin to turn over the little plot of ground by the cabin, where I plant potatoes. The first time I tried gardening up here, I was astonished. How many springs, as a boy, had I helped my grandfather plant his vegetable garden, turning over the dark soil with a pitchfork? Half a dozen at least, and I thought that it was hard work. I didn't know much. When I first broke this ground, matted with thick long grass, speckled with willows, and clumped with sage, I had to use a spade sharp as a knife. I had to shake loose the dirt from the underside of the sod, pull it from its interwoven roots, part it from its web, and then cut the taproots of the sage and willow, breaking and pulling them from the earth, so I could plant potatoes. There was no cleared ground around the cabin, which might have given me the illusion that the world was made for planting gardens, and that to eat organic spuds I, or someone before me, didn't have to wrench apart the earth. From that moment on the spade that hung on the back of the cabin became as powerful a tool as the rifle that hung inside it.

The soil loosened, I collect as many bison pies as I can find, crumbling them into the plot—one of the few gardens in America fertilized with local buffalo shit. Then, as the sleet returns, I drive north through the flurries, along the Snake River where the elk have gone. At the far end of Jackson Lake I leave the spitting snow behind, and as I drive through the lodgepole forest of central Yellowstone the sun emerges and the clouds tatter away. On the eastern side of the Divide fumaroles steam, and on the far shore of Yellowstone Lake the mountains rise white and jagged— the Absarokas. Coasting over Dunraven Pass, I park and find a comfortable nook in the rocks below the road where I set up my spotting scope and glass the great basins and meadows of the Antelope Creek watershed. Clear of snow, succulent and green, the meadows have brought Yellowstone's northern elk from their winter range, and here they're introducing their newborns to the world. Not much different from what's happening on the other side of the Divide, in Jackson Hole, except for the fact that grizzly bears live here and the elk know it.

In nervous bands the cows watch the edge of the forest while their spotted calves run among them, front legs arcing toward the ground, rear legs lifting behind them, frail as twigs, delicate and joyful. Now and then one of them will stop for a long drink, butting fiercely at its mother's udder.

They seem exuberant. Considering how they've spent the last week, maybe that's understandable. For the week following their birth, they remain bedded and hiding, so as to reduce the chance of being eaten by eagle, coyote, bear, or mountain lion. They give off little scent during this time, an evolutionary strategy enhanced by their mothers' licking them clean each day, and even eating their feces.

As I can see through my spotting scope, most of the calves seem similar in size, perhaps fifty pounds, a result of their mothers' having all come into heat and bred within a few weeks last fall. Such accurate timing is necessary if the calves will be born at the fulcrum of spring— not so early as to find intense cold and deep snow, and not so late as to miss the most nutritious plant growth, which produces rich milk in their mothers. Without nutritious milk the calves won't be able to run quickly after their moms, or grow large enough during the brief summer to survive their first winter.

Hours go by, the sun sets, and alpenglow sits on Specimen Ridge. Long before the grizzly appears I know she's there. Like weather vanes the noses of the elk point to the edge of the forest. They bark at their calves who huddle close. As the bear rambles into the open, followed by a hurrying pair of tiny cubs, the elk and their calves run toward higher ground.

Leaving her cubs at the edge of the woods, the grizzly hunts across the now-empty grass and sage, nose to the ground and zigzagging. She's looking for a calf born a little late, still hiding—head down, ears back, silent and immobile. Ignoring the distant elk, she continues along a small creek, tufted with islands of rock and grass. Suddenly, several cow elk run from the nearby trees, angling in front of the bear and trying to distract her. She swerves away from them, then just as quickly changes course as an elk calf leaps before her, materializing from nowhere. The mother grizzly takes three bounds and overwhelms the calf, chomps it dead with her powerful jaws, drops it, wheels around, and stands over it. Looking anxiously to the forest, she grabs the tiny elk by its neck and sprints toward her cubs who have been left alone for too long. A male bear, searching for an estrous female, might be about. The elk who lost her calf stares after the grizzly, her calf flopping in the running bear's mouth, then turns and joins the rest of her herd. The bear trots by her cubs and without dropping the calf leads them into the forest.

Tonight (for it's now almost dark) I'd like to follow this mother grizzly to see how she feeds her cubs. I'd like to listen to her voice as she instructs them about elk calves, and I'd also like to wander with the elk, eavesdropping on their ruminations, if any, about this event. It can't happen. For the safety of the bears all the country below me is off limits to humans. Such policies have reduced the number of bear-human confrontations, and will continue to be necessary if this place is to have grizzlies, who aren't as adaptable to civilization as black bears. But placing whole drainages off limits, a temporary solution for keeping bears safe, is really just one more symptom of human overpopulation. When it happens we become voyeurs and distant ones at that. There are ways, though, to close the gap.

Because of lower densities of grizzlies, the country closer to home isn't so heavily restricted, and when the tree-line snow melts I ride my mountain bike through the northern Gros Ventre Mountains, high into the meadows full of deep grass. Pedalling slowly into the wind, I feel my nose tugged long before I see them. I leave the horse trail, park the bike against a pine, and begin to crawl.

Soon I find matted grass and crushed lupine where the elk have made oval beds. A trampled trail leads over broken phlox and bluebell, and piles of clumpy spoor glisten and lead me on. In a lush rising meadow I find a herd of cows grazing and calling to each other. Their calves have lost their spots, and a few yearling males, called "spike bulls" because they bear two nonbranched spikes as their first antlers, circulate along the edge of the herd. Teenagers of the elk world, they can't find a comfortable place. Some stay with these female herds—their mothers of last year who are raising new calves—and some go off to be with the mature bulls. Though I search the ridges above the meadow and along the edges of the trees, I can't find any of these older males, whose haunts and survival strategy are different from the cows in the meadow. The bulls need to find the best-quality food to maximize their antler growth. Being large, strong, and having no one to take care of but themselves, they'll sacrifice a great deal of security, in terms of cover and numbers of surrounding elk, for optimum grazing.

Cows, on the other hand, nearly always choose security for their calves over rich forage, and one of the best ways to achieve that security is to congregate in big herds that can be easily smelled and spotted, yet offer a unique form of protection. As Dr. Valerius Geist explains in his book, *Elk Country*, when a cow and calf are alone in open country they can be easily singled out by a predator. But in a herd, they are surrounded by tens or hundreds of other animals whose many eyes and noses make it more likely that a predator will be noticed as it approaches. If a cow and her calf are in the center of the herd, their chance of being chosen by a predator are further reduced. Triage also comes into play. If you are a healthy cow elk the probability is high that at least one other elk in the herd will be weaker and consequently slower than you are when your herd takes off at a run. This is the animal who will be caught.

As the morning lengthens the sky becomes the same deep color as the bluebells around my outstretched arms. The earth smells of leaves, stems, and roots. The sun is warm on my neck. Lazily, I put my nose into the undergrowth, as I might into a lover's hair, and feel the arch of the knoll against my chest and stomach. I breathe deep and press the earth close. Rolling over, I chew a stem and watch the elk doing the same. On the breeze comes their musky scent—hair, ruminated forage, and the resin of the conifers in which they've bedded. Two calves stand upright, box at each other with their front hooves, drop to all fours, and gallop in a circle. With dark wet mouths and shining noses, their mothers stare at them, chew some grass, and give the edges of the meadow a long gaze. Many of the elk are lying down and partially dozing. It's the fat time of the year for them; still, they can't afford to squander their energy. The "cost of living" at this elevation, six to ten thousand feet, and at this latitude, halfway to the pole, is high and escalates with the coming of winter.

Elk live without surplus, and the best way to appreciate their situation is to consider that out of every one hundred pounds of plants an individual elk will eat in this meadow only forty-five pounds can be digested. Out of these forty-five pounds of vegetation twenty-five will ultimately be lost to the heat generated in digestion, leaving only twenty pounds to become elk muscle or to be converted to elk work—running away from me, for instance, if the wind changes and my scent is carried to them.

Finally, after much glassing, I find a couple of bulls sneaking along the tree line. Maneuvering between the spruce, they seem careful of their velveteen antlers, grey, fuzzy, bulbous, and not fully formed. The cows, of course, pay the bulls no attention, and the bulls, likewise, make no visits. Not until the decreasing daylight of August triggers their sexual hormones will cows and bulls begin to intermingle actively. Now the cows turn all their attention to foraging for their calves, eating to lactate, and the bulls forage for their antlers, intent on creating the biggest set possible by the fall rut. On first glance, such a differentiation of tasks appears to be one more instance of male vanity and selfishness. In reality, eating to build a great set of antlers is designed for the perpetuation of the bull elk's species. Big antlers help to make more and stronger elk, and how they do it is one of nature's more complex curiosities and an example of female power.

Consider that elk mothers who can divert a lot of their nutrients and energy into milk production are most successful in raising their off-spring. Large, symmetrical antlers indicate that the bull who wears them has also been able to divert much of his nutrient intake into their growth. He has found healthy forage, he has avoided injury and illness, and he has survived through winters. In the words of Geist, his antlers are "proof of health." This is the mate a cow wants, for such a male will contribute genes that will help her future daughters divert nutrients into lacta-tion—all for the good of her future calves. And it is the cow who chooses the bull, not the other way around. Although no biologist has been able to demonstrate that cows rationally select such bulls because they "know" that they will donate superior genes to their future daughters, anyone who has watched cow elk during the rut has seen them, year after year, prefer big-antlered bulls. In short, large antlers represent reproduc-tive success for cows.

For those of us with two legs instead of four, who watch from the edges and try to interpret what we see, these same antlers can represent many things: the thousands of generations of elk stretching back through mountain range after mountain range to the time when the big glaciers advanced, sea level fell, and elk first walked on to this continent—the continuity of a species made manifest; they can also represent, in their complex growth and symmetry, the beauty of the Rocky Mountain high country; and too they can symbolize what goes beyond the meat some of us bring home. When the last steak of the year is eaten, they are still there to look at, to touch, and to say all the rest. Which is why, I think, some of us put them on the wall.

I watch two more bulls join the pair I've been glassing. All four are six by sixes, which means that they have antlers with six points, or tines, on a side, the typical form of the mature bull elk. Occasionally one sees seven by sevens in these mountains or even an eight by eight in the park, where elk receive more protection from hunting, live longer, and can grow larger antlers. But I'm not looking for such an elk this year. In the course of gathering meat, I've killed a five by five and a six by six, and maybe that is enough for this lifetime. The rack of the six by six sits on my dresser, with a spray of orange leaves and a nutcracker feather on its bare skull, and sometimes on a night when I've awoken troubled, I've stood before it and held its brow tines, feeling its power course through my limbs and stop the world's swaying.

This year, as usual, I'll probably shoot a cow, which provides almost as much meat as an average-size bull who has been through the rut, and leave these less numerous big bulls to pass on their genes. In the future, as the number of hunters increases and the available habitat stays the same, or even decreases, making such altars from a thousand generations of power, or trophies to one's ego, may very well become a once-in-a-lifetime opportunity, proscribed by law and not by choice.

Then again, this year I might not shoot any elk (though I doubt it), carrying my rifle through the mountains like a vestigial organ. There have been years, when I lived in urban places and travelled to the mountains as a commuter, that I did nothing more than walk around the forests and basins, carrying my rifle a few days before putting it aside completely. I had no daily intimacy with country, the condition that I've come to believe is necessary if one is to receive life instead of merely take it.

In a line, the four bulls slip over a saddle and into the next basin, pulling at me to follow in the same way the summer earth pulls my nose down to her bosom. Retreating to fetch my bike, I make a wide circle around the herd of cows and track the quartet of animals upward through the tundra, even though I'm certain I will have to ride to the roadhead in the dark. I'm tugged by them and against my better judgment keep following. When I cross the saddle and look into the next valley they are gone, and no amount of glassing reveals them.

Over the next few weeks the fields grow tall and jungly. Lupine and daisies intertwine, aster and monkshood blow side by side, larkspur mingle with parsnip. Hiking toward tree line, I find harebell and bluebell, avens and phlox . . . purple phlox, white phlox, pink phlox . . . columbine, until mantling over a granite ledge, I catch a pale blue sky pilot staring me in the eye. Rose crown and queen crown speckle the tundra, paintbrush and dying gentian border the aspens along with that primrose bearing the loveliest of names, *Dodecatheon pauciflorum.* I swirl it on my tongue, touching it as I walk by.

Returning from the hills, I find a stray cluster of cottonwood seeds along the dirt road that leads to the cabin, and I wonder when the puffs stopped blowing. I haven't noticed the sky filled with cotton pods for days. In the dusk swallows fly above me—through the sweet yellow perfume of the Russian olive. When did *it* bloom? And when did these dogwoods turn the hillside beneath the cabin white? After the cottonwood bloomed . . . after the wild rose pinked . . . and right around the same week the olive scented the river. I noticed its perfume the night we first paddled the Gros Ventre, eddying our kayaks beneath its branches. So about ten days ago. I look up—three deer, so fluid brown they're like trout, fin through the aspen and stand hock-high in the grass; then they disappear into leafy flumes, eyes like polished river rocks.

In the morning, before sitting at the computer, I sometimes ride into the fields north of my office, an old silver trailer, worn but comfortable, and hard against the buckrail fence that marks the boundary of the park. It's a cool and pleasant way to start the day—I can watch the blue herons standing in the outflow of the Warm Springs, and follow the antelope and their new fawns through the sage. Each April the pronghorns migrate from the Red Desert, up the headwaters of the Green River, over the divide into the Gros Ventre watershed, and down to Jackson Hole. Each October they return, two hundred miles each way. Goggle-eyed, they see me pedalling from afar, stare, chew. I stop, crouch in the yellow sweet clover, and wave a bandana. Curious, they step closer, snort, canter off, and go back to browsing sage, which is what they taste like mostly.

I continue along the bumpy single track, and where it meets a smoother dirt road, named Mormon Row for the first settlers who homesteaded this side of the valley, three sage grouse erupt before my knobby front tire. They fly fast to the north, trailing liquid shit bombs from beneath their wings, and I imagine making a triple on them—*Boom! Boom!* . . . Reload. *Boom!*—which, younger, I once did not far from here. But the birds tasted so strong that, even soyed and gingered in a stir-fry, the overlay of sage burned my mouth. Still, the memory of forcing down each conscientious bite, and deciding not to shoot another sage grouse again, hasn't taken away the biomechanical pleasure of now tracing these three birds through the sky.

Did I learn this from my uncle as he crouched between my cousin and me in a duck blind thirty years ago, his hands on our shoulders while he whispered, "Wait . . . wait . . . wait," until it seemed impossible that the mallards could come any closer, and they did, cupping their wings an instant before he said, "Okay my boys, let's give it to them"? Did I learn it all from him, or does my tracing these grouse across the Wyoming sky, nothing in my hands except my bicycle gloves, lie buried in my hypothalamus like my sexual preference for women? If this part of my brain were a few microns smaller would I prefer men? Would I feel no pleasure at my imaginary tangents intercepting feathered motion in the sky? Might I preferentially think of the patterns the ripening huckleberries make in the underbrush, and the cool meanders of the stream banks green with sorrel? Might I not first imagine the dank glens in which chanterelles grow, and, drawn to Shadow Mountain, undo the stalks of fireweed, collecting their small piths until I had a pile, rather than seeing the fireweed's purple-red flower as the harbinger of fall when I could follow elk, making them into meat?

At the edge of the horizon where the grouse have disappeared, a lone bison stands, the same young bull, I think, who spent the spring around the cabin, implacable, withdrawn, and moody, a brown hump of pure hormones maturing until he can take his place in the herd. He is unchanging, ancient. His ancestors were here when elk arrived. If I didn't carry the guilt of forty million of his kind slain, would I want to eat him? I've had his meat. I know he's tasty. And this place grows him. But I never applied for one of the culling permits that were designed to keep bison numbers at about a hundred in this valley. Why keep them at a hundred when there could be thousands? One of the reasons is that the livestock growers fear competition from bison, and allege that bison transmit deadly brucellosis to their cattle, which is why, on the north side of Yellowstone, bison are shot when they wander onto private land.

True, it's a lot of good meat under one hide, but I couldn't feel honest about how I made my food if I were a hired gun for an industry whose product, beef, I won't eat anyway. I'll follow elk. This country grows them better than it does cattle, and without adding excessive fat, growth hormones, or feedlot "finishing," all of which have come with the turning of animal husbandry into an animal industry.

At this time of year the elk are hard to see. They spend the heat of the day lounging on the steep north sides of hills, deep in the trees. Oh, in the morning I can spot them crossing the hilltops behind the cabin, their tan bodies and buff rumps, for which the Shawnee named them wapiti, revealing their furtiveness, their chocolate-brown heads, manes, and lower legs blending with the pines. To watch them better I drive into the park, almost to the Tetons, where herds of female elk flow into Lupine Meadows like the morning tide, and look forever surprised at my approach. They might be matrons at a garden party, distressed and snobby, caught with their mouths full of sweet green hors d'oeuvres—why they taste so good when you grill them in the fall.

And on the way back, still early, I spy four mule deer bucks at the turnoff to my office, a perennial group whom I've watched for three years. Sleek and tumescent, flanks burnished, hooves polished, they're still in velvet and give me a superficial glance as I pass by. I wonder where they've spent the last three months since I last saw them. The largest buck walked up to the cabin in March, though I didn't know it was he. All I heard were footsteps stealthily approaching. It being after midnight, I couldn't imagine who was visiting, and the surreptitious tread, so careful and so unlike a friendly visitor, made me grab my headlamp and stand, waiting, by the side of the front door. It was cloudy and moonless, and when the footsteps halted on the step, and no knock came, I shone the light through the glass. Six inches away, enormous antlers flaring, the buck stared at me. I went to open the door and let him in, but he turned and trotted off through the snow.

Keeping their closer eyes on me, the four bucks continue to mince sage and grass. Which is why you can never tell what they'll taste like in the fall, whether you'll be eating sage-flavored jerky or grass-flavored steaks, and which is why I haven't shot a mule deer in a long time. Of course, that's only part of the reason. Making trails between office and cabin, peering in my windows, sleeping between woodpile and house, they've ingratiated themselves in a way elk never do. Wapiti gives a wide berth . . . stays wild . . . and tastes better. In fact, I've never had a bad one.

I could also say, following my Buddhist friends, Robin and Pam, that an elk provides more food per death inflicted. I could say that, but I'd be inconsistent. I shoot blue and ruffed grouse, maybe only a pound of meat per death, because there's nothing sweeter tasting in these mountains except berries, which is what these forest birds will eat in season. Plus, in my anomalous form of accounting, they are somehow even wilder than elk. No one ranches grouse for restaurants or feeds them alfalfa through the winter.

Lazily, the summer speeds by. Reading, I share the porch of my office with a string of carpenter ants, who make their way from the woodpile, across the planks, and down into a crack by the front door. Merle and his friends, Jack and Zula, doze in the dirt, the violet-green swallows spiral between the cottonwoods, Orion hunts in the grass, and from behind the school floats the turgid sound of the river, full of melt. From the sage come the liquid hammer strokes of a western meadowlark.

Dripping sweat, I go inside to make another cup of coffee, and I find a column of ants connecting cupboard and honey pot. This has become a habit of theirs. Shouting, "Okay, everybody out!" I sweep them onto the cutting board and deposit them back on the woodpile. A score, already mired in the honey, can't be saved. Like the deer mice I trap in a "Ketch All" box, some are lost despite my best intentions.

For weeks the galvanized catcher will sit empty at the foot of the stove. Then, in just a few days, it'll trap six mice, nine, a dozen—an entire new family—and I'll drive them across the river to let them go at the edge of the sage. But they foil my plans nevertheless. Once, releasing two of them, I drove off and saw in my rearview mirror that one of the mice, instead of staying in the grass, had bolted directly under the car and had been crushed by my tire. Sometimes, too, when I've gotten to the office a little late, one of these small brownish-grey mice, with big ears, doelike eyes, and trembling whiskers, has cannibalized three of its companions in the frenzy of being trapped, and will be sitting, bloated, among their chewed-out brains and dangling intestines. Which is what happened this morning. I take the survivor and the carcasses across the river, and when I bike home late in the dusk both are gone.

Wondering if it was a red-tailed or a Swainson's hawk who got an extra meal, or even one of the many Uinta ground squirrels who make the road their home, I continue up to the cabin, seeing a low form scuttling into the sage at the bend of the gulch. I hurry after it, drop the bike, and walk into the field. The badger hears me coming, turns, and lowers its head. I stop; it watches me. Carefully, we appraise each other's intent. Though I often see their holes, I rarely see the badgers themselves, and so this is a moment made luminous by scarcity. Soon, badger has enough. Turning, it waddles off, shoulders hunched.

Eating dinner at the picnic table outside the cabin, I linger through the twilight. Though it is ten-thirty the western sky is still bright, and at eleven-thirty the northwestern mountains continue to hold a red glow over their summits. Through the night a white haze circles the northern horizon. Restless, I lie in bed with the windows open, and leave before dawn, not wanting to lose part of a summer day in country so long buried in snow.

Across the valley, at the Lupine Meadows trailhead, I see a half-dozen cow elk and four very young calves walking by the edge of the forest. They pause, watching me, as I pause, watching them. The cows are the same long-necked ones who I fancy make up this herd, and the calves are perfectly formed miniatures of their mothers and aunts, except that their snouts are shorter in proportion to the size of their heads, as in the young of all terrestrial mammals. They crowd close to the legs of their moms, looking where they look, trotting at the same speed, wheeling when they wheel, their eyes wide and not afraid. They look calm and vibrant, and, at the very same moment, a little unsure. Watching them I remember when the physical world was full of unknowns, when trees, birds, flowers, cities, and the continents were nameless and everything was a surprise. The calves wheel as if newness sat behind their shoulders, and I hike up the trail feeling newness in my stride.

Through the dark forest bird song follows me, cheeps, trills, and whistles, and the "do-da-doot" of the rufous-sided towhee. As I approach the Valley Trail junction, and begin to head up Garnet Canyon to the Middle Teton, I see a young bull moose in velvet standing in the lush grass below the trail. His mouth is full of vegetation; he's brown as a tree trunk and just as still. He doesn't move a twitch. Only his eyes follow me.

Two switchbacks farther on, as the sun rises, I see a buck deer in velvet, standing against the sky at the turning of the trail, arrowleaf balsam root hanging from his mouth. He continues to feed, glancing up every few seconds as I get closer. Softly, I talk to him, and he moves off the trail slowly, his hair scruffy from moulting, his mouth continuing to pluck the greenery.

And what green! Deep, lush, moist, washed, and succulent, the valleys look like dells in Ireland, like paradise. Not paying attention to my footing, I nearly walk over a blue grouse who hardly stirs from the path. Very near here, I once caught a grouse with my bare hands, plucking him off a rock as he looked at me with his reptilian eye, then set him back on his rock where he continued his mindless clucking. Today, I don't attempt to duplicate the feat. I let the bird bob past my boots and into the understory of the trees.

Around the next bend another resident of the Garnet Canyon trail appears. A marmot, wagging her tail, scampers up a rock and stares across the valley to the bends of the Snake River . . . the hills of the Gros Ventres . . . the distant Wind River Mountains, bright with snow: the big view in the time of big light. She holds her chin in the air.

Leaving tree line, I put on gaiters and set off across the mushy snow, which grows harder by the time I reach the saddle between the South and Middle Tetons. Unexpected from the valley below, a cold breeze blows from Idaho, whisking snow crystals from the steep basins lying in shadow to the west of the range. I kick-step upwards, remembering how several years ago, as I began to cross this slope after a heavy April snowfall, it settled with a great shudder that sent me leaping for the safety of the rocks I had left. The slope didn't avalanche, and I stood there a long time, wishing to climb to the summit and ski directly from it. At last I turned back—if the slope did avalanche I knew I would never survive the twelve-hundred-foot airborne ride to Icefloe Lake.

Now, kicking steps toward the southwest couloir of the Middle Teton, I have few doubts about the safety of the frozen snow. Still, the actuaries tell us that the way we die is directly connected to the way we live. If one smokes enough cigarettes—lung cancer; if one sleeps unprotected with enough people—AIDS; if one spends enough time in the big mountains, stonefall, avalanche, or edema will likely be one's end. Or maybe not. Growing older, wiser, and more in love with life, we tend to take less chances. Of course, up here the risk never becomes as low as it is while reading a magazine at home, but that's okay. A mountain death wouldn't be a bad way to be recirculated—here in the wind, moving up toward the sky.

Between the granite walls of the couloir, cramponing over runnels of ice, I let the handholds of the rocks carry me higher. Cloud wisps unravel across sky—I look back and watch the sprawl of Idaho, tilted at an angle as from a plane, and the crazy upheaval of the western Tetons, their valleys full of snow, their sharp ridges thrusting toward hidden cirques. Higher, higher I go, the air thinner, until I emerge onto the summit ridge and scramble to the reward of view, all these snow-covered mountains rising from green valleys—the Gallatins and Beartooths in Montana, the Sawtooths far off in Idaho, the cozy Wyoming Range, bending over the southern horizon—and around me the Tetons, teachers of so many years. I feast on water and chocolate, and then plunge-step and glissade down the snow . . . the scree. When I leave the moraine and step back onto dirt, I touch it, having been granted another safe return from its airy edge. Then the cool forest . . . the mossy springs dripping . . . the sky so blue that it seems like the magic of love come true.

And at the last bend of the trail before the parking lot, I walk into a bear—a big black bear tearing apart a rotting log. He watches me as I make a wide detour around him and then goes back to his dinner. I'm just as hungry, and an hour later I'm eating elk burgers at the picnic table outside the cabin, while the sun sets over the mountain I've climbed. The rays of sunlight shoot into the sky over the central Tetons for another hour. Then the last reddish glow moves to the north, growing to a peach pink over Yellowstone. In the arctic the sun still circles the sky, but here the horizon is empty—empty, silent, and humming with the declension of evening. I stay out until dark, or rather when the stars come out to the south and overhead. To the north the solstice's white haze continues to light the horizon, and it is there in the northeast, the eternal light of June, when I finally pull my sleeping bag outside and go to sleep. At four in the morning the dawn returns, and Scorpio curls its tail over the southern hills. The birds have already begun to sing.

Week after week this blue, windless high pressure holds until, too big with its own glory, it collapses. On the day it ends the clouds build, not in increasing waves of cirrostratus from the west, which is usual, but seemingly from everywhere, filling the sky with a smokey cast. In the early evening the wind begins to blow from the east, and a soft sowing rain increases over the length of an hour until the sky turns a uniform slate grey. The rain beats steadily on the panes of my office, increasing in tempo until it lashes the windows in sheets.

A gust sweeps the rain away, and the sound of whipping sage and thrashing cottonwoods surrounds me. Overhead the sky tumbles with eerie white clouds, rolling like cannonballs toward the Tetons. To the northwest a red blotch of sky flaps. To the east from where the storm came, the sky is a bizarre, greyish-green fury, a womb of churning tempests. Gust after gust slams the trailer; the wind batters again . . . pauses . . . and rises to a higher pitch. Hail begins to pelt the roof with a metallic din—harder and harder until the trailer sounds as if it will be ripped apart. I stare wide-eyed over the top of the computer, then can stand no more. I rush outside, throw an exultant fist into the sky, and yell at the top my voice as the wind beats me with hail. I whirl, jump, shout incoherent sounds, drenched.

Suddenly I'm alone. The storm has already crossed the valley and is lashing the Tetons, now booming with thunder. In a few minutes they've become blue silhouettes as the storm spends itself behind them, in Idaho. Without changing into dry clothes, I walk across the river. On the far bank I stop in disbelief. Perfectly still in the damp air, one leaf on a small aspen tree has turned yellow. Deep in July, contrary to everything I wish, I know that summer is ending. The next morning, as if to confirm the leaf, I hear the call of a young bull elk. High and plaintive, his bugle comes again. He's experimenting a little early and not until the end of August does anyone answer him in earnest.

Then the bulls, rounding their mouths like the bell of a trumpet, begin to bugle from every mountainside—a call like a high-pitched squeal, followed by several resonating coughs, the sound signature of this place. Driving along the Grand Teton Park road, I can see them in the distance, standing in the sage at the edge of the pines, bellowing at each other while their cows graze behind them. They have shed their velvet, the richly innervated skin that has covered their growing antlers for the last five to six months. Rubbing their antlers on trees and bushes during and after the shedding of velvet has colored them a rich brown, except for their ivory points, which can be seen from afar, floating like ghostly branches as the elk move through the forest.

Long before the sun rises, I park the car, walk toward the Tetons, and ford Cottonwood Creek. Soaked to my knees and leaking water from my running shoes, I move from tree to tree, drawn by the rising squeal of one bull and the deeper-voiced response of another. Six thousand feet above us, the summits of Mt. Teewinot, Mt. Owen, and the Grand Teton turn pink, and when I look behind me a wave of carmine light breaks over the Gros Ventres. But this dawn is already an hour later than the day on which I climbed the Middle.

Staying in the pines, I look across the narrow meadow. On its right edge stands a seven-point bull with about a dozen cows. On the far left is another seven by seven with almost two dozen females. His mane is dark and matted with mud and urine; he has burly shoulders and a deep chest; his antlers, though bearing the same amount of points as those of the bull to the right, are longer and more massive. When he bugles, there is no doubt who is bigger: The three grunts that follow are rough and bass and boiling with toughness, and a cone of condensation spurts from his mouth into the cold air. Yet he makes no move to send his rival flying, and his rival makes no move to win more cows. They only nod their heads at each other, which is part of their strategy for avoiding direct confrontations.

Nodding his head moves a bull's antlers through the air, describing an arc. The larger the main beams and tines of his antlers, the greater the arc. His opponent can see the size of the arc from afar, and, remembering those bulls he has sparred with in the past, decide whether he wants to engage in a contest with his present opponent. Other indications of a rival's size can also be scouted from a safe distance: The deeper an elk's grunt, the bigger his body cavity and overall size; and the more he smells of urine, the more spraying he has done, which is another demonstration of his confidence and stature. The latter rutting phenomenon—urine spraying—is truly comical. A bull can look between his forelegs, cock his penis, and hit his neck and chin with a blast. He'll also dig wallows with his antlers, urinate in the turned-over soil, then roll on the ground. And if I can smell these bulls from several hundred yards away, each of them can certainly smell the other.

Even so the larger bull gives no indication that he will take on the slightly smaller one. There are other bulls bugling in the forest who might steal his cows while he is in combat, and being stronger isn't a guarantee that he won't be wounded while sparring. Though elk antlers grip each other when intertwined, allowing opponents to wrestle and test each other's strength without suffering a fatal thrust, a dangerous moment occurs at the point of disengagement. As the weaker animal chooses to break off the sparring and run, he has to turn, and the winner can then gore him in the side or hindquarters. Even a stronger animal can slip on loose ground or in brush and get wounded. Sparring isn't something that rutting elk totally avoid, as the annual wounds about their head, faces, and flanks point out. However, it isn't something in which they'll hurriedly engage, which is exactly the situation this morning. At least for these two bulls.

Intermittently other bugles sound from the woods and from the meadows beyond. One pair of squeals seems to get louder, and in several minutes I hear the actual clacking of antlers. The clacking grows closer, accompanied by trampling hooves. Two bulls emerge from the edge of the forest, antlers locked, directly between the two herds of cows and their respective bulls. One dark, the other light, they churn up the dust, their eyes bulging as they strain with low-pitched grunts. Pushing off each other, they disengage and stare. Each is a six-point bull, and probably would be a herd master if these other two larger bulls weren't present. Then they rush together again, uprooting a sage bush, which catches in the darker bull's antlers. He spins away, thrashing his head violently to rid himself of the bush, and the lighter-colored elk, with an opportunity to gore his opponent, merely watches. Flinging off the bush, the darker bull lowers his head, looks at his rival, and charges. Again they grapple, squealing terribly, but only for a few seconds. The darker bull pulls away, wheels, and flees. Chased by the lighter bull, he disappears into the woods.

The two herd bulls haven't stopped their bugling during the fray. Now the lesser extends his muzzle, lays his antlers along his back, and drives his cows into the pines. The larger bull bellows after him, then turns his attention to his cows. Sticking out his tongue, indicating his wish to lick, he approaches one, who turns her rear to him and walks away. When he follows, she lowers her head and sways it angrily from side to side—her signal that she isn't ready to breed. The bull turns away from her and bugles, which some observers believe reinforces the cow's dominance. In effect, the herd bull is giving her control of the situation, which younger, satellite bulls, impatient to breed, won't allow. In fact, they will continue to run her down. Thus the cow has some safety, before she comes into heat, in the harem of an experienced and more patient herd master.

When the cow approaches estrus her coyness disappears. She'll let the herd bull come close and may allow him to lick her head, her flanks, and her anus. Testing her readiness, the bull may lay his neck upon her rump and if he isn't repulsed will finally mount her. There's no mistaking his climax. He jumps up, his feet leave the ground, sometimes his spine and neck will arch. The cow is thrust forward, legs spread. If a bull is too tired from mating to be interested in a cow who has come into heat, she may rub her flank along his side to arouse him, and may even mount him.

This morning, still early in the rut, all the herd master's cows ignore him, and he spends another half hour bugling before sunlight fills the meadow. Then, as if the light were a signal to vanish into the trees, he circles his cows and prods them into the forest. For another hour his bugle, answered by calls from the surrounding stands of pine, floats up toward the Tetons. I like to think that if my hearing were acute enough, I could hear elk calling up and down the Rockies and across the highlands of Siberia and Mongolia, for the American and Asian elk are one species, *Cervus elaphus,* now separated by the Bering Sea. I can at least imagine them on this September day—the world's couple of million elk giving their all to make more of themselves—and giving us a pleasure they will never know.

F O U R

———>><<———

BY LATE SUMMER, WHEN I WALK DOWN THE HILL IN THE MORNING, frost has begun to cover the road. At its bend, where an old two-track heads into the refuge, some coyote scat lies, the frost melted around it. I kneel and take it apart, finding omnivorous remains—deer hair, the small bones of ground squirrels, and what looks like grass. Merle noses the scat and I say, "Coyoté," giving the word its Spanish pronunciation. He looks up and wags his tail. By such repetition of words with scat, and the actual sight of the animals themselves, he has learned the names of elk, deer, moose, sheep, antelope, bear, raven, and squirrel. Suddenly, he cocks his head. A moment later I hear it. The faint, fading song of a coyote over the next ridge. We listen as its bark evaporates into the increasing daylight.

A half mile farther on, where the aspens join a row of cottonwoods, stand two does and their five fawns, large ears funnelled forward. Behind them, in an open field that borders the Gros Ventre River, at least forty more mule deer graze, and one whitetail, one of the few who have begun to make their way into the valley from Idaho. Several easy winters have let the cervid population grow, and Merle, who was a deer chaser before we worked to break his habit, watches them with an eager look and a lashing tail. As I cross the bridge, a merganser paddles underneath me, craning its wicked-looking head to give me a glance, before scooting underwater. Just as I get to the trailer the nasal honks of two trumpeter swans, flying overhead, send me to work. I wonder where all of them—coyote, deer, duck, and swans—will spend their day while I sit in front of a word processor.

The sound of my building a fire and grinding coffee brings Orion meowing through the cat door from his nighttime hunting. Covered with pine needles, he jumps on the table and into my arms. He chucks his head under my chin, purrs loudly, and puts a paw on my cheek, staring at me with his enormous yellow eyes. After scratching his ears for a few minutes, I gently kid him about the mice who continue to leave their scat in the trailer, which gets me a cool, feline stare, as if to say mice are beneath his dignity. Squirming to get down, he takes a few bites from his bowl, peeks out the cat door, and is off in a streak, bound for grander deeds than mice.

It's the last time I see him. He doesn't come back the following day, or week, or month . . . until, by the arrival of autumn, I'm forced to list him as a casualty of the coyotes or the great horned owl who hunts along the river. When I sit at my desk there's no warm orange in my lap, no white paws kneading my chest, and at night, when I walk up the hill to the cabin, I hear his purrs in the coyote yips floating across the meadows and in the distant hoot of the owl.

I miss him—his intelligence, his affection, and his bravado, which was probably his undoing. He loved to ride in the car, hang out the window, and growl at moose. And how do you replace someone who spent the first weeks of his life sleeping in your arms? Merle, the big yellow dog with the brows so full of concern, and whom I found full grown, can't replace him. But then he wasn't asked to. There is no balance sheet, only a continuous departure and unexpected arrival, the flow of intimacy waxing and waning like the moon.

While I write, the front door open to the buzzing of the summer's last flies and the shouts of children returning to school, I catch the musky scent of horses in a nearby corral, and snatches from the latest controversy between my research assistant, Ruth, and our neighbor, Trisha: Ruth, a committed behavioralist, claims that children aren't born with traits— they learn them—which is why her four-year-old daughter, Anna, kept from violent toys, has no interest in guns, spears, and bows and arrows. Trisha, who might be called committed to the school of nature over nurture, believes that children come from the womb with innate proclivities, hinged closely to their gender, which is why Anna prefers dolls but why her two boys, Owen five and Peter three, make sticks into spears and willows into bows.

In Ruth's cabin and in Trisha's yurt, just a few hundred yards apart and down the path from my office, they argue this over coffee and on their walks to the Warm Springs with their kids. They are both in their mid-thirties, of the same height, with brown hair, though Trisha's is lighter and turning grey, and they even sound and look somewhat alike, though they were born on opposite ends of the continent. A kind of laconic country twang has infiltrated their speech and a kind of no-nonsense simpleness their wardrobe, which may be a function of carrying children on their backs through deep snow, chopping wood, digging in the dirt of their gardens, and walking from house to car through mud. At the same time, they are both deeply speculative, in the way people who are not professional scholars but who continue to read extensively after they have left college become keen appraisers of the daily round, filtering books through the fine and winnowing screens of their lives.

Sometimes Trisha, who worked in the bookstore in Jackson, would leave a photocopy of an essay, or a book review, or a poem on my desk, and later come over to the porch where I was reading, and say, "What did you think of that?" Then we'd sit in the sun, and talk for an hour while drinking coffee. Sometimes, too, we'd take a bike ride together, far up in the hills, and once, when my car was getting repaired, she gave me a lift back from town, driving far below the speed limit as we talked.

It wasn't a great surprise that when she left her husband, Andy, she began to come up to the cabin on the nights he had the boys. At first our two evenings a week together were a great relief—to finally express, physically, what had charged the air between us. Then the time we spent together became more frustrating than satisfying, overhung as it was by the shadow of what Trisha had quickly decided. When Andy's sabbatical in the park was over and he returned to teaching high school in Colorado, she planned to follow him so Owen and Peter could be near their father.

So we made do, knowing that the timing was wrong, but liking each other too much to break it off. Occasionally, I gave her packages of frozen elk meat, which she returned in kind with spinach and herbs from her garden. Sometimes we ate grouse, and twice geese. Owen and Pete gobbled my food, played in my trailer while I wrote, and helped me to tan an elk hide, all of which gave me the warm glow of being a provider and filled up that place that no love of work, or country, can fill.

When Trisha had a free hour we often ran along the river, or, if she had a couple of hours, we walked to Coyote Rock through the aspen, the trail leading upwards like a gilded ribbon. Only once did she see me shoot—a young ruffed grouse who burst into the air from beneath Merle's nose. When I fetched it, she knelt by my side as I held the dead bird in my hand, its wings beating spasmodically. Softly, she laid her palm on its breast and cried.

We didn't have a chance to walk farther. She had to get back to her boys. As we hiked down the trail, the grouse filling the air with silence, I thought about her sudden tears. I knew that they were mother's tears, wept for the death of any creature, especially a young one. And I thought her tears might also be for Owen and Peter, who liked to watch me pluck grouse, who would eat this one, and who someday might kill them as well, which she wasn't sure was a good thing to do. Maybe they were for me, the man who she claimed lived in the "white light" of his work, and who couldn't enjoy her for what she could give—the odd moments of the week. Maybe they were for herself, the woman who was trying to be a good mother in her own way, in a world that paid only lip service to the task.

All these possibilities surrounded me as she now walked ahead, passing through the flares of light that shone among the trees. Her jeans were frayed, her red-and-white flannel shirt ragged, and she was beautiful in the way that trees and mountains are beautiful, always with their rough edges . . . the way a child is ancient, the shadows of its eyes and jaw showing the patterns that will mark its old age.

The grouse, our dinner, lay warm against my back, and the smell of the mulched and dying leaves made me feel exposed, vulnerable to every emotion that the evening brought forth, a condition a female friend calls the "male menstruation," and which I have thought of as being perfectly transparent. The soil filled my veins. The trees conversed as I passed them. Their roots were wise. I remembered this state from childhood, lying on my back in the snow and talking with the clouds. Now my sense of being totally permeable contained an extra bit of knowledge. Each in our own way, we were doing the best we could in an imperfect and imperfectible world. Of all the things I had wanted to give her, to make her life easier, I had chosen to offer her this dead bird, which was self-indulgent to be sure, the child still needing to explain himself and win the praise of his mother. But it was also giving her this forest, or herself, or me, its blood the rough edges of us all, that evolution hasn't erased and that we remember by putting it in our mouths. My skin flushed and my eyes welled, not in frustration or impotence, but in attachment. There was no place else to be.

Dropping Trisha off in the village, I put the grouse in the frig and traded the shotgun for a rifle. The day was still early and too pretty to leave. I drove north along the Antelope Flats Road and past the turnoff to Coyote Rock, trying to visualize the elk I was about to hunt—where they might be and what they were doing, bedded, feeding, or travelling. Slowly, I let go of the many permutations of her and me, and concentrated on the country ahead.

Parking on the Shadow Mountain Road, I began to walk through the dead fireweed and fallen aspen, contouring across the slopes and into what I called my corner of inaccessibility. This was an innocuous bit of country full of deep swales and hidden creeks, bordered by private land on one side, Grand Teton National Park on the other, and protected by a forty-five-minute walk from the Bridger-Teton National Forest road on the third and fourth. Often it held deer, whom I'd never shot, and sometimes grouse, whom I had, and occasionally elk, especially in the early part of the season, whom I was looking for now, hoping that they had been pushed by hunters from the surrounding forest.

Just as the sun began to set over the Tetons, I reached an open ridge and was able to see down the valley to the village and the silver rectangle of my office-trailer . . . Trisha's yurt . . . Andy's yurt . . . Ron and Ruth's cabin . . . and across the river and up the hillside to my cabin and the few larger houses that also perched on the ridge. Behind them Jackson Peak and the snow-dusted mountains of the Gros Ventre receded into a scattering of broken clouds. The weather had bypassed the valley.

Standing against an aspen, I first glassed the parks below, seeing only a nutcracker flying. Then I turned my attention to the ridges climbing to the east and covered with aspens and conifers. Nothing moved along their crests. In another few minutes the sun touched the Tetons, irradiating brilliant orange streamers over Buck Mountain and far across the valley. For a long time, I just leaned against the tree, letting my mind clear while listening to the faraway tinkle and seep of water. When I looked east again, two elk stood on the ridge I had just glassed, their coats illuminated by the low sunlight until they glowed amid the dying aspen and yellow grass. They were about six hundred yards off and when I raised my binoculars I saw that they were spike bulls—illegal to shoot, but probably on the fringe of their herd.

Watching them drift over the ridgetop, I took my lighter from my pocket and opened its flame. It bent toward me—the wind was right. Trying to be as quiet as possible in the dry leaves, I walked across a couple of parks and up through another stand of aspen. Lying on my belly, I crawled onto the ridgetop. The elk were gone.

Another ridge, blackened from the Yellowstone fires, rose before me, and I climbed over it to peer into a valley to the south, the direction the elk had travelled, but I couldn't see them. They must have changed their minds and gone east. Nostrils wide, trying to catch their scent, I crawled that way, and over a final ridge crest.

They had disappeared. The narrow valley below me was empty.

Disappointed—in another old way I wanted to bring Trisha home some meat—I stood up and started down the far side of the ridge, intending to make a big circle back to the car. I walked perhaps seventy-five yards when I saw half a dozen elk grazing below me in the very bottom of the valley, along a dry streambed. I lay on the ground and moved my binoculars from one shape to another, seeing a four-point bull among his cows.

Creeping through the grass, I reached a stand of aspen, cutting the distance to the bull to slightly under two hundred yards. As I tried to get even closer, the fallen leaves and the brittle stalks of parsnip gave me away. The bull, who had been chasing off a forkhorn, a young, two-point elk, glanced up. Despite the aspen behind me, confusing my silhouette, he stiffened. He knew something on the hillside wasn't as it had been the last time he had looked.

I brought my feet in front of me, dug my boots into the grass, and put the crosshairs on his chest. The light was growing ever dimmer, and his antlers looked small. In fact, he was just the sort of supernumerary bull that most biologists would say ought to be "harvested," if one were going to kill a bull elk at all. But of course, he wasn't a supernumerary, for there wasn't a more mature bull around—otherwise he wouldn't have had these cows. The elk below me was an average four-point bull who had done good in his own little valley, a little on the small side to be sure, but wooing cows as if he'd done it forever, lording it over the two-pointers, *his* supernumeraries, and full to the brim with his September hormones, a major player in his out-of-the-way forest . . . a survivor.

Uneasy and like a single animal, the herd started moving toward the woods. I kept the reticle on the bull's chest as he climbed through the spruce, his brown mane made darker by the forest's shadows. Twice he paused, giving me a chance to shoot, but there were branches obscuring him. Then he came out in a meadow beyond the woods, more than three hundred yards from me. The crosshairs shook a bit, straying from his chest, so I took off my pack, laid it on the grass, padded it with my stocking cap, and lay behind this makeshift rest with the rifle lying across it. Through the now-steady scope I watched the bull lower his neck and thrust his muzzle at a cow, who scampered away. Then he turned on the annoying forkhorn and chased him. Swinging his head in suspicion, he looked back at the hillside where I lay, holding the crosshairs steadily over his back. He was 350 yards away, a shot I knew I could make, for I had made it before—both on paper at the rifle range and while crawling toward distant antelope on the plains. In fact, as usual before hunting season, I had practiced for weeks with this rifle in my office—taking a break from writing, aiming at a knot on the wall, letting out my breath, and marking the click of the firing pin as the crosshairs hung steady on the knot, until I was certain that I wouldn't miss on a standing animal.

Thinking of how I wanted the meat, and what a wonderful opportunity this was—fairly close to the road, and gone only a couple of hours from the house—I pushed the safety forward. But there were so many cows to be had this year, every year—and the season on cows would open in November and stay open until December 10. In fact, if one wanted to play God-the-Wildlife-Manager, he would shoot nothing but cows until the bull-cow ratio came back to its historical balance. If I didn't squeeze the trigger, perhaps next year this elk in my scope would become a five by five—wooing cows, chasing off smaller bulls, and passing along some of his survivor genes. And of course it was only September, and I knew that he'd probably breed some of these cows in the next few weeks. Did I want to terminate that?

September. It was, at last, September. If I shot him, it would be all over: the dawns to come and these twilights, the long, long walks through the country, the dead parsnip in the frosted meadows, and the musky smell of the bedded elk in the trampled grass. All over for another ten months . . . and all before I had watched and listened and smelled enough to be engaged with the season.

I unloaded the rifle and closed the bolt. Then I returned the crosshairs over the elk's shoulder, let out my breath, and squeezed the trigger. Without the crosshairs quivering in the least, I heard the click of the firing pin. Then I lay there as it grew dark, watching the four-point bull and his cows climb over the ridge crest and disappear into the next valley.

Now, IN THE EARLY MORNINGS, I CAN HEAR THE POP OF GUNFIRE. Sometimes it will be directly south of the cabin, in the hills of the refuge, and other mornings it will come from the north and west, in Grand Teton National Park. This morning it is from the park. As I drive to town, to service my seized-up computer, I see the small orange signs, posted around Antelope Flats and along the Gros Ventre River Road, indicating which areas of the park are open to hunting and which are closed. For days there have been pickup trucks parked the length of the road, with hunters sitting in the front seats waiting for the elk to migrate from the park, across the Gros Ventre River, and into the National Elk Refuge. Sometimes I have seen a hunter dragging an elk to the road. This morning I see no carcasses, only hunters in their vehicles and one empty pickup. I suspect that the gunfire must have come from somewhere on Blacktail Butte, and that the hunters who own the empty pickup actually got out of it, walking a mile or so from the road and up into the forest.

I always find it interesting to speculate about what sort of people these hunters are, and what brings them here from all over the country to sit by a road and watch for elk. During the last few days I've gotten some insight from a survey done by Stephen Kellert at Yale's School of Forestry and Environmental Studies. Sampling hunters across the nation, he found three significant types.

Those he called "Utilitarian/Meat Hunters" were more than likely raised in rural areas and primarily interested in harvesting meat much as one might harvest apples or soybeans. They had little interest in the living animals themselves or the environment they inhabited. Indeed, hunting just to be outside, without the possibility of "harvesting" an animal, was not appealing. This group comprised 43.8 percent of the total hunters in the survey.

"The Nature Hunter," while representing only 17.7 percent of the survey, hunted most often and was demographically the youngest. As a group they knew the most about wildlife, and their goal was to be intensely involved with wild animals in their natural habitats. Motivated by genuine affection for wildlife, they were faced with the paradox of killing creatures they loved.

The third category, the "Dominionistic/Sport Hunter" constituted the second largest category, 38.5 percent of all those who had hunted during the last five years. They often lived in cities and savored competition with and mastery over animals in the context of a sporting contest. However, their knowledge of nature and wildlife was very low. The only group surveyed by Kellert whose knowledge about animals was equally low was the antihunters.

As a category these animal welfarists fell into two types. The first, the Humanistic Antihunter, had a strong emotional identification with animals, typically pets, and identified, anthropomorphically, with the fear, pain, or suffering they imputed to hunted animals. The second, the Moralistic Antihunter, took the position that hunting was ethically wrong and fundamentally evil. Perhaps the clearest statement of this position was written by Joseph Wood Krutch, who said, "Killing 'for sport' is the perfect type of that pure evil for which metaphysicians have sometimes sought. . . . The killer for sport . . . prefers death to life, darkness to light." Interestingly enough, only 4.5 percent of the antihunters sampled objected to all forms of hunting, including hunting for food.

Still another study I've looked at, done by Robert Jackson, Robert Norton, and Raymond Anderson at the University of Wisconsin, found that many hunters went through five phases during their lives. Initially, those in the "shooter stage" revelled in opportunities to discharge their firearms many times. Moving on to the "limiting-out stage" they found satisfaction in the numbers of animals taken. In the third phase, called the "trophy stage," hunters believed selectivity of paramount importance, passing up what they considered animals of lesser value. Evolving into "the method stage," hunters then invested heavily in equipment and discovered pleasure in "how" the hunting was done—calling ducks or bugling elk, for instance, or using primitive weapons such as the bow and arrow. In the final "sportsman stage," the mellowed hunter was satisfied merely to be outside and gave up control of the world through pyrotechnics, accounting, collecting, or methodology.

Looking at the fellows sitting in their pickups and drinking their morning coffee, I say, "Utilitarian/meat hunter, limiting-out stage." Which is, of course, too simple and discounts a lot of their individuality. Once, wanting to know more, I stopped and asked a hunter standing by his truck why he chose to hunt from the road and in the park. He was from Arkansas, with a three-day beard, heavy wool pants, and a black-and-red hat crowned by a pom-pom. He was staying in a motel in town, and was one of those likeable people who maintain good cheer even when things are not going their way—the clear weather had moved no elk. He told me that he liked the park hunt because it was easy, and that he could see all this "purty" country without actually getting into it, which he wasn't sure he would like to do alone because he didn't know it. He also mentioned that the success rate in the park was pretty high. He was right on at least one count—ease. Legally, hunters have to walk only four hundred yards from the road to discharge their firearms. When I checked several days later, he had gotten no animal but maintained that he had had a thoroughly good time. In fact, he said that next year he would reapply for a park permit, and he hoped that those who wanted to end hunting in the park didn't succeed.

He had little to fear. The park hunt—liked by those who partake in it, often deplored by those who don't—will no doubt continue. It's a messy way of dealing with too many elk, but like many of our imperfect compromises, which have been created as by-products of good intentions, it has been difficult to replace by anything less problematic.

The good intentions occurred when Grand Teton National Park was enlarged in 1950, incorporating the grand vista of low hills and sage prairies to the east of the Tetons. This country happened to be a historic elk migration corridor between the elk's summer range in the park, the Teton Wilderness, and southern Yellowstone, and their winter range in the National Elk Refuge. As a way to control elk numbers on the refuge, as well as for that mixture of food gathering and recreation we've named public sport hunting, elk had been hunted in this corridor for years. Hunting in this corridor would now be illegal under the International Treaty for Nature Protection and Wildlife Preservation in the Western Hemisphere, which prohibits sport hunting in national parks, and which the United States signed along with seventeen other nations in

1942. So as to continue to manage this particular elk population (the language of the enabling legislation says, "to protect the population for future generations"), the state of Wyoming licensed hunters, and the secretary of the interior deputized them as *national park rangers*. Thus, the hunters I see parked along the Gros Ventre road are legally "deputy rangers," and what they're doing is legally a biological cull, not a sport hunt. The park calls it a "reduction," and in keeping with the "reduction" versus the "sporting" theme, doesn't permit black powder weapons or bows and arrows to be used.

Those who find these machinations both incongruous and distasteful point out that national parks were created to preserve ecosystems as they existed before the arrival of European civilization and that such wildlife manipulation is a violation of this mission. Unfortunately, most parks, even those that have been enlarged, haven't been made big enough to preserve the summer and winter habitats of their large migratory mammals. The high summer range may be sufficient for a particular species; the low winter range, where people have built their homes, then becomes the limiting factor on a species' numbers. This has been the case in Jackson Hole where since the early 1900s an increasing portion of this crucial winter range has been developed and now stands under cattle ranches, the town of Jackson, and its adjacent suburban neighborhoods. Indeed, the National Elk Refuge was established in 1912 as a way of preserving the last of this undeveloped winter range so that elk could be maintained in their historic numbers—another good intention whose largesse wasn't quite ample enough.

The 24,700 acres that were eventually set aside can't accommodate the entire herd on natural forage, and a winter feeding program, also begun in 1912, continues to the present. Elk are fed about eight pounds of alfalfa pellets per animal per day, depending on the severity of the winter. Feeding generally begins in January and is terminated in March or April. So far so good. However, to keep disease such as scabies and brucellosis to a minimum, to prevent range damage to the refuge, and to control the expenses of feeding elk (about $250,000 annually), the U.S. Fish and Wildlife Service, which administers the refuge, and the Wyoming Department of Game and Fish, which also shares the feeding costs, have decided that no more than seventy-five hundred elk should winter there. One of the easiest ways to control elk numbers is to shoot them, utilizing public hunters. Hence the cull.

And one of the two legal places to cull these park elk (the other is the refuge itself) has been in their migration corridor through Antelope Flats and across Blacktail Butte—the country that borders my village and that is also visible from several of the park's paved roads.

Hunting elk from horseback or on foot, up in the mountains, is one thing, and hunting elk from a pickup parked along the tarmac is another—even in the eyes of a lot of meat-eating Wyomingites. Consequently, the cull takes its share of yearly licks from an array of detractors. Its members claim that they're not against hunting "per se," but that this roadside aberration should be halted.

Can't be done without compromising the health of the herd, rejoin the agency biologists, explaining that to continue to feed elk on the refuge, while not culling them, would be neglectful of the welfare of all the elk who spend the winter there. The inevitable increase in elk numbers would spread diseases and degrade both the winter and summer ranges.

So don't cull elk, counter the more extreme animal welfarists, but let's discontinue the feeding program and allow elk to forage on the refuge's currently available winter habitat. This plan, which might be called the hands-off management approach, would temporarily create a large winterkill and habitat degradation, until the herd achieved a balance with its winter range. Nothing prevents such a plan being implemented except the fact that such a winterkill is politically and economically unacceptable to the local community, as well as to many observers far and wide. The elk bring in millions of dollars of revenue each year as the region's premier big-game animal, as well as its most significant wildlife tourist attraction. Thousands of hunters travel to Jackson Hole each fall, and increasing numbers of tourists come to the valley to observe elk bugling. In the winter visitors ride horse-drawn sleds onto the refuge where they watch and photograph elk at distances of only a few yards. Letting the herds starve to death, when they have been historically fed, is simply not going to happen.

A third management option would be to cull the herd only in the refuge. In fact, culling is presently practiced on the northern half of the refuge by licensed public hunters who participate in a weekly lottery during the regular and park hunting seasons. If their tag is drawn they can hunt, by foot or by horseback, on the northern half of the refuge. It is their gunfire I sometimes hear right behind my cabin in the early morning.

There are those who, in principle, don't object to such culling on the refuge, but who find it immoral that the cull is conducted by individuals who derive enjoyment from their participation. Far better, they say, to have trained, dispassionate, wildlife biologists from the U.S. Fish and Wildlife Service do the culling and donate the meat to the needy. Others, however, will object. Foremost are the public hunters, who don't want agency people taking over a cull that provides them with food and recreation. Secondly, no matter who did the culling, animal welfarists would find it heinous that elk are shot on lands designated for their protection. (It must be noted that no one ever said individual elk were going to be protected, only the species. And in this respect, the refuge has fulfilled its mission, helping to maintain the species in its historic numbers.)

Yet another solution to this thorny problem would be to stop both culling and feeding while also returning the southern end of the valley to winter range by razing the town of Jackson and the surrounding housing developments and ranching lands. As might be expected, the local chamber of commerce, as well as most property owners, haven't been supporters of this measure.

None of these unpleasant measures need be instituted, say another contingent of the let-nature-be school, if we would only restore the elk's historic predator, the grey wolf. Such a movement is underfoot for Yellowstone National Park, so why not for Grand Teton National Park? For one, Grand Teton is a far smaller park, and its western boundary lies not far from agricultural communities. To the south are fairly dense human and livestock populations. Why bring back a predator who will almost immediately be tempted by dogs, cattle, and horses, and who will have to be controlled as well? But such reasoning misses the more relevant point. As Bruce Smith, the elk biologist on the refuge, has pointed out, "Wolves would not control elk numbers." Weather, and its effects on forage and animal health, is the primary regulating factor. The wolves would only be beneficiaries of severe winters, while helping to dampen the fluctuations in the elk population over long periods of time.

In short, it appears that we're stuck with this cull, which is more than messy and controversial. Some think it has become inefficient. Elk have learned to migrate through the park at night, significantly reducing the number killed during some years, so that by mid-winter eight . . . nine . . . ten thousand elk—from the park *and* from the surrounding forests— are lining up for the refuge's dole. To counter their nighttime travel, managers have suggested that elk be hunted in the western portion of the park before migration took place; but only Congress can open that part of the park to hunting, and the likelihood of that happening is slim.

To complicate matters even further, more elk are shot on the surrounding Bridger-Teton Forest before they can migrate to the feedground in an attempt to keep refuge numbers at seventy-five hundred. Over the past thirty years, this forest segment of the Jackson elk herd has been culled at a rate greater than its annual rate of increase, as compared to the park herd, which has been culled at a lower rate than its yearly increase. It is this forest segment of the herd that everyone would like to see grow. But because too many park elk arrive in the refuge, these forest elk continue to be targeted. In reality, this is a simplified version of a more complicated story. Because the Forest Service has permitted extensive cutting and road building in its holdings, these forest elk have been made more vulnerable.

The mixing of elk from different herds on the refuge is also the reason why contraception of the herd—called for by some animal rightists—is a difficult strategy to undertake. On the refuge, it is impossible to know which is a park elk and which is a forest elk; nor would contraception of thousands of animals be an easy matter. On the summer range, where the herds are separated, contraception is also an impractical solution to keeping the population in check. Individual elk are widely scattered, making their capture and handling beyond the financial means of the federal and state agencies, as well as for any animal welfare group, none of which has offered the money to begin such a program. It also must be noted that contraception can cause wildlife deaths, as handled animals die from stress. Though relatively benign, it is another form of wildlife manipulation serving a human vision of an ecosystem.

So the cull continues. Unlike shooting bison on the refuge, which was challenged and successfully terminated by animal welfare groups, the legality of thinning elk in the park and refuge remains untested. However, if push came to shove and an animal rights organization *did* place a referendum on the Wyoming ballot, calling for the end of the park hunt, what would I do? I think about this possibility as I drive home with my jump-started computer, and finally decide that though I'm no fan of the cull I wouldn't vote for its termination, though I would try to make it less visible by not permitting cullers to sit in their vehicles or shoot within a half mile of the road. In this way, it might be made more like hunting in the mountains. Predictably, biologists in the agencies tell me that these "aesthetic restrictions" may reduce the cull's effectiveness even further, creating an even more crowded situation on the refuge. Perhaps.

For now, these two reforms of the cull are the best I can offer with the evidence I have. No matter what is done—close-to-the-road management, far-from-the-road management, or no-cull-at-all management—elk are going to die. The hands-off policy temporarily increases the winterkill and consequently the coyote and raven populations. Hands-on tactics keep elk steaks on the table, photographs on the wall, and give some people the illusion that they're doing some good by saving elk from the "cruel" death of starvation. Of all the arguments for the cull, this is the lamest. Elk have starved with grace and dignity for thousands of years, and don't need Florence Nightingales with rifles to sanitize their deaths.

I guess if we were truly responsible, we wouldn't put much emphasis on any of these management schemes. We would deemphasize our manipulation of wildlife for their purported good, and proceed headlong and without delay on what would really benefit them—manipulating ourselves. It is we who need birth control, not animals.

Driving along the river, the aspen grey and austere, I pass the same half-dozen pickup trucks and a few new ones, waiting out the afternoon. They make me think of one more suggestion: make hunter-education courses mandatory for everyone, no matter how long an individual has hunted, and increase their length and rigorousness until they resemble those in central Europe, where prospective hunters must not only demonstrate expert shooting, but also must spend up to one hundred hours studying wildlife biology and forestry before they are granted the privilege of hunting. Presently, hunter safety courses in North America average thirteen hours for the United States and eighteen in Canada, and are devoted predominantly to the subject of safety. That wide open, tortuous country called "ethics" is dispatched of quickly. On the average but an hour and a half is devoted to such topics as patience, compassion, and respect, qualities that informed hunter-gatherers for millennia.

In a black Ford pickup a lone man drops his binoculars from his eyes as he catches my car in his peripheral vision. There is nothing to indicate that I am a hunter—no orange cap on the dash, no gun rack across the back window, no NRA sticker on the vent, just a scruffy, long-haired man in a worn, blue pile jacket, driving an old beat-up vehicle with local plates. He raises his left index finger and gives it a little tap toward me—

"Take 'er easy," and a little more, a book as thick as *War and Peace,* describing this cold afternoon, and those big granite mountains with their cap cloud of pewter grey . . . his sitting, my driving, in the midst of all this country filled with elk. I tap my right index finger back. Acknowledged.

As I come around the road's eastward bend, I look up to the forested ridges of Turpin Creek, and wonder if the swirl of clouds hanging over their summit means departing or lingering weather. Lingering, I decide, feeling the low pressure sit in my ears. If we get a few inches of snow I might hunt in the morning, climbing up to Turpin's ridges and across some hidden parks where I've rarely seen another person. Staring at a sucker hole in the clouds, and thinking about whether to enter Turpin Creek from its bottom or climb around to its top, I get the creepy feeling of déjà vu. The cool, diaphanous light along the edge of the cloud has reminded me of someone's smile. I cycle back through my recent memories and find the serene face of Chukinima Rimpoche, a Buddhist holy man in Nepal, whom I sat before not long ago. He told me, with a compassionate smile, that for every fish and animal I had killed—mindfully or not—I would have to be reincarnated as that creature before moving on to a "higher life."

Slowing down at the post office, I sample being an elk—bugling my heart out to the sky . . . licking my calf . . . feeling the shock of a 30-06 bullet. Then I try on being a trout, finning in the Gros Ventre and being yanked into the air. How about a goose flying up the Snake, honking over the oxbows, and tumbling suddenly from the sky, never having heard the ten gauge that sent me flying out of my temporary goose life? I think I could do it. Such karma seems no worse than being struck by lightning in the Tetons, and far better than being bumped off for my billfold in L.A.

The clouds continue to build, and the sucker hole loses shape, here a minute, gone the next, just like the enigmatic smile of the Rimpoche, and the Buddha painted on the wall behind him. Of all the words attributed to Siddhartha, my favorite remains those that he uttered on his deathbed as his disciples, despondent at losing their teacher, leaned close. "All compound things dissolve," he said. "Become a lamp unto yourself. Work out your own salvation diligently."

THE NEXT DAY THE WORLD BEGINS TO TURN WHITE. BETWEEN THE cabin and the car an astonished crisscrossing of deer tracks and scuff marks lies in the scant half inch of snow. I scuff it as well, kicking snow spray at Merle who jigs and laughs, then grows still, head cocked to the gulch below. A young coyote howls, "Yip-yip-oooooo, yip-yip-oooooo," over and over, his voice quavering between delight and perplexity. Merle wags his tail and whines happily. On the hood of the car we find the imprint of a deer's nose, scenting in a semicircle above the radiator cap, and when I look west to gauge the weather, I see the mountains shining a dull pink, appearing to have grown in height while sinking remotely into the distance.

Too many thoughts swirl in my head to go hunting. I build a fire in the wood stove and watch the flames blossom around the logs. Feeling their warmth on my face, I put a finger to the end of a log, oozing moisture and sap as the flames engulf it. Scorched in the Yellowstone Fires and cut in Ditch Creek, these lodgepoles now heat my writing room—xylem to ashes. Is that all? Didn't they hold soil in place, provide homes for woodpeckers, owls, and pine martens, and pump oxygen into the atmosphere? Didn't they stand and sway in the wind for themselves? I think of the grove of great spruces at the mouth of Death Canyon, where I sometimes run and sit, looking up their enormous trunks, six feet in diameter, to where they move silently against the sky. If a saw or ax were put to these monarchs, wouldn't they feel something? Is grandness in a life-form the quality necessary for us to imagine that it has feelings? These days, I doubt it. Poinsettias, poppies, and milkweeds exude latex, thick, milky, and often poisonous, when bitten by an insect. The latex kills the predator or glues its mouth shut. By analogy don't the lodegepole, the lily, and the blade of grass feel something when they are cut and trampled? Perhaps their response, maybe no more than a small cry, is noted only by the most sensitive.

This plants-have-feelings argument won't wash with most of the Western world, which lays the stimulus-response reaction of plants upon the doorstep of tropism. However, in other cultures the sentience of the plant kingdom is acknowledged, alongside that of animals and even mountains and rivers. The anthropologist Richard Nelson, in his book *Make Prayers to the Raven,* recounts how the Koyukon Indians of northwestern Alaska return birch chips to the forest after they have made snowshoes rather than burning them in a fire, which they believe would be disrespectful to the birch, one of the more powerful spirits of the forest. Believing that the world watches their actions, they see themselves as moving through a forest of eyes and never truly alone. At every moment the world must be treated with respect. Is this any more foolish than respecting a God who sits in an unverifiable heaven and judges our actions? This morning, listening to the pine pop and snap, I don't think so.

Tea made, the wood stove chugging, I lean my chin in my hand and stare at the computer screen. On my fingers I can smell elk breakfast sausage, and I imagine some part of his digested flesh charging my synapses when my hands start to move over the keyboard. I even wonder if he-in-me might be measured. After all, testing for toxic substances has grown sophisticated enough so that the E.P.A. can detect one part in a quintillion—less than a tablespoon of a compound dropped into the Great Lakes. Could we devise a test that would detect the venison my great-grandfather ate resident in my bones? Or one that might locate the ancient compulsion to hunt what the land grows hiding in the spirals of my DNA? The woman who pulled me from my mother's womb found my umbilical cord wrapped around my neck and my face an anoxic blue. Fact of birth. The old wisdom, though, says that such a strangled child must tell stories.

Today I do as the sky grows darker. Snow falls from late morning until evening, and when I head to the cabin I leave the car parked below, thinking that I won't get it off the hill if it blizzards. As Merle and I cross the river and walk along the cottonwoods, three dark shapes bound from the windrow of trees, bounce twenty yards, leaving puffs of snow, then stand looking at us. The wind lashes across the treetops; snow stings my eyes. Far above the clouds there is a full moon, and its light casts a seashell white through the storm. I can see the deer's noses, nibbling at my shape. But the wind blows directly from them to us, perhaps 40 miles per hour. "Easy," I say, as much to them as to Merle, wagging his tail wildly. We continue past them as they stand in the lee of the trees— they'll be sleeping here while I sleep in the cabin. After a half minute, Merle and I look back. They're still watching us—three abreast, heads turned over their shoulders.

In the dawn, the light is opalescent and grey like smokey pearls, the air filled with snow. With visibility cut to a hundred yards this is the center of the world. Though I can't see them, I feel the mountains surrounding the cabin, encircling and holding me. Then I recall what the Oglala Sioux Holy Man, Black Elk, said about this country. "The Power of the World always works in circles, and everything tries to be round." He lived not that far to the east of here, among these horizons.

I listen to the wind—another of this place's sound signatures in addition to elk bugles—and to my dog's dream yips from the bedroom. After a while I begin to read *The Tuning of the World,* constructing my understanding of the morning from its printed words and the sounds of the storm. The author, the musicologist R. Murray Schafer, recounts how he once asked his meditating students to hum what they considered to be the tone of "prime unity"—that sound which arose from the very center of their being and against which all other sounds could be measured. One might think such a sound would be the rhythmic beat of waves on a seashore, or the sound of wind in trees, or perhaps seasonal bird song. But it wasn't. In America Schafer discovered that most students hummed B natural, which happens to be the resonant frequency of our 60-cycle electric current. In Europe, students hummed G sharp, the resonant frequency of that continent's electrical wiring.

I listen to the hot water heater give its final eccentric shudder and grow quiet. The frig, too, has become silent, and I shut off the light by my side, the baseboard heater, the ceiling fan, and the stereo, which isn't playing but whose digital clock still emits a faint glow. Now there is only the wind, the grey light of the sky, and my dog's soft breathing. Yet, if one wanted to make the case, latent industrial noise could be said to surround me: A sensitive ear might hear the milled logs, so warm and honey brown, still screeching from the saw cut; the frig and stainless steel sink were bent and pounded into shape; the woodstove forged; the carpet dyed in a vat of petrochemical brew.

Perhaps the stillest points can only be found outside. I hear them
when I plunge naked into the Gros Ventre, when I walk from the house
and pee naked under the stars, when I hike far into the mountains . . . as
I'll do when the storm ends. I turn the light and ceiling fan back on, and
watch its slow spin. Then I follow its grey cord connecting it to the
ancient, ivy-twined chandelier, and to the rest of the house's power system. From the circuit breakers on the back side of the cabin the power
line goes underground and joins a distribution system that branches out
across the valley from the substation at the village. From there a trans-
mission line heads across the Teton Valley Ranch, traverses the gulch
below the cabin, crosses the Elk Refuge, and interconnects with a
higher-voltage power line that passes through the Snake River Canyon
on its way to the Goshen Substation near Shelley, Idaho. Owned by the
Utah, Idaho, and Bonneville Power Companies, this hub collects electricity from a grid stretching across the Northwest—federally owned
dams in the Columbia and Snake River basins, as well as from the Jim
Bridger coal-fired plant near Rock Springs, Wyoming. In the summer
the Palisades Dam, which is located on the Idaho-Wyoming border, and
which is primarily an irrigation dam, provides most of the power for
Jackson Hole. However, starting now, in the winter heating season when
power use rises, it's more than likely that the Goshen Substation is actually getting some of its electricity from the Jim Bridger plant. Then its
emissions, scrubbed though they are, escape into the atmosphere and add
their incremental bit to the nation's smog and acid rain. So aren't our
increasingly cloudy skies, acidified lakes, and salmon going extinct in
the dammed Columbia, all partly my responsibility?

I hold the thought while looking at the painting hanging above me—
a grizzly and her cub ambling out of an alpine valley in Glacier National
Park. On my bedroom wall hangs another famous mountainscape—
Ansel Adams's photo of the Tetons taken from the Snake River Over-
look. As if having mountains outside the windows weren't enough, I
want to bring them inside, read and sleep under them when I'm only
separated by the distance across the valley. Along with my own photographs, they are my cave paintings, my endearment for this place. But
important though they are, they're trapped within their own two dimen-
sionality.

Walking into the bedroom, I stand before the dresser and the large
antlers of two years ago. I can still smell them faintly—hair and bone and
a trace of dry meat. I run my fingers over the tines and clasp them.
Listening to the soughing of the wind, I think of where I will go when

the storm stops, my mind flying over ridges and into valleys, and sensing, like an elk, where the elk will be.

When Orion rises over the mountain called the Sleeping Indian, I leave, driving until the Ditch Creek road becomes too snow clogged to go on. A mile of dark cold walking brings me to the gate where I usually park. Though not legally designated wilderness, as is the country south of Gros Ventre River, the Ditch Creek drainages have been put off-limits to vehicular traffic by the Forest Service and the Wyoming Department of Game and Fish to restore wildlife habitat. The gate forms more than a physical barrier. It creates an emotional boundary, the world behind it unfolding at a speed that humans can assimilate.

Up to my shins in new snow, I pass the steep side creeks where I have surprised deer on early mornings, the golden aspen leaves thick on the earth. Sometimes, during buck season, I have seen antlers and followed their bounding through my rifle's scope. The deer have always seemed too fleeting, and the possibilities of the days ahead too certain, to risk firing. It is what makes being a resident so attractive. The hurry disappears and there is always another day to see another deer or elk, to walk to the river and catch some trout, to pick huckleberries.

Where the old road turns east, going through a clear-cut, I remember another snowy morning, dark and glittering with starlight like this one, when I walked softly into a herd of bedded elk. They sprang up before me, twenty dark shapes against the forest, standing and unsure. I listened to their puffs of breath trying to get my scent, then, one after the other, they wheeled and tramped into the woods.

Soon, not far from that traditional bedding area, I find tracks—cows and calves, and one set of prints larger than the rest, moving south over a ridge and down to a pond. I follow them under the very first light of the sky, thinking of how many spoors I have followed along this ridge, and how once, catching up to a herd on the last day of bull season, I crept upon them, looking for antlers. I saw only one set, which might have been a forkhorn (legal), but then again might have been a spike (illegal). Just as they caught my scent and began to run, I saw the telltale fork in one beam of the young bull's antlers, threw up the rifle as he bounded across the sage, and pressed the trigger following his bound. I knew instantly that I had shot far over his shoulder. I remained kneeling, smelling their musk and fear on the morning air, and feeling hot shame wash over me, for I had broken an accord: to put everything else aside—especially to whom I would pridefully tell the news—so that walking among elk was allowed by them; to be so calm that they stood momen-tarily unafraid and perhaps willing to be taken; and, equally important, so that there was enough time to apologize. Of the necessity of these last few but interminable moments, I have no doubt, for they are what make hunting more than murder or the inattentive harvesting of a "natural resource." They are the bedrock of our oldest relationship with animals.

When people evolved a conscience, understanding for the first time the death that ran the world, they could no longer be one with all its other creatures—living in innocence of our mutual dependence, and killing without remorse. Call this our first guilt, or our first responsibil-ity, states of mind that perhaps evolved after emigrant humans entered landscapes whose large animals had never before seen an erect predator. In New Zealand, Polynesia, and on the North American continent but twelve thousand years ago, there is ample evidence showing that our newly arrived prehistoric ancestors did a thorough job of eliminating species who were tasty and easy to snare, spear, or run down—the giant, flightless moa whom the Maoris took in great numbers; several species of flightless, gooselike Hawaiian ducks called *moa-nalo;* and mammoths and ground sloths from Wyoming to the Grand Canyon. At some point, though, in some cultures more than in others, these same hungry, im-pulsive, and nomadic hunters became resident ones, witnessing the de-cline of the game who had fed and clothed them. In some societies an ethos of restraint was passed down. From this restraint, this guilt, this self-interest—call it what you will—and in Africa and Asia first, Europe second, and in Australia and the Americas last, grew the painted cave walls, the shrines of piled bear skulls, and the many worldwide prayers, lofted on smoke and chanted to every animal soul killed for food and clothing . . . prayers for forgiveness and rebirth, prayers given in thanks for those lives who made human life possible, prayers offered in sadness for the web enfolding us all. It is the recognizance of those sacrifices made, and the respect for those creatures who made them, that became our first accord with animals and that made hunting a holy act.

The modern mind says it was not an accord at all, for the animals themselves had no part in its making. The ancient mind, used to seeing animals permit themselves to be taken, would disagree. It is impossible to decide which mind holds the more accurate version of what took place. Perhaps the accord really was no more than self-deception on the part of ancient hunters, fostering one of grandest rationalizations of our species, that we were being given a gift because of our mindful behavior. Still, having watched deer and elk stand motionless before me, after I have taken the time to enter their world, I too would disagree with those who say that it has been all a sham. But I may be one of the last who is duping himself.

Of this, though, I'm certain. When the minds who made that careful entrance became engaged in other tasks, the actual or invented circle that contained both people and animals—as both dependents and donors of life, as fated cohorts—was broken. It has yet to be restored, and on a worldwide scale more than likely never will.

Down to the pond I hike quietly, the stars vanishing until only Orion, hunter of the sky, walks before me. Then he too disappears into the pale blue morning. Up through a wide ridge of conifers, I follow the tracks as they mix with those of several moose, fresher than the elk. Coming to a small clearing, I spy a dark shape and I slip behind a tree to watch. Attacking a downed log, a young bull moose pirouettes in the snow. His antlers are small and silly looking on his large body, and his head is covered with wood chips. Butting the log a few times, he turns quickly, his feet jigging happily like a jaunty prizefighter doing a fast two-step, then he attacks again, muzzle full of snow, ears full of chips. I walk along the edge of the clearing, making a wide detour around him, but he sees me anyway, and glances up with the amazed and sheepish look that surprised moose can wear, seeming to say, "Oh, no, a man with a gun!" He trots a few yards, stops and looks back, just to make sure his eyes weren't playing tricks on him. The shock flashes across his face again. "Yes! Human!" His long black legs lifting clear of the snow, he disappears into the forest.

Following the elk tracks through the cold forest, I think about how easy it would have been to have shot this moose and carried the meat out surreptitiously. On how many days would it have been easy to shoot deer and elk, sheep and bison, and get away with it? The pitifully small fines and too few wardens spread over so much country aren't a deterrent to those who contemplate poaching. They have never concurred to the agreement by which the rest of us abide: to shoot only those species for which we have bought a license and only on the days legally set aside for hunting them.

On the surface it appears that the hunting community is composed only of these two members—the poachers and the law-abiding citizens. But there is also a third group of individuals carrying guns out here, a subset of the law-abiding class. These people tend to reflect more on what they're doing, and how they do it, so that eventually some of them don't do it at all, or at least don't participate in what others would consider perfectly legal. Believing that what goes on between a hunter and his or her country can't readily be shared, most of these hunters hunt alone, which makes it difficult to know their rituals.

One person with whom I do walk a few days each fall is Bob Ciulla. Once a professional hunting guide, now a builder, he has the sharpest eyes of anyone I know and is inspired to look. In fact, he's one of those rare individuals who on foot and without the use of dogs has actually spied a mountain lion. Thin and tan, with a gentle smile and rim of curly hair, he hikes through all the seasons, wearing binoculars, finding shed elk antlers, photographing sheep, and in the autumn carrying his rifle for weeks without loading it. Last year, he and I stalked a bachelor group of bull elk, including a couple of six by sixes. Getting close, we raised our rifles only to watch them trot away with great stateliness. Neither he nor I said a thing, but I knew what both of us felt: for one, how many antlers does one need to collect; and two, that shooting in the middle of the season would have been dumb, for then our being out in the country would have been over, *out in it* being a strange turn of phrase that aptly explains being outside one's daily shelter while being completely immersed in the tasks of an old home.

A few weeks later we stalked a half-dozen cows and he shot one. When we walked across the draw to the great animal sprawled on the blood-stained snow, he said, "This is the part of getting meat that I hate." He cleaned her through her backbone, which is not how I do it, but which was neat and effective. We do many things differently. I was standing off a ways with the pile of meat when he laid her head at the base of a tree, knelt before her, and placed an evergreen sprig in her mouth, his face tender and utterly sad. He has watched too long not to be conflicted when taking . . . receiving their playful lives.

Cutting back into the meadow, I find the elk tracks still climbing through the forest. They meander along a series of hidden ponds, zigzag through some blowdowns over which I have to climb, and descend a steep, exposed meadow falling into a stand of aspen and a tiny stream. Here, many years ago, I shot a five-point elk on Halloween, the last day of the season. He was bedded in the thick spruce below the aspen, and I had tracked him and his cows for miles through the snow, creeping the last few hundred yards like a lynx. One cow after another emerged from the spruce, twelve in all, crossing this field, and he followed. I had a bull tag and I shot him.

The rut hadn't been over for very long, and he was still thin from breeding and not eating, yet more enormous than I could at first comprehend. I sat by his head, held his antlers, and thought about the magnificence I had taken out of the world. The ridge where we sat opened upon the Snake River plain and the Tetons marching to the north, bright with snow. Older than either of us, they hummed, wrapping elk and man together.

I can never pass the meadow without sitting here, just below where he fell and where I left his hooves, arranging them as they had run in life—fore in front, rear to aft—a cairn now long gone. "May you run long in field and forest," I said over them. "May your kind run long. May we run long together." I don't know from whom I first heard this. I heard it coming out of my mouth the first time I killed and said farewell to an elk. I heard it in the hum of the mountains, teaching me what to say.

They hum now, mixing yes and no equivocally, humming from everywhere so the exact source is hard to place, the hum itself hard to hold in its slipperiness, retreating as I cock an ear toward it, coming closer as I try not to listen. It's the hum of being out in the country, which isn't a model of what is. It *is* what is . . . at least in this place.

Climbing through the spruce and lodgepoles, I let the tracks go across a saddle and down into the Middle Fork. I know I won't catch the elk who made them. I continue up through some cliffs and finally reach the summit above Tangled Creek. Many trails cross here. In the summer I lay down my mountain bike and eat lunch. In the winter I ski up the east side, circuitously, avoiding the avalanche danger. In the fall I cross over many times, going from one drainage to the next, glassing the basins, and stopping for a cup of tea. I can see from the Wind River Mountains to the Absorakas, from Yellowstone through the Tetons, and south to the Snake River Range—snow, granite, and mute dark conifers, a special place still doing what it has been doing for a long, long time, and now buried in its winter snow. I know that its workings aren't the workings of many places in this nation or in the world; but they are the workings of many others—central Idaho, the mountains of Montana, Alberta, and British Columbia, the Yukon, Alaska, the slickrock of Utah and Arizona, the open spaces of New Mexico, and how many hollows and forests in New England, the North Woods, the Appalachians, how many bayous? The country is big, but most of us now live in cities, where what *is* is very different. Both places exist and whether we experience one or the other is determined first by the circumstances of our birth and later by what draws us, the equality we try to create in civilization, or the cycles we come to accept in nature. There are some who would have it all one way. However, there seems to be room for both.

I look at the rifle in my hands—walnut stock, blue-black barrel, telescopic sight. Its ancestry is more closely connected to the industrial world than to any spear a hunter-gatherer carried across this country. Yet what it does in my hands—kill wild animals for food—is connected to our ancient relationship with the earth. I look over the morning clouds flowing down the valleys, and let my eyes climb to the ranges of conifer forest rising into the silver-and-yellow bands of sky to the east. The elk who live in these forests, the blueberries who grow in its understory, the streamside lettuce I put in my salads can't be grown by anyone. True, blueberries are cultivated, and elk are ranched in many places, but they aren't the same blueberries and elk as these wild ones, though they may bear the same genetic makeup. Wild elk, along with all the other creatures and plants of nature, are what the earth still provides from her initial grace. They can't be planted or harvested or ranched; they can only be received. Whether the means of receiving them is a spear, a gun, or one's plucking fingers matters less than the state of mind moving hands to action.

THE DAYS GROW COLD AND CLEAR, AND ELK ARE EVERYWHERE. I SEE them on the Sleeping Indian in the last light of the day, I see their prints crossing the snowy Ditch Creek Road, and Bob and I watch them on the west side of the Snake River, just inside the Grand Teton National Park boundary as we sit on Breadloaf Mountain, just outside the boundary. We have canoed down in the late afternoon, made camp in the willows, and climbed up the steep ridge. At dusk twenty elk—cows, calves, and young bulls—prance from the forest, safely inside the widely spaced but clearly visible metal stakes. Several more herds appear along the marshy bends of the river as the night falls, and geese fly from Yellowstone, honking and setting their wings.

One cow elk, curious but hesitant, walks very close to the boundary, and I watch her, thinking about whether I will shoot her if she crosses it. Three hundred yards off and from a good rest—why not? But I know I won't. Tonight I'm only "out looking," just as canoeing down the river I wasn't really hunting either. In both cases there would have been no stalk, which is what forces me to accept the elk's medium—smell, sound, and presence. The last is a difficult phenomenon to grasp, but you can understand it if you've sat under a tree, and looked up to see a great horned owl staring down at you. Or, leaning against a boulder, you've felt eyes behind your head. You turn—there's a cougar, lying on the rimrock, observing you. Presence.

During the following weeks I go out in the mornings and hunt the Ditch Creek drainages. In years past I have taken horses into the less roaded country along the Divide, but such hunts are a big to-do with trailers and panniers, and one pair of boots for riding and one for hiking, and the stock to feed and water, and a lot going on that isn't tied to what I do each day. I think of the cabin and the trailer as where I camp, and going hunting close by them as part of what I do while being home.

A three-hour loop takes me up Tangled Creek, over Moose Mountain, and down Hidden Ridge to the car. None of these names can be found on any map; they are my names, given over the years and for my use alone, which is the privilege of those who currently walk the country. They will die with me, just as the old Indian names for these places almost completely died with them. In fact, most of us can't even imagine that this continent, so seemingly blank when Europeans arrived, had already been explored and populated, and that nearly every ridge, valley, and swamp, every peninsula, beach, and cove—where people lived, gave birth to children, hunted, gathered plants, and died—had been named, with affection, with humor, and in memory of hard times. It wasn't a "wilderness" when Europeans first sighted it; it was *home* to a multitude of peoples, a revered and cared-for home.

Walking down Hidden Ridge, I find the prints and the beds of elk melted in the snow, elk pellets scattered over the pine needles, and the smell of elk lingering in the cold morning air. Sometimes when I'm up here, I hear a faint shot from a distant valley, and sometimes I catch a flash of blaze orange moving on a far ridge, and occasionally I see boot prints crossing my trail of the previous day. But almost always I'm alone, as today, and it makes me think that hunting, sifting along through the trees while talking with the country, can only really be done in land this quiet.

The broad top of Hidden Ridge narrows, and its sides fall into two parallel draws. Walking along with the cold southwest breeze in my face, I try to watch both sides of the ridge simultaneously, which is impossible, so I stop every few steps to search the trees to the right, and then to the left.

As I leave one stand of pines and begin to cross a hundred yards of steep, snowy meadow, I see seven cow elk standing at the very edge of the trees on the opposite side of the draw to my left. They are looking directly at me, and with no place to hide I stand perfectly still. They are about two hundred yards off, and I think that if I sit in the snow very slowly, and then quickly shoot I might get one of them. But they're close to the trees and could be gone in an instant. I could wound one.

They wheel and disappear into the forest, and I climb into the draw and go up the other side, where I find their tracks and begin to follow them through the woods. Their tracks are widely spaced and don't slow down for four hundred yards. Even then, they remain in a trot. Knowing I won't catch them, I dawdle, pondering, as I often do when I've had the opportunity to shoot and don't, how I came to the decision. Today, it was a quick but intricate train of logic, having its origins in my long-standing feeling about what sorts of pain can be sanctioned. Mulling over this question was what, at first, caused me to abandon hunting, and, upon further reflection, brought me back to it.

Bullfighting, cockfighting, dogfighting . . . shooting live pigeons and prairie dogs for "sport" and money . . . dropping cosmetics into rabbits' eyes so humans can have nonirritating and frivolous products . . . keeping calves in stalls for tender veal, and chickens in crowded, filthy boxes to increase production . . . wounding elk through carelessness—all of these examples, and thousands of others whose common denominator is disrespect, seemed to me to be gratuitous forms of pain that are best removed from the world. Different from them is the instrumental pain caused by the honest biological clamor of our guts' wanting to be fed and which seems irreducible.

Once, in an attempt to outwit this pain, I became a vegetarian, and stayed one for quite a while. But when I inquired about the lives lost on a mechanized farm, I realized what costs we pay at the supermarket. One Oregon farmer told me that half the cottontail rabbits went into his combine when he cut a wheat field, that virtually all of the small mammals, ground birds, and reptiles were killed when he harvested windrow crops like rye and sugar beets, and that when the leaves were stripped from bush beans all the mice and the snakes who were living among them were destroyed as well. Perhaps he exaggerated; certainly he hadn't taken a census of his fields' small-animal populations. Nonetheless, from boyhood, he had seen many animals being killed as he made America's food. Because most of these animals have been seen as expendable, or not seen at all, few scientific studies have been done measuring agriculture's effects on their populations. Those that have been done demonstrate that agricultural lands often act as "ecological traps," attracting birds, for instance, who begin their nesting only to have machinery pass over the land, destroying their nests and often the birds themselves. This is particularly true in the case of alfalfa, grown to feed livestock, but it also happens in corn, soybean, and spring wheat fields. When one factors in the lives lost to pesticides, the toll is enormous, and includes those species not commonly thought of as "pests": Canada geese, mallards, great blue herons, phalaropes, larks, waxwings, warblers, hawks, gulls, squirrels, and cottontails, to name a few species listed in one study that assessed the hazards of organophosphate pesticides on wildlife. And as one biologist told me, when you find dead birds, you're only finding what's been "hit over the head with a baseball bat." You don't see, except after several years, the decline in reproduction among these bird populations, which these pesticides also cause. Raised on a farm in Iowa, he went on to say that current agricultural practices, particularly combining, left the earth a "biological desert." Our fields might be brimming over with wheat and corn and soybeans, but unless we began to leave habitat for wildlife—stubble, hedgerows, and ditches—we were going to find ourselves in an austerely quiet world, as silent as the silent spring about which Rachel Carson warned . . . unless one counted the growl of tractors as song.

Such data, scanty as it is, addresses only the lives lost on the farm itself. When our produce is transported along the interstate highway system, birds . . . deer . . . skunks . . . raccoons all get flattened. Who hasn't witnessed the carnage? And this doesn't even begin to count the animals lost to the development of the oil fields themselves, the transportation of petroleum across tundra, mountain ranges, and the oceans, and in the wars fought over that oil. In short, being a supermarket vegetarian didn't take me out of the web in which animals are constantly dying to feed humans, it merely put their deaths over the horizon, making them, in the bloodless jargon of cost-accounting, externalities.

When I looked into that web, so full of pain, I came to see that my killing an elk each year did less harm, expressed in animal lives who I believe count equally, than importing the same amount of vegetable food to my bioregion. That didn't ease my conscience; but it did make the choices clearer. And just to be sure I wasn't kidding myself, I called the College of Agriculture and Life Sciences at Cornell University and asked Dr. David Pimentel, who has analyzed the fossil fuel costs of agriculture, to help me calculate the costs of some of the foods I was eating. When I was done, the numbers confirmed my intuition.

The 150 pounds of elk meat I get from a yearly elk costs the planet seventy-nine thousand kilocalories of fossil fuel energy. This takes into account my driving to and from my cabin to nearby roadheads, the energy it took to produce my automobile as well as the rifle I use each hunting season, and the cartridges that I hand load but whose components I buy. It also reckons the storage costs in electricity to freeze the meat in my chest freezer, a cost that decreases over the second half of the year when some of the elk has been jerked, and I can put the remaining meat in the freezer of my refrigerator, which is running anyway. It doesn't take into account the cost of producing the paper in which I wrap the butchered elk, or the plastic wrappers that the butcher in town uses when, occasionally, I have had to leave on a research project while the elk I had killed hung and aged, and I couldn't return in time to cut and wrap the meat myself. Nor does it take into account the other food I might eat besides elk, which powers me while I'm hunting and has a fossil fuel cost to produce as well, and it doesn't completely account for the winter feeding habits of the different elk I have shot. If an elk spends its winter on the National Elk Refuge, where it is fed alfalfa pellets spread by tractors, its fossil fuel costs rise. If it eats baled hay delivered by horses, on the upper Gros Ventre feedgrounds, its cost decreases. If it goes to neither area and spends the winter foraging in the Gros Ventre valley, its fossil fuel cost is zero. I have no way of telling what an individual elk I shoot in the fall has done the previous winter. I believe that over the years I have shot elk who have wintered in all three locations.

On the other hand, if I consume the equivalent caloric value of 150 pounds of elk in the form of Idaho potatoes, cultivated just on the other side of the Tetons, planet earth expends 151,000 kilocalories of fossil fuel energy, mostly in the form of the machinery used in planting and harvesting, and transporting the potatoes themselves. The fossil fuel cost of a calorically equivalent amount of rice and canned pinto beans, grown through the intensive use of fertilizers and irrigation, and imported a thousand miles from California, is quite a bit more—477,000 kilocalories. And as worldwide evidence has shown, as fossil fuel costs rise, more wildlife dies. I'm not saying I've totally given up eating Mexican food. But after doing my cost accounting, I found myself pressure cooking more dried pinto beans, and eating more elk and vegetables grown closer to home.

I realize that I could buy more organic produce, the environmentally sound choice of the conscientious consumer. However, in Jackson Hole, as in many small towns far from agricultural lands and interstate highways, organic produce isn't available with any regularity. I guess I could drive to Idaho Falls and pick it up, but that would increase its fossil fuel cost. Others who don't know this climate have suggested planting a garden that would remove me from the loop of agribusiness costs entirely. But, in this country, a garden that was supportive of a person's nutritional needs year-round would need a greenhouse, and for the long cloudy spells when solar heat wasn't available, it would have to be heated with fossil fuel or wood, the latter adding to the smog that plagues the valley during winter temperature inversions. Another externality.

One way to avoid using wood, or more fossil fuel, would be to plant an outdoor garden of potatoes, a high-altitude crop to be sure, which is exactly what I've done. In fact, my research assistant, Ruth, a gardener of some renown, helped me to figure the fossil fuel costs of organically growing 360 pounds of potatoes to replace my 150 pounds of elk. Forty-two thousand kilocalories was the sum, she said, a savings of thirty-seven thousand kilocalories and nearly one-half elk life per year. But she was quick to point out that the vegetables I saved for compost contained fossil fuel energy that hadn't been figured in her equation. She also pointed out that I would have to expand my little potato plot to .02 hectare, and that increasing the area cultivated would displace some wildlife from what had been its browse. What contribution this particular .02 hectare makes to the local deer and bisons' yearly nutritional requirements I cannot say. It is clear, though, that if enough people put .02 hectares into cultivation wildlife will suffer. And the costs of a garden don't stop here. The plot has to be watered, and the pump operating my well uses electricity, which of course has those costs associated with dams and coal-fired plants. There's also the small matter of keeping the Uinta ground squirrels, who range around the cabin by the hundreds, from eating every seed, shoot, and leaf. Fencing works, if the small-mesh chicken wire is placed well beneath the ground, but the wire, too, has its manufacturing costs in a mill far away, which I've never calculated. Often, the wily and persevering rodents manage to dig beneath the barricades, and the deer just leap over the fence.

Cats and dogs on patrol help to keep the squirrels scarce. But then one has merely shifted the burdens of squirrel control from live traps, or a .22 rifle in one's own hands, to the jaws of one's pets. Orion and Merle have never seemed to mind the duty. When my cat was alive, he would pile ground squirrels on the front step of the cabin, his record being five in an hour, and Merle continues to chase ground squirrels with never-ending glee, pouncing on them in a cloud of dust and flying sage, shaking their little bodies wickedly, and dropping them in the dirt, his tail wagging. There have been moments, watching my potatoes making their way up through the earth, when I have felt the complexity of this world hold my conscience in its claws. Which hasn't felt exactly bad, only humbling. Maybe that is what prey feels like when it finally stops struggling.

Despite these imperfections, planting an organic garden remains a less-harm solution to the conundrum of staying alive, and is one that I'll continue to pursue without giving up hunting what this bioregion grows. I'm not convinced that becoming an organic farmer is the way back to some innocence we have lost, or that it is the single-handed means by which we'll create a more conscientious future. Nor will I move away and become an organic farmer in a temperate climate better suited for agriculture. I'm attached to these cold places, still singing of glaciers and big mammals, and in my bones I know that farming has abandoned a connection to them, a relationship of provision by uncultivated land, and concern for that land by its inhabitants, that seems clearest while hunting well.

I believe that before the invention of agriculture hunter-gathers felt the same way about their country, later called "marginal" by those who tried to hoe it, and build on it, and own it. Hunters never thought in this way. Wandering seasonally, they didn't own more than their clothing and tools, and they certainly didn't own fenced-off pieces of the earth. Not owning land, or cultivating it, or building more than temporary structures on it, the ancient hunter-gatherers didn't have to protect it from wildlife, or, for a long time, from other roaming peoples who had their own territories. They ate the wildlife and plants it produced without substantially altering the landscape, and when they turned to agriculture as a way of supporting denser human populations, their worldview began to change.

Agriculture invested land with labor, which is different from wandering curiously, the hallmark of hunting and gathering. Land became valued by the time invested in its tillage and the return it produced. It became a human creation—loved for its melding of culture with nature—a concept that is markedly different from believing land to be out of one's control and intrinsically sacred. Not having to follow wildlife in an unencumbered fashion, farmers could accumulate possessions, and with possessions came the need for insurance—police, armies, and warfare—what we call history, and what I've thought of as our straightening the world into rows.

Having engineered our world for centuries, can we now learn from the inadequacy of our results and love the original, tangled world that remains, stepping off our civilized margins occasionally, and allowing ourselves to be enfolded in its crooked angles and ambiguous harmony? It is the experiment I have been trying, out here in the country, hunting; but it's certainly not one whose broader ground rules I invented.

In terms of an ethical imperative it was Aldo Leopold who first gave clear expression to the idea of our becoming more equal partners in the larger community composed of humans, animals, and landscape. Beginning his professional career as a forester in Arizona and New Mexico, he went on to write the first game-management text and eventually a slim volume of essays, A Sand County Almanac, in which he melded biology, ethics, and politics, counseling a less domineering role for humans in nature. Published in 1949, the essays describe what Leopold called "The Land Ethic."

"A thing is right," he wrote, "when it preserves the integrity, stability, and beauty of the biotic community. It is wrong when it tends otherwise." Such communities could not be created, said Leopold, until people changed their role "from conqueror of the land-community to plain member and citizen of it." He had learned these lessons firsthand when, thinking he was benefiting deer herds, he helped to exterminate predators in the Southwest. Only later did he see the same herds increase enormously, destroy their range, and starve. Agreeing with his idea of preserving the whole of a biotic community . . . a bioregion . . . an ecosystem—all three terms are currently used, but perhaps in this case a more apt name would be "my home"—I have judged hunting by this standard.

Obviously, shooting hurriedly, wounding, and losing a single elk, as I could have done this morning, wouldn't have markedly decreased the wholeness and continuity of the Yellowstone ecosystem. In fact, it would have provided an extra meal for some magpies and other scavengers. However, if enough people shoot indiscriminately, wounding and losing elk until the hunting season closed for the year, or they kill one, then the following hunting seasons will have to be shortened, or closed, to allow elk numbers to recover. More lost elk means that scavengers may temporarily benefit, but the elk population, as a whole, won't, nor will the country, and nor will its people. Those people who would have eaten elk, and who now cannot hunt because of closed seasons, may eat more beef or more vegetables, and eating more beef may contribute to more cattle being kept in cruel conditions, overuse of the range, and deforestation abroad, while consuming more vegetables increases the likelihood that other wildlife will become side-effect casualties in agricultural communities far away. And the people themselves will then be eating food that their bioregion doesn't grow and may become even more disconnected from the place in which they live and less likely to care for it. They will have lost what has been—for Leopold, for me, and for hunter-gatherers stretching back into the millennia—the foundation of an ethical relationship between people and their country, between culture and nature, and that is mindful participation.

This argument may seem farfetched (and it doesn't even begin to address how such participation harms *individual* creatures while preserving the integrity of their species), but it's used to point out the subtle webs of cause and effect that, until recently, most of us have been able to ignore. In elk's clothing, it is the old tragedies of the commons argument, in which the single sheep herder adds another animal to the commons, sacrificing everyone else's and his own future good for short-term profit. Regulation—local, state, and federal—can prevent the commons from being degraded by overuse and pollution, but there are many commons that are still, in large measure, outside of the regulatory loop. The ocean and the atmosphere are two examples; hunting mindfully is another.

This overall belief, concerning itself with preserving the integrity of a natural community and its resident species over the needs of any of its individuals, is known these days by the terms *holistic* or *deep* ecology. The argument of the deep ecologists won't fly, however, with many academic philosophers who believe in the individual rights of animals, rights postulated on the intrinsic evil of pain, and the prima facie duty of moral beings—people—not to cause pain to *any* sentient creature. This school of thought claims that deep ecologists are really "environmental fascists"—people who, because of their good-of-the-ecosystem beliefs, might judge a rare wildflower, a snail, or a spotted owl more valuable to the biotic community than humans, and so get rid of humans to save the flower, the mollusk, or the bird.

Since such triage rarely occurs, the proponents of animal rights maintain that deep ecology is, in reality, a muddle of hypocrisy. (It must be mentioned that, in the case of the spotted owl, a judgment for the animal has occurred on a modest scale, the endangered owl and its set-aside habitat having kept loggers from their livelihood in portions of the Pacific Northwest.) However, taken in the strict terms of the sentient tradition of animal rights, this accusation is in most instances true; but it is an accusation that overlooks the almost innate and irremediable speciesism of all species, including our own, and which operates in the animal rightists themselves.

In this case I'm using the word *speciesism* without its usual negative connotation of "racism" or "sexism." I'm giving it the implication of familial love. When push really comes to shove, and a choice must be made instantly and on a gut level, the animal rightist also reverts to this sort of familial love of the species, and first scoops up the babe in front of the oncoming car and then worries about the puppy. To make the case more graphic consider your child, and a neighbor's child, in front of the oncoming car, or abducted by a kidnaper, or in a burning building. Whom do you save first, if you can't save both? A heartrending choice. But probably family. This may be why people have eaten animals for millions of years, and, for the most part, haven't made a habit of eating each other.

Another group of academicians also finds the reasoning of the deep ecologists unsound, saying that it confuses fact and value, *is* and *ought.* In other words, what one *ought* to do as a moral agent cannot be derived from the ecological facts of what constitutes a healthy, natural ecosystem. If one does make such a derivation, as Leopold did, one has crossed a logical bridge between biology and ethics, which simply does not exist. On the other hand, some deep-ecology philosophers point out that the bridge is in fact quite intact, but merely omitted in practical argument. Though this debate can be heavy going for the nonacademician, it really is the crux of the matter, and one that can be expressed in plain language: If the world *is* a jungle, *ought* we participate in it?

For most of us this isn't even a question. We participate without thinking. Even Jains—an Asian vegetarian sect whose members wear gauze masks so as not to inhale and kill an insect or microbe—can't escape from inadvertently taking some forms of animal life when they eat crops others have grown. Yet, even though we participate in this "jungle," few of us would make the simultaneous claim that the Holocaust, the genocide perpetrated by the Khmer Rouge, or drive-by shootings in our inner cities have the slightest resemblance to what goes on, of necessity, as we and animals ingest others to keep functioning. One sort of death is fundamental and necessary; the other is malicious, twisted, and unnecessary.

These are clear distinctions. The greyer cases arise when we turn to how "necessary" food is produced. Does a free-ranging, adult steer qualify as a suitable candidate for "necessary food," whereas the calf, chained in its stall so that its flesh can become tender veal, fails the test, being as it is no more than a fillip for the jaded palate? How about geese who are force-fed to produce pâté de foie gras, or, a more down-to-earth example, the countless, penal-colony chickens crammed in their boxes so Colonel Sanders can keep America licking its fingers? Is the elk shot by me any more or less a necessary death than these or that of the thousands of rabbits and mice inadvertently destroyed in the process of growing and harvesting my organic, all natural, oat bran breakfast cereal?

I would argue that making clearer, more compassionate choices from such a multitude of daily options is the most important task of our lives, and is precisely what the poet, Robinson Jeffers, gets at when he says, ". . . morality/Is not an end in itself: truth is an end." And a poignant one it is. The elk in the forest, the tuna at sea, the myriad of small creatures lost as the combines turn the fields, even the Douglas fir hidden in the walls of our homes—every day we foreclose one life over another, a never-ending triage, a constant choice of who will suffer so that we may live, bending a blue note into the neatness of morality. It is this tender pain between species that is the plasma bearing us all along.

Given this condition and my final inability to escape from it, I decided to go back to hunting . . . hunting because it attaches me to this place and the animals I love, asking me to own what each of us ought to own in some personal way—the pain that runs the world. And hunting elk in particular because they are the loved totem of my home . . . because this home makes them and leaves them free . . . and because eating them does nothing to increase the aggregate pain of the world. In fact, by attaching me lovingly here, the relationship between elk and me decreases it.

All of this I have known most keenly walking in this forest, with the wind in my face, and pine in my nostrils, and snow under my boots. None of which means that someone else, trying the same experiment, would have reached a similar conclusion about how to treat animals. In the end, I think you have to *listen,* and if you can't *listen* to the quiet sadness of this world, a lifetime of roaming the outdoors, or thinking in libraries, is not going to tell you that the country is you and you are it, and when you cause it to suffer needlessly then you have broken a cord of sympathy, which is a much more demanding tie to nature than any system of ethics.

The elk prints emerge from tree line, cross the windswept southern flank of the ridge, circle around the basin, and head toward Turpin Creek. On the saddle separating the two drainages, the elk themselves stand and watch me. Six hundred yards off. Having hunted this far, I simply watch them. The ballistic Hail Mary has never been part of my repertoire.

They turn and disappear into the next valley. I have a suspicion that most of the other elk in Ditch Creek have gone there also. The upper parks of Turpin Creek are farther from the road and more secluded. I tell myself that in the morning I'll get up early and hike into Turpin. But several days go by, and the snow grows crunchier, before I find the energy for a four A.M. start.

E I G H T

—>><<—

WHEN I FINISH MY CHORES—THE KINDLING SPLIT, THE CLEAR PLAS-
tic insulation put over the cabin's windows, the studded tires mounted
on the car—the temperature has fallen to its late November lows. As I
leave the cabin my face stings in the fifteen below air, and as I put my
pack in the car, I see an enormous shooting star fall from the dark and
glittering sky. It falls straight as a plumb line, down to the notch where
the Gros Ventre River emerges from the hills, and as it falls it seems to
float, like a phosphorescent flare. Then it vanishes over the horizon. I
recall how the Bushmen believe that such a star means that one of them
has fallen over and is lying in the dark, waiting for the star of the morning to show them the way. I never have had the same mournful feeling
about falling meteors—my experience has been that good luck has followed my seeing them. But this star fell directly into Turpin Creek, and
perhaps spoke for the elk I think I will find this morning.

   In the first light, I hike up the west ridge of the drainage, feeling the
sweat dampen my shoulders against the small pack, which contains my
food and extra clothing. Across the Snake River plain, the very summits
of the Tetons, like the lips of a seashell, turn a pale, soft ivory. When I
look into Turpin Creek, I can just begin to make out its boggy meadows
narrowing into a canyon along whose rim I climb. On the far side of the
gorge, parks rise into stands of fir and pine, and I pause, search with my
binoculars . . . walk on . . . glass. Almost immediately, I feel elk in the
air, elk on the wind, and elk moving, and all the thoughts of the last
weeks—how I hunt, and why I hunt—become lost in just the hunting,
my thoughts, and pondering, and calculation left behind with the darkness and the shooting star.

Upward I climb, the travelling becoming easier on the ridge crest where the prevailing southwestern wind has packed the snow into the consistency of concrete. A cornice spills over the ridge to my right, and I stay away from its edge, not wanting to break through it and fall into the valley below. Shivering in the wind, I stop, putting on a jacket and hat. As I dress I see them on the opposite side of the valley—three cow elk walking through a park, going from the aspen on its south margin to the lodgepole pines on its north. The pines merge into firs and spruce, which descend the steep slopes to Turpin Creek. I suspect the elk are going into the trees to bed, where protected by the crunchy snow they'll be unapproachable.

They're a little more than a mile away, line of sight, longer by the way I must go—down into the valley, across its bottom, and up the other side—and at the speed they're travelling, I won't have enough time to stalk them. The grey sky has turned the faintest blue, and I know that the elk will vanish into the conifers before I can cover the distance. In fact, it's impossible to get off the ridge through the cornice.

I continue climbing north, and a few hundred yards farther on, still watching the elk across the valley, I notice four or five more cows in the park just above the first three. They're obviously part of the same herd; but these animals graze calmly. Their easiness, and their sense of security in their high, high meadow, makes me feel that my chances of reaching them may be greater than I at first thought. They are probably not used to people climbing after them.

In another few minutes I'm able to find a ridgelet leading through the cornice and down to the valley floor. There I follow moose tracks through the willow and across the frozen creek. On the other side of the valley, I climb steadily through the forest while trying to keep my breathing quiet. A half hour later, near the meadow in which I first saw the three elk, I stop and wait, feeling my pulse drop its cadence. A few stalks of grass stand in the snow before me, not moving in the least. I rub some of the grass seeds between my fingers and toss them into the air. They fall straight down. Picking the dullest-looking snow, which is the softest, and keeping to the trees, I creep upward. As I near the edge of the the meadow, I kneel, then lie in the snow, and crawl forward until I can just see over a snowdrift. The meadow is empty.

Crawling higher, I find the tracks of the first three cows, heading into the stand of conifers through which I've just climbed. I cross their trail, pass through another stand of aspen, and find the meadow in which I saw the half-dozen cows. It, too, is empty. Their many tracks have trampled the snow. Kneeling, I take off my glove and touch some droppings. They're soft and warm.

For a moment I think of tracking these elk into the forest but the snow seems far too noisy to do this successfully, and the top of the park beckons. Walking through the frozen crust, I angle toward two lodgepoles that form a gate leading to the next meadow. But I go no more than fifty yards before seeing an elk behind them. Its head is down and it is intent on its grazing. I step right, putting the nearer tree between the elk and me, and walk directly toward the trunk where I crouch among its branches, getting some of their resin on my face. I let out a quiet breath, look up at the sky, then peer through the needles. The elk is a spike bull—illegal. I watch him as he grazes toward the pines. Just ahead of me more tracks head in that direction. When the bull walks behind a few aspen, I start to follow the tracks, taking one careful but noisy step every few seconds.

At the edge of the lodgepoles, I stand for a long time, nostrils wide, sucking the air. Musky, the smell comes, vanishes, stays. Elk. I slow my pace to almost no movement at all.

Drifting among the trees . . . pausing . . . waiting . . . I hear the crunch of a footstep ahead of me. I pause, waiting to hear it again before taking a step of my own. Crunch . . . I take a step and wait. Not forty yards off and a little to my left stands an elk, its ruddy hindquarters and left flank facing me. I remain motionless—watching and waiting, and barely breathing—for it to raise its head. It's another spike bull.

I stand while he paws the snow and grazes. A red squirrel scampers in a tree above me, but, inexplicably, this habitual watchman of the woods ignores me. Then I spot another elk, perhaps fifty yards off and to my right, appearing and reappearing along the forest edge as it grazes. It wears no antlers. Then I spot a fourth elk, closer to me and a much clearer shot. I look at it through the rifle's scope. But it's the first spike bull whom I saw.

Waiting, I listen to the nearest elk chewing. When he takes a step, crunching the snow, I take a step toward the cow. But slowly, ever so slowly, she recedes from me. I go to a knee, and try to sight on her. Fallen logs block my view. I stand again, move slightly left, which is even worse for a clear shot. I have to wait a long time before an elk footfall lets me move back to the right. She is now screened by many thick branches.

Several minutes go by and I hear more elk in the distance . . . in the thicker trees falling steeply to the headwaters of the creek. But I see no way of getting closer to them. The spike bull is twenty-five yards off, and in another two steps I'll be within his circle of awareness. Without scent or sound from me, he will sense my presence. Moving only my eyes, I watch the cow elk reemerge from the trees and stand at their edge. She is large and without calf.

Slowly, she angles away from me. In a few more steps she will be gone from sight and down the steep north slope. In the many miles walked this fall, among all the elk I've seen, she has become the possible elk—the elk approached with care, the elk close to home, the elk seen far enough into the season so that soon the season will be over . . . the elk whom the morning, the snow, and the elk themselves have allowed me to approach. Only the asking remains.

"Mother elk," I say. "Please stop." I speak the words in my mind, sending them through the trees and into her sleek brown head. She crosses an opening in the forest, and there, for no reason I can understand, she pauses, her shoulder and flank visible.

It is a clear shot, though not a perfect one—I have to stand at full height to make it. But I know I can make it and I say, "Thank-you. I am sorry." Still I hesitate, for though I can lose myself in the hunting, I have never been able to stop thinking about its results—that I forget it's *this* elk rather than *that* elk who is about to die; that it's *this* creature whom I'm about to take from the world rather than some number in an equation proving the merits of wild-food harvesting over being a supermarket vegetarian; that this being before me—who sees, who smells, who *knows*—will no longer be among us, so that I may go on living. And I don't know how to escape this incongruous pain out of which we grow, this unresolvable unfairness, other than saying that I would rather be caught in this lovely tragedy with those whom I love, whom the ground beneath my feet has created alongside me, than with those far away, whose deaths I cannot own. Not that I think all this. I know it in my hesitation.

Still she stands, strangely immobile. I raise the rifle, and still she stands, and still I wait, for there have been times that I have come to this final moment, and through the air the animal's spirit has flown into my heart, sending me its pride and defiance, or its beseeching, frightened voice, saying, "I am not for you." And I have watched them walk away. She sweeps her eye across the forest and begins to graze down the north slope, exposing her flank for one more instant, and allowing me to decide. I listen, hearing the air thrum with the ambivalence of our joining, about which I can only say, once again, "I am sorry." As she disappears from sight, I fire behind her left shoulder, the sound of the shot muffled by the forest.

Then she's gone, and the woods are alive with the sound of hooves and branches crashing. I run forward, seeing a dozen cows and an enormous six-point bull stream from the pines and climb into the upper meadow, full of aspen. They pause and look back at me, but I can't see the elk I fired at. For one instant I think of shooting another cow as they stand and stare—the easiest shot imaginable. But I know I hit the animal I shot at.

As I start forward, the elk wheel and run up through the white trees, their tan rumps bobbing. Then they disappear into the next stand of conifers. In a few more steps I see an elk lying in the swale below me, her legs tucked under her, her head erect. She jumps up and moves off at an ungainly trot. I fire, and miss, and she disappears behind a small knob of pines that juts into the aspen.

I climb over several fallen trees and find her lying not thirty feet away, her head turned over her left shoulder, great brown eyes utterly calm. My heart tears apart.

I shoot and she drops her head. As she kicks her final shudders I go to her, sitting with my hip against her spine, my hand on her flank, feeling her warmth, her pulse, her life, changing states. She is enormous, and beautiful, and my throat constricts. Her right cheek lies on the snow; her nose is moist; her eye stares into the heaven, now blue with the morning.

She kicks several more times, gasps once, and lies still, a great, reddish-brown creature, her rear legs straight, her front ones tucked under her. There isn't a speck of blood anywhere.

After a few minutes I take off my pack, unload the rifle, and lean it against an aspen. Then I sit on a log, all the concentration that produced this death gone, and I just watch her—her brown mane, her dark legs, the taut muscles under her ruddy haunches. Beyond our grove of pines is a small meadow. It runs to the edge of the slope and falls like a waterfall of white snow to the headwaters of Turpin Creek far below. The opposite hillsides rise abruptly—bare aspen, grey cliffs, a burrow in the snow that must be a coyote den, a summit line of green spruce.

I pour a cup of tea, and after a few sips begin to feel it warm my insides. Holding the cup to my mouth in both my hands, I see my face reflected on the surface of the tea and my dark brown eyes, always so full of yes and no. I set the cup on the log and sigh.

Taking out my knife, I slit the hide on her belly. Using my fingers

under the knife as a shield, so as not to cut her viscera, I open her perito-
neum and go inside her up to my elbows. As I puncture her diaphragm,
steam emerges around my shoulders with a gasp. Cutting away her heart,
I feel hot blood bathe my arms, which is what the old hunter-gatherers
knew when, in a cold, cold world, they found improbable warmth . . . life
. . . in the bodies and blood of mammals.

After I pull out her stomach and intestines, I open her pelvic girdle
with the saw, being careful not to rupture her bladder or rectum. As I
start skinning her I discover a piece of meat on my finger. I put it in my
mouth, chew it, and swallow it. She tastes like warm, raw elk.

It takes about an hour to skin her, and as she passes under my hands
I note what she is as food—the layer of white fat on her hips, which is
good for frying pancakes and for mixing into pemmican; the steaks decreasing in tenderness from the loins to her rump; the burger, jerky,
kabob, and sausage. I smile because I can feel saliva lubricating my
mouth. Going in the other direction, I smell what she has been—her hair
smells of pine, her meat of grass, her fat like the undersides of rocks.

Then I saw her into quarters, the hardest job, and the warmest. I'm
down to my shirt as the sun begins to shine into our snowy north-facing
dell, and the temperature feels as if it finally goes above zero. I hang her
two hindquarters in a nearby aspen that has been tilted over by the wind.
I also hang her shoulders there, and put each side of her rib cage on a
downed aspen. Then I fold the hide and place it alongside the rib cage.
The liver and heart I bury in the snow so the Canadian jays, already
pecking at the fat around her intestines, will leave them alone.

I wash my hands with snow, have another cup of tea, then I take her
hooves and place them on a nearby rise that looks north across the valley.
I place her head on top of her legs. Her eyes have sunken a bit forward and
are no longer wide and glistening. Sometimes I have used the head,
boiling off its meat and eating the tongue. Today I don't. Kneeling by
her hooves and head, I stroke her long brown hair and say a few more
words.

When I rise and walk back to my pack her smell follows me—my
hands are covered with her pine-scented musk. I take my pack and rifle
and go back the way I came, following my tracks a short distance then
angling away from them on the north side of the slope. Descending into
thicker forest, I find a dozen elk beds. Backtracking their spoor, I find
myself in the meadow where the elk grazed as I first noticed them from
the opposite side of the valley.

Going to the spot where I first saw the young bull, I track my own prints into the woods, a distance of not more than two hundred yards, though it took a half hour to stalk it. At the place from where I shot, I examine how my footprints stepped back and forth as I tried to find an opening. Standing in the last prints I made before jumping into a run, I find the tunnel through the boughs, raise the rifle again, sight down the opening, and one more time replay the shot, wondering how it could have gone high. I let the sight follow my heartbeat and know how it happened—having deliberated so long, I hurried through that fraction of a second in which I should have been patient and steady. It's no excuse. It's what happened this year.

Walking back into the meadow I'm surprised by the suddenness of the Tetons—right there, standing over the next westward ridge. For hours I had forgotten them. To the south lies the gorge of the Gros Ventre River, and rising from it the Sleeping Indian, heavy with spruce, shadowed, mysterious. I stop, cock an ear. Faintly . . . growing louder . . . moving down the river, comes the out-of-sync honking of geese, sweet and floating up the creek, while behind me a raven caws, having spotted the pile of entrails.

In the afternoon, accompanied by Merle, I return with a toboggan, and I'm startled to find that the liver and heart have already disappeared to a coyote. A line of paw prints and a bloody drag mark lead into the woods. Merle, overwhelmed at the smell and sight of so much meat, lies somberly, his golden brow furrowed, as I lash a quarter to the sled. Then we slide it down to the road, the first of what will be several trips.

The stars are out when I finally hang the quarter on the north side of the shed by the trailer. Tired in every joint, I stop at Trisha's yurt to tell her the news. Her boys are visiting their dad, and she asks if I would like some dinner. She wears sweatpants and a T-shirt, and still has on her snowpacks. I wash my hands while she cooks a pot of spaghetti and asks me about the elk—particularly did she fall right over? When I tell her the story she says, "I wish it didn't seem so unfair, using guns." Stirring the sauce, she pushes her gold-grey hair from her eyes, which are wet.

Feeling my own eyes well up, I gently toss my head to the package of turkey sausage defrosting on her counter.

"I know," she says, "I know," and closes the subject.

While I finish my dinner she makes up her bed.

"I think I may go up to the cabin tonight," I say, putting the plate in the sink.

"Are you still in Turpin Creek?"

I nod and she sighs.

Driving up to the cabin, I think about what a long day it has been, and how it isn't over yet. Putting on a warmer coat, I walk under the Milky Way—up the road to the top of the hill, and back toward the Gros Ventre, until I see a shooting star, and find this elk, wandering in the hum of the sky, and in the steady tumble of the distant river.

"I HAD POLAR BEARS AND GRIZZLY BEARS AND BLACK BEARS AND pronghorns and African lions and Bengal tigers," says Wayne Pacelle. "I mean I could go to 'B' in the encyclopedia and I would just hit a certain page and open the book and I'd come to a certain animal whose particular history I had memorized."

We're driving inside the Beltway, heading toward Wayne's Silver Spring, Maryland, home. It's Super Sunday and we've spent the morning standing in the cold outside of a local market named Magruder's, protesting their selling "genuine trophy-mounted buffalo heads" for fifteen hundred dollars to promote today's Super Bowl between the Washington Redskins and the Buffalo Bills.

Wayne, the twenty-six-year-old director for the most well organized and vocal antihunting organization in the United States, The Fund For Animals, is tall and darkly handsome, and has the politician's device of leaning back and sticking out his center to create a podium from which to look down at you. Unable to project himself from the passenger's seat of the rental car that I'm driving, he projects his voice, which is resonant and refined. "So I've always had an affinity for wildlife, and the direct assault made on that wildlife by hunters and trappers has always infuriated me. Even when I went out on a couple fishing operations, just when people were fishing you know, I was disgusted and so appalled by the animals suffocating in the air. I was less than ten."

His black hair falls to his dark eyebrows; his nose is a little too fleshy to be classic; his lips are sensuous; a hint of beard stains his cheeks and strong chin, and he wears jeans, running shoes, and a comfortable blue shirt. Across the back of his high-collared, black coat the words SEA SHEPHERD CREW are written. The *Sea Shepherd* is the vessel that has gone around the world, sabotaging whalers and disrupting seal hunts.

"At the same time," he says, making sure that I don't misunderstand him, "I don't have a hands-on fondness for animals. I did not grow up with dozens of dogs and cats as many people did. To this day I don't feel bonded to any particular nonhuman animal. I like them and I pet them and I'm kind to them, but there's no special bond between me and other animals. The reason that I campaign on the issue of animal rights is that I intensely dislike suffering, and the fact that humans unnecessarily perpetrate suffering on animals. It's more of an intellectual/philosophical motivation than it is a hands-on one."

Abstractly motivated though he may be, he knows his politics. When Cleveland Amory, the founder of The Fund For Animals, offered him the position of executive director three and a half years ago, Wayne told the senior member of America's animal rights movement that he had no salary requirements and no constraints on his travel, or the time he would invest. The only thing he wanted to do was develop a national antihunting campaign. "Both Cleveland and I noted," he says, "how the hunting community, in particular the outdoor press, overreacts to everything. We thought that even a limited amount of activity would generate a fire-and-brimstone response from them which would serve our purpose. As the issue is discussed, especially in an unintelligible way, we win. When issues aren't discussed the status quo is retained."

Capitalizing on America's increasing urban populations, who have little day-to-day intimacy with wildlife, he has successfully halted proposed hunts through the courts and the ballot, most notably in California. He also has organized "Hunt Sabs" in the East, sabotages or disruptions of legal hunts on public lands, the object of which is to scare animals away from hunters while simultaneously talking to the hunters about the wrongness of what they're doing. He's been arrested fourteen times, not only for civil disobedience associated with animal rights causes, but also for antiapartheid demonstrations while he was a Western history and environmental studies major at Yale. He has always been acquitted or has had the charges dropped. Wondering if he is a self-made social reformer, or if his parents were also active in the movement, I ask him about his background.

He lets out a small laugh, points to the tree-lined, semiurban streets through which we're driving, and says that his boyhood home in New

Haven was cut "of the same cloth" and had a "multiethnic" background. His father was a schoolteacher and Italian, his mother a secretary and Greek. He grew up in a large, extended family, none of whose members spoke against hunting. "They just didn't do it," he says, adding that his training in political protestation was born when he began to fight his mother's attempt to get him to go to church. "That was where I perhaps developed the limited persuasion abilities that I might have today." Smiling at this bit of self-deprecation, he adds, "I argued vociferously that it was much more meaningful for me to watch Aquaman who led all the animals against the villains than it was for me to be bored while someone spoke literally Greek to me. That cartoon was my favorite. I don't know if you remember it. It was the aquatic equivalent of an *Animal Farm* situation where this guy would fight bad guys by sending out this signal to sea horses and dolphins and sharks, and they would all fight against the villains."

At his house, a white brick just off one of the main arteries leading into Washington, D.C., we find Gretel, a feisty dachshund, and Reiley, a thin black lab, languishing on a dilapidated sofa. They jump up to greet us, and true to his word, Wayne ignores them, mentioning, as he goes to the telephone answering machine, that Reiley steals his socks and that both dogs are vegetarians—he points to a case of canned food on one of the end tables. The animals belong to his housemates, both of whom are workers for PETA (People for the Ethical Treatment of Animals).

While he listens to his messages, I look around. The backyard is full of leaves; the kitchen looks as if it's rarely used; hardwood stairs lead to the second-floor landing where a poster of two forlorn canines and a primate says VICTIMS OF VIVISECTION. A disheveled bathroom stands between the two closed doors. The third bedroom is Wayne's. It retains the air of a college dorm.

A closet disgorges suits and rumpled clothes onto the floor, a double bed lies unmade, and a file cabinet holds a small tape cassette player. A large desk is covered with newspapers, and above it hangs a photo of a breaching grey whale. On the opposite wall is a poster of a mountain lion that says, FOREVER WILD AND FREE CALIFORNIA COUGARS—a memento to Wayne's greatest achievement, the stopping of mountain lion hunting in California.

He joins me as I look at his overflowing bookcase. Moving aside a few magazines, he pulls out a copy of *Without Consent or Contract,* and finds the passage that he has mentioned he wants to read to me. " 'For 3,000 years—,' " he begins, " 'from the time of Moses to the end of the seventeenth century—virtually every major statesman, philosopher, theologian, writer, and critic accepted the existence and legitimacy of slavery. The word "accepted" is chosen deliberately for these men of affairs and molders of thought neither excused, condoned, pardoned, nor forgave the institution. They did not have to; they were not burdened by the view that slavery was wrong. Slavery was considered to be part of the natural scheme of things. "From the hour of their birth," said Aristotle, "some are marked out for subjection, others for rule." ' " Closing the book upon his finger, and giving me a direct look, he adds, "The same can be said of animals."

Opening the book again, he runs his finger down an accompanying table, "Chronology of Emancipation 1772–1888." The first date is when Lord Chief Justice Mansfield ruled that slavery was not supported by English law, laying the legal basis for the freeing of England's fifteen thousand slaves, the second marks Brazil's being the last nation to free its chattels.

"Social change proceeds like evolution," he says, "sometimes slowly and other times rapidly in punctuated equilibrium, just as Stephen Jay Gould proposes for biological evolution." Giving me another deep look from under his thick brows, he adds, "What we're now seeing is a period of rapid social change with regard to animal rights."

That point made, and his messages collected, we drive across town to a Super Bowl party given by one of his fellow workers at the Fund, Heidi Prescott. As Wayne directs me through a maze of suburban housing developments, I tell him that I'm still puzzled by his being committed to animal rights without having had any hands-on relationship with animals. He says that isn't exactly true. There has been one pivotal experience—his watching wolves and moose interact naturally on Isle Royale. Though he never actually saw a wolf while on the island, he came to believe that "animals could live without being manipulated by people." Thereafter, natural regulation of ungulates and prey, with humans trying their utmost to be no more than observers, became the management model he has advocated.

"Do you think that people were once a natural, interactive part of their ecosystems?" I ask.

"Maybe before the invention of agriculture," he says.

"Do you think that it's possible for modern people who hunt to have a respectful relationship with landscape and animals?"

"There's no question that the shooting of some animals can be a sustainable activity," he says, gliding off the question. "I consider it more relevant to ask, 'Is it necessary as a management tool?' and I think in almost all circumstances it's not a necessary component to have a generalized sport hunting season. I'm not saying I don't believe in management. I firmly believe in management. But I think that lethal controls should be the last course, and it should be management on a nuisance basis, and only after animals have been identified as causing some problems."

"That's not what I asked."

He looks at me eagerly, eyes bright. He has told me that he has looked forward to our meeting and our engaging in one of his favorite pastimes, "polemic."

"What I mean is, would you let people hunt for food if they did it respectfully?"

"Well, it's a good question," he says, pondering what he's about to say. "I think that I would campaign against it. Yes, I think that I would. I believe in a majoritarian democracy. I believe in a market-oriented society as a political, economic philosophy, but it needs to be tempered. And I think that we need to have tolerance for minority views and minority rights, but I think that people cross the threshold when they harm others."

"So harm is the bottom line?"

"Yes. At baseline I'm against cruelty. I embrace the ideas of Henry Bergh who founded the ASPCA in 1866. He was an individual who stepped out of societal standards, and said we want to stop something that is going on. I consider myself following that tradition and taking it a step further, that is, establishing legal protection for animals, which is a logical extension of liberalism."

Feeling that we may have some common ground, I explain my least-harm theory to him, whereby a person hunting in their bioregion causes less harm to sentient wildlife by hunting some large food animals than by importing the equivalent amount of vegetable food produced through the use of fossil fuels. I also mention that I think this is quite in keeping with Tom Regan's "miniride principle." Tom Regan is the philosopher from North Carolina State University who has written one of the most closely reasoned books on the subject of the interrelationship of people and animals, and who represents the scholarly side of animal rights as Wayne represents the political. In *The Case for Animal Rights,* he describes the miniride principle, short for "the minimize overriding principle," as that situation in which "we must choose between overriding the rights of many who are innocent or the rights of few who are innocent, and when each affected individual will be harmed in a prima facie comparable way." When these conditions are met, "then we ought to choose to override the rights of the few in preference to overriding the rights of the many."

"That's very interesting," says Wayne, clasping his hands and for the first time appearing truly uncomfortable at hearing an argument that, couched in rightist terminology, still produces a conclusion through which some life is harmed. "I've never heard it put quite that way, and I would like to hear what Tom has to say about it."

"I would too."

"We'll call him tomorrow," says Wayne.

"Excellent."

"In the meantime, I will say that . . . take a right there. No, no. After the stop sign. I'll say that agriculture is the way of least harm, light agriculture, organically produced, and an agriculture that is in the appropriate region, not the California desert."

"But being a farmer doesn't give me the same feeling about living in the place I live."

"I don't care how you feel," he says flatly. "I care that animals are being harmed."

I nod.

"I also believe in interstate transport of food items," he continues. "I believe in providing that food to people in other regions where it cannot be locally produced. My ethic is not a local food production ethic. It's an interlocal, interstate, and perhaps an international system of food distribution to allow people to tread lightly on the planet, and it should be a food production system that is as energy efficient as possible, and hopefully one day it will be an energy-based system that's not driven by fossil fuels."

"But are you a proponent of endless agriculture for endless people?"

"Oh, no, no. I don't believe in the green revolution as a means of feeding the world, and I certainly don't plan to have children. I take it as a very serious personal responsibility not to put another consumer on this planet."

After stopping for potato chips, pretzels, and beer, and making only two more wrong turns, we find Heidi Prescott's town house. She's the national outreach director for the Fund and is famous—the first person to go to jail for animal rights. Rustling leaves with her feet during a public hunt at a Maryland wildlife management area, she was fined five hundred dollars under a state law that forbids the harassment of hunters. Refusing to pay the fine, she spent fifteen days in jail, which opened her eyes to the plight of inmates.

Heavy set, jovial, and blonde, she has told me, "If I gave up animal rights and zero population work, I'd go into prison reform." At twenty-nine, she's already had her tubes tied for four years and declares that "she's never regretted the decision." After all "population is the bottom line."

She leads us down to her finished basement where a TV blares and food has been laid out on a table alongside it—vegetarian chili, chips, salsa, soft drinks, and beer. As we watch the Redskins demolish the Bills, Peter Wood, one of Wayne's housemates, and a worker for People for the Ethical Treatment of Animals, joins us. An abrasive New Yorker with stickers like MEAT STINKS and FUR IS DEAD plastered on the back of his Ford Bronco, he has been upset with Wayne for allowing my visit and letting an enemy in their camp. Sitting on the edge of the couch, with Wayne between us, he now leans toward me and vents. "Tell me," he says, his eyes blazing, "do you get pleasure out of killing? I lead a normal life. I have a good time. And I don't have to kill things."

"No, I don't get pleasure."

"Then why do you do it?"

"For food."

"I eat vegetables," he snarls, "and I lead a normal life." Unable to stay in the same room with me, he stalks upstairs.

"Peter has a rough edge," says Wayne.

In a few minutes he returns, sits down with ill-concealed agitation, and demands, "Do you hunt with a gun?"

"You bet."

"What's the sport in that? Why don't you use a bow and arrow?"

"I thought you guys were against primitive weapons because they're cruel."

Muttering something under his breath, he gets up and leaves.

"You know you walked into the belly of the beast here," says Wayne.

We don't stay until the end of the game. Wayne has work to do at home in preparation for an upcoming lecture tour. While I unroll my sleeping bag on the floor of his bedroom, he makes a few phone calls then comes upstairs in a chatty mood. Sitting at his desk, he asks about the trophy hunters with whom I've travelled—where do they come from, what do they do for a living—seeming to file what I tell him in some mental folder for future use. He notes with particular relish that all the trophy hunters I accompanied are members of Safari Club International, as if this is exactly what he expected.

Then he picks my brain about the Greenlanders with whom I lived. After hearing about their seal and narwhal hunts, he says, "I'm not going to say that I support what they do, nor will I say that I oppose it. I will say this: I can understand that they want to retain their distinct cultural food-gathering activity. But does someone in New York City have an obligation to buy a sealskin coat or a fur coat to keep that market alive?"

This seems like an excellent phrasing of the issue, but I'm too sleepy to continue the discussion. It is now past midnight.

"But why do they stay there?" he asks. He is wide awake and fired up for talking.

"What?"

"Why do the Greenlanders stay there? What's the name of the place—" He pulls at the air with a hand.

"Kullorsuaq."

"Yeah. It seems like such a barren place to live."

Of all the questions we've discussed, this one seems to have the most obvious answer. I say, "It's their home."

He shrugs and turns to the stack of newspapers on his desk. Long after I've fallen into fitful sleep, I hear him turning the pages of *The New York Times* and *The Washington Post*.

The alarm wakes us in the dark and Wayne marches off to his shower. Other than brushing his teeth, he claims showering to be his only form of ritual. When he's done I have to hurry, for we're already late and the day is tightly scheduled: a lecture at the Duke Ellington School of the Arts in the morning, followed by a radio show, followed by campaign work at the Fund office, followed by a dinner meeting with a potential donor.

He's in uniform quickly—light-charcoal-grey suit, raspberry-colored tie, pinstripe shirt, black belt, and matching dress shoes. In case I mistake the origins of his belt and shoes, Wayne points out their synthetic composition, saying that they're as stylish as any leather product, and adds that all the cosmetics, shampoos, and detergents in his house have not been tested on animals. He wears a plain gold watch and his dark brown eyes are fresh and clear despite his few hours of sleep.

He drinks no coffee; he has no breakfast; we drive directly to the high school, climb a tiled stairwell, and not long after rolling out of bed he faces a dozen sweatshirted, leather-jacketed, gum-chewing, Walkman-listening seniors, in a class called "Alternatives to Violence." There are several white students in the class, the rest are black. The young women have hairdos sculpted into daggers and sit with their heads cocked over one shoulder; the young men slouch in their chairs, their Reeboks crossed; they call out their names: "Elston, Camise, Jason."

"Hey," says Wayne, putting a little jive into his fine Yale accent, "did we do it to those Bills?"

"Yeah, man! Oh, yeah! Redskins wo!" Shouts and cheers.

He's got 'em.

"How many of you have seen *E.T.*?"

The entire class raises their hands.

"Who can tell me what it's about?"

After the class makes a group effort to summarize the plot, he says, "Well what if an extraterrestrial decided to come to earth and eat us, or wear our skins for clothing? Would that be right?"

"It'd be wrong to skin and mount us," says one tall fellow without raising his head from hand, "but if they can't eat nothing else that'd be okay."

"But what if they had a choice," says Wayne. "What if they could eat corn? Does might make right?" And he dives into his statistics about the meat industry, not the Fund's major target, but, as he has told me, one that these high school students can relate to better than the issue of hunting wild animals.

"Six-point-six billion," he says in a loud voice, "Billion-with-a-*B* animals killed in the U.S. to feed humans who can eat other things. Thirty-four million cows, eighty-five million pigs who are more intelligent than dogs. How many of you have a dog or a cat? Can they think?"

"You bet! Yeah, man!"

"Five billion—BILLION with a *B*—chickens, two hundred million animals shot by hunters, seventy million animals used in labs, fifty million killed in the fur trade."

He stares at them in their leather jackets, the juice of their breakfast McMuffin still on their lips, and says, "Is palate preference a sufficient reason to take the life of an animal? That's the question you're going to have to answer." If there were a jury rail before him, he would be leaning on it. He looks over their heads, takes a breath, and goes on. "What a social change movement is about is altering what exists right now. It's changing things for the better and tradition is no defense. Like when some people decided to end slavery in this country others claimed *tradition* and *need.* But some people . . ."

As he leads into his favorite analogy of slavery, a few of the students slump in their chairs, others look at their hands. Wayne starts to go red in the face. "What was decided," he says, looking flustered, "was that one group couldn't control another." Avoiding the words *black, white,* or *slavery,* he crawls from this mucky ground and wends his way back toward the safety of *E.T.* "So I ask you, Would extraterrestrials recognize that there is no difference between themselves and humans?"

Seventeen minutes before his scheduled radio talk, we hurry from the class and I take him across town.

"You always drive this slow?" he says, looking at his watch.

"You bet. You know where I live a person could hit an animal."

He cocks his head as if I might have really landed the blow on his jaw, and counters by saying that it was actually his Yale college classmates driving too fast through the countryside, and endangering the lives of animals, that was one of the many motivating factors that brought him to animal rights.

"You never drive fast?"

He lets out a sheepish smile and admits that sometimes he does, especially during hunt disruptions where timing is critical, and he might have to do a U-turn, accelerate from zero to fifty in a few seconds, and try to catch a hunter going into the woods. As he tells me this, his voice grows excited.

Despite my abiding by the speed limit, we reach the Silver Springs, Maryland, office of the Fund one minute before the scheduled radio talk. Wayne slides behind his desk, takes a deep breath, and calls the radio station.

"Hi Ray. Wayne Pacelle here. I know, I know. We made it in time. I wouldn't forget you, Ray. Never. Never. Hello. Hello. Yes. Let's begin the discussion with language and how our language is peppered with references to animals. We shoot the bull . . ."

With a great deal of oratorical skill, and employing the same devices I've watched him use in videotaped debates—burying callers in figures, politely but repeatedly defaming the opposition, and belittling the historical contribution of hunters to wildlife conservation—Wayne begins to get the Fund's message over the airways.

"It's a two-billion-acre country," he says briskly, "and there are roughly seven hundred million public land acres. The Bureau of Land Management is two hundred seventy million acres. The U.S. Forest Service manages one hundred ninety-one million acres. The National Park Service manages eighty million acres. The National Wildlife Refuge System, administered by the Fish and Wildlife Service, has ninety million acres. That is the bulk of land. And the only direct *hunter* contributions to *any* of that land are the three point five percent of the National Wildlife Refuge System, so about three point five million acres. And I don't think that three point five million acres is important."

The caller says something and Wayne replies, "Yes, I think a lot of those lands are vital, and I don't discount the significance of those particular lands. But let's face it, public lands protection is not hinged upon hunter contributions." He now tallies up the lands purchased by the Pittman-Robertson Act, an 11 percent excise tax on firearms and cartridges, which hunters are fond of claiming to be one of the most powerful tools for wildlife conservation in America. Only 4 million acres, says Wayne in the disdainful tone he uses for accomplishments that hunters point to with pride. Then he adds in those lands purchased by duck stamp money, another 4 million. He accounts for lands bought by "so-called conservation groups" like The Rocky Mountain Elk Foundation, 3 million acres, and, to be generous, throws in another 5 million purchased through state hunting licenses. "When we add it all together," he says, "hunters have contributed fifteen point five million acres, and it's a two-*billion*-acre country. If that's doing the trick for wildlife, then you know that's magic."

During a commercial break, I ask Wayne if he realizes that it was a hunter, Theodore Roosevelt, who expanded the National Forests to 150 million acres, and it's these forests that are now home to most of the large mammalian species of the continent as well as being the headwaters of our cold-water fisheries. In addition to creating five national parks, where hunting was prohibited, Roosevelt also inaugurated the National Wildlife Refuge system, eventually setting aside fifty-three of them. I also mention that another turn-of-the-century hunter, George Bird Grinnell, was responsible for creating Glacier National Park.

"And the list is longer," I say. "Wouldn't you call that a direct contribution by hunters, created to halt the excesses of the market hunting that preceded them?"

His hand over the receiver, Wayne says, "Of course. Of course."

"And don't you think it's a little unfair to say that it's a two-billion-acre country, when more than half of it was already developed before the word *conservation* had entered anyone's vocabulary?"

He smiles, and goes back on the air.

"*Tradition?*" he bays. "What has *tradition* got to do with suffering?" And for the next few minutes he talks about how hunters have "massacred, butchered, slaughtered, and mown down animals."

At the next break, he turns to me and says, "You'll probably hear me repeat myself. But repetition will indelibly imprint the audience."

When a caller asks him about the Fund's contributions to wildlife, Wayne mentions its fifteen regional offices across the country, its three animal sanctuaries, one six hundred acres in extent, and its spaying and neutering work.

During the next break, I ask him how much wildlife habitat The Fund For Animals has actually preserved.

"Zero," he say. "Our mission is advocacy."

On and on the calls go: "The Fund takes no organizational position on the sale and use of firearms. . . . We're opposed to greyhound racing. . . . No, I won't campaign against fishing in the sense of imposing legislative activities against it. But I personally don't do it and don't like it. We have to set our priorities because there's a whole world of animal abuse out there. We focus on the shooting of terrestrial animals. . . . Well, that's what makes the world go round. Hunting is a subject of spirited debate, and if society says that it doesn't want the recreational killing of wildlife then we should do away with it, just the way we've done away with cockfighting and dogfighting. Thank *you.* And *thank-you,* Ray. Always. Always."

While Wayne has been on the air, the rest of the staff has continued to work. The basement suite is divided down the middle—Heidi and D.J. to the left, Wayne and Vicki to the right, the fax and coffee machine in between. Their offices hum with the ring of telephones, the flash of the photocopier, and the clack of a printer. Heidi calls to raise volunteers to protest a coyote competition shoot in Pennsylvania on Saturday, and to ask others to drive to Virginia on Thursday, the day after tomorrow, to testify about a proposed tundra swan hunt. D. J. Schubert, a quiet young biologist in sweats, works at a computer writing a memo about the shooting of bison, whom the livestock industry claims carry brucellosis to cattle as they migrate from Yellowstone National Park. He travels to Montana frequently, trying to haze bison back into the park so they won't be shot. Recently, while following a herd across the Yellowstone

River, he was swept into rapids and only saved himself by a strong swim to shore. Now he looks tired. He has been working until four A.M., and sleeping on the office couch, in an attempt to find a legal loophole to end the Montana cull. Vicki, a friendly, dark-haired woman, answers the phone and shuttles calls to the appropriate person. Every bit of wall is covered with a planning map, a cartoon, or a poster. HEAR PACELLE IN IOWA ON HUNTING, declaims one; another recounts the confessions of a recovering hunter; on Heidi's door hangs a photograph of a man lashed to the front of a car while a deer drives him away.

"Look Leo," says Wayne from his office, "we gotta get back on bears. In '94 we'll do business."

"No I don't think you'll have to go to jail," says Heidi into her phone.

D.J. clicks away on his keyboard in the computer room.

"Vicki," calls Wayne, "get me a '91 annual report."

Seated cross from D.J., I watch a video of the *Sally Jessy Raphael* show. A panel of hunters, including the rock star Ted Nugent, face a panel of antihunters, including Wayne and the founder of The Fund For Animals, Cleveland Amory. The discussion breaks down into a shouting match, both sides calling each other names, with Sally trying vainly to keep order.

Looking groggy and rubbing his eyes, Wayne walks into the computer room, and says, "I'm tired." Noticing the video I'm watching, he says, "That was not one of our best moments."

After another minute of watching the free-for-all, he suggests calling Tom Regan, and we go to his office where he places the call, switches on the speaker phone, and introduces me.

Tom's voice, quick, precise, and scholarly, fills the room. From his photos, I imagine him in his North Carolina office—a mid-fortyish professor and activist with a round face, a trim grey beard, and a full head of grey hair.

When I explain my energy analysis to him, and suggest that hunting large mammals in one's bioregion adheres to his miniride principle, he says, "That's a good question and it shows a very deep reading of what I said, and that's unusual and I value that. Are you saying that eating vegetable food could cause greater harm to whom?"

"To other wildlife, caused by the whole system of fossil fuel production and transportation, and mechanized farming."

"Let me try this answer and see if it makes sense." Rapidly, he enumerates the meat industry, animal research, and subsistence, sport, and recreational hunting, and describes them as practices that can't be defined without saying the words *and an animal gets killed.*

When I point out that the same could be said for agriculture, he agrees, "no question about it." Then he goes on to say that our job isn't to ignore this fact, but rather to stop supporting those industries and practices that directly kill animals while, at the very same time, striving to reform those practices which aren't directly in the business of killing animals but whose side effects do. For example, agribusiness and the cotton industry, which in the process of creating benign products have absolutely devastating effects on land, water, and wildlife.

Wondering how we can feed a world population moving toward 10 billion without continuing to usurp wildlife habitat and using some machinery, I ask him if he doesn't think that it's impossible to eliminate side-effect deaths to wildlife. He says that "as a conscientious vegan," one can "support local farmers doing low-scale organic farming. I'm not saying this is going to be possible throughout the world but it is the step to take."

Then he adds a gracious note. "There's a lot of anthropology going on here, and there's a lot of sociology, a lot of class stuff, a lot more than a philosophical argument. The whole gestalt of rural people, their whole way of viewing the world is radically different from somebody living in Washington, D.C., and the more we understand the other layers of it, the more we can practice 'hate sin love the sinner.' Even if we disagree with the other person, we must affirm that person's humanity, and not get to the point where we can confuse that person's character with that person's actions. Good people can do bad things. Even if we disagree morally with them about what they're doing, many of them are still good people. That's a tough thing for the animal rights people to keep in mind, but I think it's true."

Another of Tom's arguments, which has puzzled me, is the one in which even the most committed animal rightists seem to favor humans over animals when the chips are down. Tom calls these situations "lifeboat cases," and in *The Case for Animal Rights* he describes them like this: Four normally intelligent and relatively good humans (no Adolph Hitlers, no Idi Amins) are in a lifeboat with a normally intelligent and friendly dog. There's room for only four and all will perish if someone isn't thrown overboard. Who goes? The dog, says Tom, explaining that "all on board have equal inherent value and an equal prima facie right not to be harmed." He goes on to say that the case wouldn't be any different if it were four humans and a million dogs. The rights view still implies that the million dogs should be thrown overboard and the four humans saved.

When I recall the lifeboat case to him, and say that his choosing to save humans in this way seems to demonstrate his speciesism, he contests my point by reminding me of what he has actually stated in *The Case,* which I'm holding in front of me. I reread what he has written: "Death for the dog . . . though a harm, is not comparable to the harm that death would be for any of the humans. To throw any one of the humans overboard, to face certain death, would be to make that individual worse-off (i.e., would cause *that* individual a greater harm) than the harm that would be done to the dog if the animal was thrown overboard." To make things clearer he now says, "If you had four normal human beings and a severely retarded one, then you should throw the retarded human being over. And if you had one normal human being, three very severely retarded human beings, and a bright dog, then you should save the normal person and the dog. So it's not a case that you judge who goes on the basis of species identity. It's really a question of taking that individual seriously and trying to be fair to everyone involved in those perilous circumstances where you save the best you can."

We have been on the phone a long time, and Wayne's dinner appointment is drawing closer. I don't have time to make the point that always haunts me when I play with these theoretical exercises, for instance, take two normally intelligent mothers, and their two healthy children, and put them in the lifeboat. One has to go, who goes? Take four good humans and one friendly, bright dog, *loved* by one of the humans. Who goes? There is no fair way to choose, other than drawing straws.

We sign off with many thanks, and as we put on our coats I say, "I bet you there are a lot of dog owners out there who would save Fido over some normal, bright, and perfectly moral human being they didn't know."

Wayne, giving a sigh that seems to express the frustration he feels each day as he campaigns against the illogicality of human attachments, says, "I know that's true."

The sky has grown dark and reflects the pink glow of the street lamps. After a half-hour drive, we park the car in a downtown garage, and walk to City Lights, a Chinese restaurant that serves vegetarian food. There Wayne is scheduled to meet a potential donor, Melanie Roberts. She's from a foundation in Texas, and he would like "to establish a relationship with her." As the traffic light changes, and we step into the crosswalk, a woman in a fur coat angles in front of us. Wayne takes a couple of fast steps, leans forward, and says, "Disgusting coat. Disgusting." The woman shivers, hunches her shoulder, and hurries on.

On the far side of the street is the magazine store where Wayne and I have stopped over the weekend so that he could study the hunting periodicals, plot strategy, and let his "blood boil." It was there, leafing through photographs of dead deer, that he told me, "The definition of obscenity on the newsstands should be extended to many hunting magazines." Now a woman in a grey coat with a white fur collar makes the mistake of walking out of the periodical store, directly in front of us.

Wayne catches up to her and asks, "Is that a real fur collar?"

She won't look at him, but does answer. "Yes."

"Don't you care about them?" he chides.

"I couldn't care less."

Taking long strides, he follows her.

"That's a pity you couldn't care less."

Shaking her head in fury, the woman crosses to the opposite side of the street.

"How come you don't do that to people who wear leather shoes?" I ask as we continue toward the restaurant.

"Because people who wear fur certainly know about the cruelty. They know that the animals are killed just for their fur, and it's a pure matter of style, not function. Leather is a by-product of the meat industry, which is largely accepted in this society." After we pass a few storefronts, he says, "I don't like doing this—heckling people. I really don't. I'm much more comfortable with trying to enact laws and having rational discourse about the fur issue, and to discuss things on their merits. But at some point the animal rights movement is no different from other social movements. One has to use so-called 'guerilla tactics.' One has to have an element of direct action and confrontation. And I think that the fur issue is one that requires some activity on the streets. I don't use spray paint. I don't consider it traumatic or terroristic to tell someone what they're doing is cruel."

"At what latitude would you stop heckling people for wearing fur?"

He looks at me as if I've asked a stupid question.

"You know, like some Greenlander driving his dogsled across the pack ice."

He gets my point and says, "At every latitude where people of Western society are wearing fur and they have alternatives."

It's still early in the dinner hour when we arrive, and the hostess, a stunning Chinese woman in red, gives us our choice of tables. Wayne opts for the downstairs room, which he says will be quieter for his meeting.

As we take our seats and Wayne's eyes follow the hostess across the room, I say, "About fishing . . . do you avoid campaigning against it because there isn't a ground-swell movement in our culture to eliminate it?"

"That is correct."

A plump waitress, dressed in a tight blue dress, takes our order for an appetizer, and when she leaves, he continues. "We're out to minimize suffering wherever it can be done, and wherever our limited resources can be utilized most effectively—abusive forms of hunting for now, all hunting eventually."

"And fish aren't furry and cute."

He hesitates a moment, then says, "That's right."

"How about pets, Wayne? Would you envision a future with no pets in the world?"

"I wouldn't say that I envision that, no. If I had my personal view perhaps that might take hold. In fact, I don't want to see another cat or dog born. It's not something I strive for, though. If people were very responsible, and didn't do manipulative breeding, and cared for animals in all senses, and accounted for their nutritional needs as well as their social and psychological needs, then I think it could be an appropriate thing. I'm not sure. I think it's one of those things that we'll decide later in society. I think we're still far from it."

The dumplings that we've ordered arrive quickly, and when we open them we discover that they're filled with meat. Wayne drops his chopsticks as if he's touched acid, and calls after the waitress, explaining that we can't eat these, and that we ordered vegetarian dumplings. "Those special order make," she says, "take much longer."

Wayne says that's just fine, we'll wait. Looking at him dubiously, she takes the plate away.

"They eat a lot of pigs in China," I say, pushing him.

"Clearly," he says, "there are other cultures that are using animals very intensively. Right now, in our society, our cultural standards dictate activity to mitigate the impact on animals."

Knowing that my next question will get no slack either, I say, "Would you consider that there might be different cultures in the U.S.? That Wyoming isn't the Beltway? Tom admitted that."

"Absolutely," he says in his deep voice, which lets you like him even while he's disagreeing with you. "Absolutely. But even if people have distinctive aspects to their life-style, they adhere to certain fundamental tenets and are part of the society. If they want to be part of our society then they choose not to murder people because it happens to be their prerogative, they happen not to cannibalize other people because it's their preference. To me there is no apparent logical distinction between other basic standards in society and the use of animals."

The hostess, pointing from the doorway, shows Melanie our table. A willowy blonde with milky skin and a pleasant Southern accent, she's dressed in a rich suit and wears a large diamond ring. The director of the Summerlee Foundation, which has the diverse goals of supporting animal welfare as well as the research and preservation of Texas history, she is taking a workshop here in the capital, and is staying at the Ritz-Carlton, which she points out has presented her with an ethical dilemma—being in the nonprofit sector and staying at such an expensive hotel.

After Wayne introduces her, and we search the menu and order, she asks about the various preserves the Fund operates and Wayne describes what I've heard him often repeat: the animal rehabilitation center in southern California, the six-hundred-acre animal sanctuary in Texas, and a rabbit and woodchuck sanctuary in South Carolina. Melanie is interested in sanctuaries because she is currently working on a project to rescue animals from the Panama City zoo, where several species are being ill-treated years after the war has come to a close. Two crocodiles have had their eyes poked out. A chimp has died when its keepers gave him drugs and alcohol. One male lion out of a pride of three has died.

Wayne closes his eyes and says, "Oh, my god. That's hard for an animal lover to hear."

The animals still can be saved, says Melanie. A sanctuary in northern California is willing to take them. But she's been unable to get an air carrier to fly them without charge beyond Miami. United Airlines has discontinued their wide-body jets on that route, and the person with whom she spoke at Delta was positively rude to her. Wayne wishes that he could help her, but he doesn't have the means to charter a jet. Melanie nods understandingly and says, "If there were only more people of good intentions." Wayne replies that they just need to be motivated, and she's doing a fine job of that.

She smiles at his flattery and admits that she tries. But sometimes she is frustrated by people who seem so contradictory. The president of the Summerlee Foundation, for instance, is a hunter. Wayne rolls his eyes.

"But he's just a deer hunter," she qualifies, "and is able to hear our side of the story." Then she mentions a veterinarian whom she knows. "He's donating his time at zoos taking care of wildlife, doin' a wonderful job. Yet he also works at CDC, doin' AIDS research, and he experiments on chimps!" She shakes her head in disbelief.

Wayne furrows his eyebrows and joins her dismayed head shaking. The conversation can go no further. The waitress slides several platters on the table—sweet-and-sour tofu, a couple of spicy vegetable dishes swimming in rich sauces, and our tardy dumplings.

Melanie says, "This is excellent vegetarian food."

Wayne says, "I thought you'd like it."

We eat for a few moments, then with shy excitement she says, "My son, you know, is four and a half, and my husband who is a vegetarian is trying not to influence him, so he gives him hamburger. And my son, he says, 'That's cow, I don't want it.' "

Smiling, Wayne says, "Well that's being very neutral."

"We are not complete vegans," she adds. "My husband still eats seafood, and I occasionally eat shrimp."

Wayne opens his hands and clears his throat.

At curbside, he flags down a taxi and Melanie gives him a hug. As we head for the car, he says, "All part of the job." Then we drive crosstown to a mall where he needs to do some clothes shopping for his upcoming lecture and debating tour. Tomorrow we're on the seven o'clock jet out of Dulles, and tomorrow evening he will debate Jerry Hart, the head of the United Sportsmen's Council, at the University of Colorado in Boulder.

Taking glittering escalators and passing pizza and cookie booths, we find a men's store and Wayne buys a ten-pack of socks and three bags of Jockey underwear to replace what Reiley, the black lab, has eaten. Looking in a nearby mirror, he runs his hand through his hair and wonders if he ought to catch a haircut this evening. I tell him that he looks fine, but he insists that he needs to look clean-cut for his debate with Hart. When he asks me what he should wear, I say, "Casual shirt and jeans."

"Can't," he says. "I'll look too young and I want to present a certain image. It's got to be a suit and tie."

Going down the escalator, the mall empty and quiet, he says, "You know, I've really enjoyed your visit."

This stroll through the mall and our drive back to his house will be our last one-on-one. He has work to do at home, and after the Boulder debate I'm returning to Wyoming.

"I've been thinking about that lifeboat scenario that you and Tom talked about," he says. "What if it was just you, me, and a guy from Safari Club International in the lifeboat, and one of us has to go. Who would you throw out?"

I think a moment, then say, "That's a hard question, Wayne. I wouldn't want to live with either one of you." I smile but tell the truth. "I guess, though, I'd dump you overboard."

He looks hurt. "I thought we've had a great dialogue during the last few days. We have our differences, that's true, but we agree on so much—ending the competitive shooting of wildlife, for instance, the evils of the meat industry . . ."

"What we disagree on is pretty fundamental. Your mission is to end *all* hunting in your lifetime, not just the egregious kind."

He opens his hands in his wonderful politic gesture, so Latin, so endearing, so like a Godfather saying, *"Paesano,"* while having put a contract on you. "But why would you throw me overboard instead of the guy from SCI?"

"You're young, Wayne. The SCI guy would more than likely be old. I dump you overboard, he dies, soon I have the lifeboat to myself, and maybe someone I can live with drifts along."

Wayne throws his head back and laughs from his belly.

At CU he flattens Hart. The head of the United Sportsmen's Council has obviously never watched Wayne debate. Wayne opens with jokes and patter, Hart with a serious monologue. Wayne is twenty-six, wears a black suit and red tie, and is only beginning to put on weight. Hart is in his fifties, paunchy, dressed in a sport shirt, and looks like he just came from the bowling alley. Wayne has a tidal wave of figures proving that hunter's have done little to conserve wildlife. Hart does nothing to refute these figures, or show the significant historical contribution of hunters. Wayne repeats, over and over, the words *egregious, despicable, disgusting, shameful.* Hart can find no way to counter this bombast. When Wayne asks him if he will stand up and oppose activities such as the annual prairie dog shoot for money in Nucla, Colorado, Hart can only say that those competitions are choices individuals are free to make. He comes off looking as if he will endorse anything if it has the word *hunting* attached to it.

At the end of the debate, members of the audience mill around their champions. Hart is surrounded by men, Wayne by a bevy of young women. He shakes hands, gives hugs, clasps his hands behind his back, and says, "Yes, yes, yes," smiling.

When he looks up, I wave from the stairs of the lecture hall. He disengages himself, climbs up to me, and pumps my hand. "Thanks for coming," he says in his great public voice. "It's been productive."

"Same here."

Then he leans close and lowers his voice. "If the rest of the hunting community was like you, I probably wouldn't be campaigning."

"Give me a break, Wayne."

"No." He shakes his head sincerely. "It's largely the egregious things that draw me out of the woodwork." Then he pumps my hand again and walks down to the crowded front of the theater.

Driving to the airport, I wonder if he could say that to the millions of hunters across the land who put some meat on the table, and have no interest in vaporizing prairie dogs or in collecting endangered species, all those hunters who have never heard of the difference between gratuitous and instrumental pain, but who seem to be able to make the distinction between using a living creature for target practice and hunting for food. I wonder if he could compromise with those who live in different webs.

T E N

━━➤✕◄━━

On sunday we go to church, gathering in a small yurt around an iron stove burning hot. A half dozen of us, naked, sit on the smooth benches as the steam wafts around us. We have come from the yurts and cabins nearby, from the science school up the road, and from the town of Jackson, downvalley. The smell of sage and pine fills the air.

A heavy man with a great hairy belly begins to make a sound like wind in a canyon, like erupting lava. There are no words, only the resonance of his furry chest. From across the fire, a red-haired woman sings like a coyote when it's moaning soft and high, which is the sound of so many Indian songs.

It is so hot on the bench above the fire that I jump off and kneel by the door, where a crack of vapor enters the sweat. I pour water over my head, the water of the nearby Gros Ventre River, and kneel with my fingers curled in the small, smooth river rocks that serve as our floor. I curl my fingers down to the dirt underneath them, the fire roaring hot in front of my face, a circle of feet and legs and thighs receding into the steam. The man's voice, melodious and lovely, like sunlight in aspens, turns into words. "With every breath we choose, make us as true as you. How you sustain us, we know not why. Make us as true as thy . . . thy . . . thy . . ." The words begin to come out of my stomach, all sound, coming out of the rocks and up my legs, the sound of roots.

When I go outside snow is falling from a grey sky. The wind blows from the southwest, and I stand naked facing it, letting it dry me. My hair stands up; the layers blow away. What better soap than sweat; what larger thanks than song?

After skiing on the hills across the valley, and watching the dusk fill with snow from a high place, we return and cook a meal that, like so many meals these days, has three alternatives: pasta and vegetables for the vegans; pasta and elk for the wild-meat eaters; pasta and beef for those who will eat most anything. Though these fine points of behavior have come to the country, dietary preference has never been a contentious issue in this group. Other ties run deeper . . . ones of home and its care.

I have seen these faces at public meetings, speaking against the many development proposals that encroach on the open spaces of this valley and its surroundings—extension of the airport's runway, a new bridge over the Snake River, a widened highway in the Snake River Canyon, and oil development throughout grizzly country. On other occasions, some of these folks have spoken for the restoration of wolves to Yellowstone and for limiting overall growth in Jackson Hole. In either case, my friends have supported limiting options for people and increasing habitat for wildlife, which of course increases another sort of option for people, the possibility that they might enjoy more wildlife. I think it is hard to calculate what fraction of their prohabitat position is strictly for the good of wildlife and which is for their own future enjoyment as birders, photographers, fishermen, and hunters. The two are so inextricably intertwined that they can't be readily separated. At times, there's nothing that can be said about this connection except in song.

Through the dark, and pelted by thick snowflakes, Merle and I climb the gulch, heading for the cabin at the top of the ridge. Leaving my circle of friends, I wonder, as I occasionally do, why I've put myself up here, the hermit on the hill. Nearing the cabin, and momentarily lighting my headlamp to walk over the drifts, I see coyote tracks and remember why. Here, the rest of our community comes closer.

Directly in front of the cabin I spot the green glow of a bison's eyes. I shine the light away, wait a few moments, then say, "How 'bout letting us pass?" Cautiously, we move by his dark shape and bass rumbles.

When I get under the blankets and pull the long-haired elk hide over me, I can still hear him rooting in the snow and snorting. My legs begin to jerk reflexively from the many turns, and gradually I feel them walking . . . walking in a drifting, disembodied way. Then they become part of my body as I hike upwards through the pines. The snow has melted and I climb through a deep forest toward a swale at tree line. I know there is a small hidden pond in the swale, and around it is a herd of elk, many cows and a few bulls. I know this because I can feel them there.

Crawling in the duff, I bring my head slowly over some exposed tree roots and see elk before me, around me, moving everywhere, big dark shapes in the trees, along with their calves of the year. I raise the rifle, wanting to fire, but also wanting to wait. Some of the cows run around the pond and others swim across it. Standing, I walk among them. They aren't afraid, and behind me one of the cows rubs her flank against me. She doesn't smell like elk—dry and musky. She smells washed and clean. When I turn around, she drops her coat and becomes a naked woman, pressing herself to me and pushing me down. Her skin is the creamy color of wapiti rump, her breasts are small, and she points to the elk who trot around the other side of the pond with their young calves. Their breasts are bigger. Her nose is thin, her eyes large; her hair is wild and filled with twigs. She looks like a nomad from the center of Asia, young, perhaps enormously old.

Nodding to the valley, she says that she will visit me. Without speaking English, or even using words, she has sent this thought into my mind. As she bends her head to my chest and tries to take off my shirt, I lift her chin. Her eyes are wet and shining, and I can't tell if she is about to laugh or to cry. I put my hand behind her head, pulling her face toward me for a kiss, when I see the elk hide under my nose in the dawn.

NOTES

PAGE NUMBER

11. [When I was a child] Knud Rasmussen, *The People of the Polar North,* J. P. Lippincott Company, Philadelphia, 1908, p. xix.

13. [There are men] Knud Rasmussen, *Across Arctic America,* G. P. Putnam's Sons, New York–London, 1927, p. 229.

13. [For myself] Ibid., p. 230.

14. [I can describe the scene] Gontran de Poncins, *Kabloona,* Reynal & Hitchcock, Inc., New York, 1941, p. 303.

15. [highly complicated and meaningless observances] Rasmussen, *Across Arctic America,* p. 128.

15. [Look . . . snow and storm] Ibid., p. 129.

15. [You see, even you cannot answer] as quoted in Ibid., p. 129–131.

16. [The greatest peril of life] as quoted in Ian Stirling, *Polar Bears,* The University of Michigan Press, Ann Arbor, 1988, p. 31.

19. [I had to give him a few blows] Finn Gad, *The History of Greenland, vol. II,* McGill–Queen's University Press, Montreal, 1973, p. 86.

19. [usual method] Fridtjof Nansen, *Eskimo Life,* Longmans, Green, and Co., London, 1893, p. 307.

19. [slothful and brutish . . . wandering and unstable] Ibid., p. 106.

20. [Give us this day] as quoted in Sam Hall, *The Fourth World, The Heritage of the Arctic and Its Destruction,* Alfred A. Knopf, New York, 1987, p. 111.

30. [What this means] Stirling, *Polar Bears,* p. 206.

36. [You earth,/Our great earth! . . . The great sea/Moves me!] as quoted in Peter Freuchen, *Book of the Eskimos,* Fawcet Premier, New York, 1961, pp. 206–207.

58. [All true wisdom] as quoted in Rasmussen, *Across Arctic America,* p. 381.

63. [It keeps me crying baby] The Supremes, "Come See About Me" on stereo cassette *Supremes Greatest Hits,* Motown Record Company, 1967.

64. [As I sat eating the rotten fish] Rasmussen, *The People of the Polar North,* p. 338.

65. [Let us be without day] Knud Rasmussen, *Greenland by the Polar Sea,* Frederick A. Stokes Company, New York, 1921, p. 29.

69. [on dark nights] Odell Shepard, *The Lore of the Unicorn,* Avenel Books, New York, 1982, p. 20.

72. [when a captive bull narwhal vocalized] John K. B. Ford and H. Dean Fisher, "Underwater acoustic signals of the narwhal (*Monodon monoceros*)," *Canadian Journal of Zoology* 56: p. 559.

94. [individual who has made the greatest] dinner program, thirty-second annual award dinner, Weatherby Big Game Trophy, December 1, 1988, Newport Beach, California.

96. [knew not what . . . stink pretty bad around the edges] Jack O'Connor, *Sheep and Sheep Hunting,* Winchester Press, New York, 1974, pp. 246–258.

104. [Through our labors] William J. Morden, *Across Asia's Snows and Deserts,* G. P. Putnam's Sons, New York–London, 1927, p. 385.

104. [the peak experience] see Abraham H. Maslow, *Toward a Psychology of Being,* second edition, D. Van Nostrand Company, New York, 1968, pp. 71–102.

104. [Sitting on the rock] Charles Sheldon, *The Wilderness of the Upper Yukon,* Charles Scribner's Sons, New York, 1911, pp. 214–215.

105. [the high altitudes are a special world] George B. Schaller, *Mountain Monarchs,* The University of Chicago Press, Chicago, 1977, pp. 336–337.

105. [Possessed of keen sight] John Muir, "The Wild Sheep of California," *Overland Monthly,* 12, April 1874.

105. [the noblest form of sport] Theodore Roosevelt, *Hunting Trips of a Ranchman, Ranch Life and the Hunting Trail,* National Edition, Vol. 1, Hermann Hagedorn, ed., Charles Scribner's Sons, New York, 1926, p. 173.

105. [Homeric . . . the muscular skills of the hero] Joseph Wood Krutch, "The Barbarian Mammal," in *The Great Chain of Life,* Houghton Mifflin Company, Boston, 1956, p. 101.

136. [been somewhere and done something] Aldo Leopold, *A Sand County Almanac,* Oxford University Press, London, 1975, p. 169.

136. [We patronize them for their incompleteness] Henry Beston, *The Outermost House,* Ballantine Books, New York, 1971, pp. 19–20.

137. [We need another and a wiser] Ibid., p. 19.

169. [stiff but fair . . . devastating to Mr. Asper . . . these items] Sentencing Statement, December 14, 1990, Judge Muir, United States District Court for the Middle District of Pennsylvania, pp. 2, 4, 7.

180. [The valley produce(s)] Osborne Russell, *Journal of a Trapper,* University of Nebraska Press, Lincoln, 1965, p. 18.

190. [cost of living] Valerius Geist, *Elk Country,* NorthWord Press, Inc., Minocqua, Wisconsin, 1991, p. 139.

191. [proof of health] Ibid., p. 69.

211. [Utilitarian/Meat Hunters, The Nature Hunter, Dominionistic/Sport Hunter] Stephen R. Kellert, "Attitudes and Characteristics of Hunters and Antihunters," *Transactions of the North American Wildlife and Natural Resources Conference,* #43, 1978, pp. 412–423.

212. [Killing "for sport"] Krutch, "Reverence for Life," in *The Great Chain of Life,* pp. 147–148.

212. [shooter stage . . . sportsman stage] Robert Jackson and Robert Norton, " 'Phases,' The Personal Evolution of the Sport Hunter," *Wisconsin Sportsman,* November/December 1980, pp. 17–20.

222. [The Power of the World] Black Elk as told through John G. Neihardt, *Black Elk Speaks,* University of Nebraska Press, Lincoln, 1972, p. 194.

237. [A thing is right . . . from conqueror of] Leopold, *A Sand County Almanac,* pp. 204, 224–225.

240. [morality/Is not an end] Robinson Jeffers, "Curb Science?" in *The Double Axe,* Liveright, New York, 1977, p. 164.

254. [miniride principle] Tom Regan, *The Case for Animal Rights,* University of California Pres, Berkeley, 1983, p. 305.

263. [all on board have equal . . . death for the dog] Ibid., p. 324.

TED KERASOTE has written about nature for a variety of publications, including *Audubon, Outside,* and *Sports Afield,* where his EcoWatch column has followed the many issues of wildlife and wilderness conservation. He lives in northwestern Wyoming.

ABOUT THE TYPE

This book was set on the monotype in Garamond, a typeface designed by the French printer Jean Jannon. It is styled after Garamond's original models. The face is dignified, and is light but without fragile lines. The italic is modeled after a font of Granjon, which was probably cut in the middle of the sixteenth century.